Wheeling
& Dealing
In My World

Including
World War II Memories

Maury Feren

Editing by
Joanne Fenton Humphrey

Editor
Joanne Fenton Humphrey

Book Design & Photography
Ron Humphrey

Windjammer Adventure Publishing
289 South Franklin Street, Chagrin Falls, OH 44022
Telephone 440.247.6610 Email windjammerpub@mac.com

DEDICATION

No man lives alone. Once you become part of a family, your life is changed forever. I will never forget my mother's warning after I was married: "You are now three," she said. "How could I be three?" I answered. "It's only Bess and I." Of course, she envisioned the family that was yet to come, a far-reaching conclusion that would change my life in every way.

There is no question of the role my children played in my life. They were and are my life, and the decisions I made were based on my relationship to each of them. Their story of our relationship will have to come from them. For me, the most important thing was to give them love, to instill in them my beliefs and my moral values, to protect them, to gain their respect, and to make them proud that I was their father.

This book is dedicated to my children, grandchildren, and great-grandchildren: To my daughter, Shelley and her husband, Marty Yonas; their daughters, Debbie Yonas, and Lorrie van Buskirk (husband, Bobby); great-granddaughters Becca and Lindsey van Buskirk. To my son, Dr. Alan Feren, and his wife, Carol, and their daughter, Amy; their son, Michael and his wife, Lisa; and their children, Alya and Asher Feren.

My wife, Bess, and I were married for sixty-seven years. Unfortunately, she suffered from Alzheimer's disease the last eight to ten years of our marriage. Obviously, this brought many changes in our life. Bess was not only my wife, a mother, grandmother, and a great-grandmother—she was all those things and more. She was made of love and the family was the most important part of her life: She gave her heart, her soul and every part of her being. Bess was also a very important, creative part of the gift basket business and I will always say that she helped to make me the man I am. After all is said and done, this book is affectionately dedicated with love to Bess. I couldn't have done any of it without her!

ACKNOWLEDGEMENTS

I would like to thank Joanne Humphrey, my editor, and Ron Humphrey, photographer and book designer. I feel so lucky to have chosen Windjammer Adventure Publishing to produce my book. Ron and Joanne have been so helpful, warmly critical, and honest. This book could never have come to being without their love, friendship and critical eyes. I am indebted. Gratitude also goes to David Levey, friend and critic, who helped to make this book happen; and Kathy De Long, whose advice and expertise made me aware of what I needed to do.

I offer my appreciation to the United Fruit and Vegetable Association; and to Jeff Sanson of the Sanson Company, who was a supporter and enthusiast of my work. I must also thank my brother, Hal (deceased), and my brother-in-law, Sonny (deceased), who helped me become the produce king of my day; because of their love and devotion, the M.B. Feren Produce Company was a great success.

Thank you Joe Cavalier for your help; Lee Wolf for your antique cars; Larry Morrow for all you are and all you do, my life long friend whom I love; Michael Settoni, who is unforgettable; Laura Taxel, who took time off to help; and Fred Griffith for his friendship and support for so many years.

TABLE OF CONTENTS

February 2010: Maury's place of business was
at the far left. He sold it in 1968.

February 2010: This is Maury at his original warehouse at
the Northern Ohio Food Terminal, which he sold in 1968.
"The best years of my produce career were spent here."

AN OVERVIEW OF MAURY'S CAREER

Maury often talked about the way his life turned out. "Luck of the draw," he said. He also claimed that he has had several different lives. He spent thirty years as a wholesale produce merchant. His intense interest in all things green helped him rise to the top of his field.

In 1950, Maury developed a fruit basket company; even from the business's conception, he learned to utilize epicurean foods, exotic fruits, and cheese and wine to their best advantage. His extensive knowledge enabled him to become an instructor at John Carrol University, teaching courses about wine and gourmet foods for thirteen years in the Continuing Education Program. The Feren Fruit Basket Company became the leading fruit supplier in the greater Cleveland area. The business was sold to Fisher Fazio Company in 1968.

Maury was determined to become an authority in the produce field. For fifteen years he wrote a weekly column in the *Cleveland Plain Dealer* entitled, "In the Markets." He wrote occasional stories for the *Catholic Universe*; the *Cleveland Jewish News*; the *Grocery Spotlight*; *Cleveland Magazine*; *Supermarket News*; and *Restaurant Hospitality Magazine*. For fifteen years he also wrote a column for the *Produce News*, a nationally distributed industry newspaper that covered growers and shippers; this column, "Thinking Retail," was the first to recognize the expectations of the consumer. It received local and national attention. He published a book, *How To Save Money on Fruits and Vegetables* in 1968.

Maury's radio career, with a call-in program giving market reports two to three times a week, began with Big Wilson. Big Wilson always made sure that Maury's segment of the program had plenty of humor. Bill Randle, the most popular WERE host of his day, also made sure that Maury's food reports were heard three times a week. In 2000, the Radio Broadcasters of the Air honored Maury. As of March 2010, Maury's radio show is still on the air on Saturday morning, from 8AM to 9AM, on WERE 1490.

Appearances on television soon augmented the radio

shows: Paige Palmer; Ghoulardi (Ernie Anderson); then regular presentations on the *Morning Exchange* with Fred Griffith. Maury became a weekly food reporter on AM Cleveland, and Channel 8 News, also appearing on the *Mike Douglas Show*. In the 1980's he became an "Action Cam" reporter for Channel 5.

Beginning in 1990, Maury produced his own Saturday afternoon television show on WVIZ, *Maury's Market,* featuring the foods of twenty-seven different ethnicities. This series ran through 1993. He was also a restaurant critic for *Cableview Magazine,* from 1985-1996.

First TV program on food in greater Cleveland, 1955.
Maggie Byrnes, the host (left), Maury (far right).

Maury taught about wine and epi-
curian foods at John Carrol University in the mid and late 1980's.
This painting won first place in
the Chagrin Falls Art Show.

A Message From Fred Griffith

Whenever we watch TV these days, we will see people cooking. Chefs show off their skills; creative food experts share their recipes. We learn about the importance of good food in our lives. When we first started on our TV program, *The Morning Exchange,* in the early 1970's, we sometimes had cooks on the program. I became comfortable with food and cooking on TV.

That was a long time ago, but Maury Feren was ahead of us all. No one has done more in his whole professional life, nor has been more devoted to understanding food. No one was more of a pioneer in getting good food to be served in wonderful creative ways—and no one will ever break his record as a broadcaster on this important subject.

Maury Feren loved that role and you knew it when you watched him work on TV, helping us understand his ideas. With this book we will be able to learn more about the importance of food as well as more about this leader in our lives.

Fred Griffith
Cleveland, Ohio Television Personality

Maury filming *Maury's Market* on WVIZ TV, one of
twenty-seven original telivision programs he hosted.

Maury hosting *Maury's Market* on WERE AM, January 2010

WHY WRITE AN AUTOBIOGRAPHY?

I suppose this book began in my mind long before I sat down to write it. It is difficult for anyone who does not understand why writers say there has to be day of reckoning; in my case this had to be story about why it all happened, the way I saw it. I realize that writing about my life is going to be harder to do than I planned, for it is only natural to color things the way I think I experienced them, and not the way they were. At first I thought I might use a diary as a basis, but then I realized that I did not have enough material to bring it to life. There were other possibilities, of course, but they, too, had as many loopholes as the diary. I discovered unhappily that I would have to use a different approach, and that it would be more difficult.

What I'm really trying to say is that I've had this book within me for many years. I didn't realize the form it was going to take, or where it was going to go, but I felt that I have something to say, important enough to tell the world about it. I came to this conclusion much later than I should have.

My experiences during World War II were a vital force that made me into the human being I am today. Fortunately, fate was kinder to me than most, giving me another chance to live. Those years are so far away now, I almost think of them as a part of another life. In fact, it's hard to believe I was once another kind of guy—and he was a soldier. A completely different person?

I have made a study of myself and I know positively that there were certain things about me that people either liked or disliked, and I was determined to use that knowledge so that I would improve. This was what I always strived for, and if in the course of a bad day I would have a few setbacks, I would always accept the fact that I was basically in the process of learning. It took me many years to overcome some of my deficiencies of character, but at least there was gradual improvement. I think it was Churchill who said, "Until the whole man is able to cope with life, relieved of the constant pressure of the sex drive, will he have the freedom and the ability to analyze the world and its affect upon him." I suppose this is really true. In fact, today I am just beginning to see the light!

One of the things I learned too late in life is that some of the greatest ideas an individual may have are not unique, nor do they belong only to him, for no matter where you may go you will find there are many "cries in the night" that are expressing the same ideas as you. And I thought I was so extraordinary!

Anyway, this is the book I always wanted to write. The fact that it is about me doesn't make me egotistical; if I had chosen to write about a fictional character, I might have had a lot more fun imaginatively, but it would still have turned out to be the same story—just about me! So why not tell it the way it really happened, and let the chips fall where they may.

Maury giving an acceptance speech;
honored by Israel Bonds, 1990.

BEGINNING AT THE BEGINNING: A LITTLE ABOUT MY EARLY YEARS

Any story has to begin with a background of environment and heredity. In my case, both were important influences in my life. Today there is not enough emphasis on the closely-knit family and its relationship to society; in my childhood my family was probably the most important aspect of my life. Today that world seems far away, but when I think back I am aware more than ever how important those days were in the formation of my personality.

My father, Max, and my mother, Fanny, were both immigrants from the old world, Russia and Romania respectively. They spoke English well, although they used Yiddish in our home whenever they wished to discuss things privately while the children were present. In our faith, we were considered to be Orthodox Jews, although there were some practices that were open to interpretation. Both of my parents were intelligent and knowledgeable about the world, community affairs, and current events. They were interested in theatre and appreciated music and some of the arts—though there was little time for those things in a world in which there was a constant struggle for survival.

I always remember the emphasis my mother put on books and how important it was to her that I read them. It was not enough to go to school, for that was only a part of studying. Time was to be used advantageously and wasting it was frivolous and a terrible loss; oftentimes I find I have a feeling of guilt when I waste time. My mother's lessons have remained with me all these years. She constantly goaded me on to higher goals. Her aim in life was solely to give her children the opportunities that were not available to her in her youth. Her life had been a hard one, having migrated from Europe to New York at an early age.

Her father was a teacher and a learned man, known as Reb Dovid. He made his living teaching Hebrew privately for very small fees. Although teaching has always been a Jewish man's position of respect, the pay was never very good, nor has it improved comparatively today.

How can I describe a man like my grandfather when he only came into my life for one short summer, so many years ago? Yet, there are some distinct images that are as vivid as the days we spent together: Grandfather was a tall, thin figure of a man, six feet or more, with the passage of time inscribed on a face that generated love. His graying beard covered most of his face, and his curly hair always seemed to need more trimming, though it was never actually straggly or unkempt. The kindness in his face was reflected in the softness of his voice; I could feel his gentleness whenever I came near him.

Oftentimes, I think back to my childhood trying to figure our why the personality I have developed the way it did. Perhaps in today's society I may not have done as well, faced with the kind of competition our energetic young people must face in every aspect of daily living. I suppose the competition was just as tough in my early days, but the method of evaluation was a little different. Life in the "good old days" wasn't that good when I analyze it closely, but there were many things about it that made me think so. In any event, my childhood seems so distant and far away, I wonder if there ever were such a time, and if so what was it in reality?

In the Jewish religion a boy is considered to be a man at thirteen, at his Bar-Mitzvah. It never seemed logical to me to assume that a thirteen-year-old is ready to accept the responsibilities of adulthood. (As a matter of fact, I wonder how ready he might be at eighteen). But in my own case, the turning point towards manhood occurred during my thirteenth year. I don't think I became a man at once, but it was a big step forward for me because I was compelled by necessity to adjust my attitudes and behavior to a changing situation.

Summer was never usually a time for studying, but since Grandfather was only visiting his son, my Uncle Louie, for a short visit, it was a matter or necessity that daily study become the rule: There was a morning and an afternoon session, and even though Grandfather considered them too short, they generally lasted an hour. Sitting there beside him, under the blue sky and afternoon sun, his pleasant voice chanting with me the songs and prayers of our people, I could only react pleasurably. I know of very few boys of thirteen who would have enjoyed Hebrew study, but under Grandpa's tutelage it didn't seem half bad.

The syllables or sounds that he sang indicated the intonation and pattern of the music. These chants represent a way of life that goes back a thousand years or more. There is one major distinction, and that is the key of each accented syllable never changes, only the style—as interpreted by the Orthodox or Conservative sects—may change. Nevertheless Grandfather represented "learning with dignity" and his life was one that we all look back at with pride.

"Ma" is the only way I addressed my mother—not "Mom", not "Mother"; those were fancy names and sounded strange. She was the oldest daughter of a family of six, in a strange new world that left few choices for her. She began work in a dress factory at an early age, working long hours, as did thousands of others, for very poor pay. She met my father at what was then considered a late age, marrying him in New York City when she was twenty-eight years old. (This may have been a psychological block in their relationship, because he was a few years younger, and I often wonder whether it did make a difference in their marriage). Pa was the more integrated of the two into American life in the big city. He was a bright, vibrant-looking man, who spoke English well because he had migrated from Russia to London many years before he came to the United States.

My father's daily contact in the business world was an asset he used unconsciously, and he capitalized on his worldliness, even though he never achieved any financial success or recognition in his field. He, too, loved books and liturgical music and had an excellent background in Hebrew and the teachings of Torah and Talmud. His voice was melodious, and his renditions at the holiday Seder table were a joy to all who heard him. His prayers were always letter-perfect and he could "doven" (pray) with the best; this was an ability that few men possessed, even in those days, and Ma loved to listen to him. It was he who instilled in me the appreciation for the inspiration and beauty that one could derive from Jewish music, especially if it were sung by a true "Chazan."

There were Cantors and Chazanim, and if you were an expert like my father, you knew exactly what to look for. A Chazan had to meet specific requirements, and from discussions with Pa, I learned what made the difference: A Chazan was the Hebraic term for a Cantor, but there was a distinction made to determine a man's ability; a Chazan was the intimate term for a sweet-singing Cantor. In fact, there were not any great Cantors in Cleveland at that time, for the best singers remained in New York, where they could use their talents more fully. A big day in our town came when a noted Cantor came to Cleveland to give a concert. If finances enabled us to attend, this would be an event comparable to going to the opera today. (If this whole discussion seems irrelevant, I assure you it is not, because I still have strong feelings about cantorical music. I have many records that I play during my moody periods because of their emotional sensitivity, and I attend occasional concerts whenever possible).

Ma and Pa were the two balancing factors that developed my personality, giving me different perspectives of the world as it appeared to them. Oftentimes I try to compare my relationship with my parents to my relationship with my own children. What did they do that bound me so to them, and why were the things they felt so important to me? How does it compare with my own relationship to my family, and why was it so different? Was it better to be so close, and yet respectfully distant? I cannot remember ever being whipped by my father, nor do I think this would have made any difference to me in our relationship. All that I remember was that they commanded respect, and that their word was the law in our home. My two brothers and sister lived in the same house, with the normal family problems and minor age differences. Harmony was the major key to the little happiness that came our way.

Thirteen years old, and what a new world I was entering. A lavish Bar Mitzvah? No, but one that would meet all the requirements of those times. I had studied, having been tutored by my grandfather from New York, who represented to me the epitome of Jewish learning. Many of my friends attended Hebrew school, but of those I still know today, there are only a few who can read the language, even at the simplest level. In fact, although my knowledge of the essentials of Judaism was minute, it seemed significant in later years when I compared it to modern Jewish education. This is not an evaluation of my Hebrew school and its teachers, for I certainly was not the epitome of a good student, but I can honestly say that the richness of my Jewish heritage was a part of the way I lived. Being Jewish was something one lived and felt, and in our home it permeated every room, as well as every fiber of my being. It was not a question of what benefit Jewishness would bring, but rather it was a way of life as natural as the air I breathed.

My father was the religious representative in our home. He could "doven" like a rabbi, perhaps better. The words he uttered were distinct and melodious, and they seemed to flow with ease. Here was a comfortable approach to contemporary living that met all of the requirements we needed to live. It was as simple as that. The fundamentals were never questioned: If the law required that we observe two days of Rosh Hashanah (New Year) and eight days of Passover, so it was. Every major holiday had its place and we played our part, no questions asked, however it is most interesting that we were not Sabbath observers. The Sabbath was not given the importance that it seems to hold today, probably because my father—and many other Jewish immigrants—had to work six days a week in order to make a living.

There were many religious practices in our home that were Orthodox in their most primitive form. For example, the practice of "Schlugging Capora" with a chicken—whirling it round and round over your head and then throwing it into a corner of the room—took place before Passover. This ritual, whose significance escapes me, originated in Europe many years ago.

Things came to a complete standstill at each major holiday, and there was no work allowed for anyone in the family: no writing, no cleaning, no riding buses or any other form of transportation, and no business contacts. There was a finality about this that left no room for negotiation.

Every day in our childhood was a struggle. There was always a shortage of money in the household, and it was only during the summer months that we managed to show the financial results that gave my parents the courage to continue on. I don't think life was too much better for most families. We were all in the same boat. I can't remember ever going hungry, but there were certainly times the choice of food could have been better. (I have never spoken of this in the many years since then).

I must mention my role as a choir singer at the old Jewish Center Temple, on Grantwood Avenue, in the East 105th Street area. It was there that I completed my education in religious music, learning to love the beautiful melodies of my people. Male choirs were the feature of the day, and the participants' ages ranged from nine to thirteen, with some strong older voices. The plaintive melodies of the Jewish religion are symbolic of the plight of the Jew in exile; the music expresses all of the longings of the Jew for Zion, a homeland. Only those who understand this underlying theme can appreciate the depth of emotion that is conveyed. My participation in the choir lasted about three years, from age eleven to fourteen, with many hours of practice devoted to it. Dan Frohman, the choir leader, was a difficult taskmaster who required perfection from us. He raged and foamed at us continuously, attempting to relay his enthusiasm to us. My participation as a singer in the choir was meaningful. It was a time of trial and tribulation and the throes of growing up. A new world had opened up to me, and I was happily a part of it. Each of my brothers sang in that choir simultaneously as boys, and in their later years as well. Hal, the youngest, was also a soloist who thrilled his listeners with beautiful renditions of "Rachamono" in his sharp, clear, alto voice.

After singing with the choir for several years, I was selected for small parts in the Yiddish Theater. What an experience that was! Live theater with all the great actors of that era! I doubt I would be as impressed today as I was then, but the $2.00 per performance was a major inducement—as well as my ambition to become a singer.

During this period, one of our choir singers, Billy Sherman, began his career as a theater performer doing regular renditions "Mammy" and "Sonny Boy," imitating Al Jolson. I was always envious of him because he seemed so sure of himself. Besides, he had the opportunity to do what I always had hoped I could do: become an accomplished vaudeville performer. But alas, my enthusiasm for music was short-lived. My voice began to change, and instead of resting it during that period, I continued to sing. That was disastrous for me, for everyone in the music field knows that it is wrong for a growing boy to sing while his voice is in the process of changing. For many years I blamed Dan Frohman for the ruination of my voice, but I finally came to accept it since I am a man who believes in Fate (called "Bashert" in Yiddish). I suppose it was predestined.

The Jewish Center was not only a place to sing in the choir, but it was the hub of the active Jewish Community. There were many small "shuls" or synagogues that ran from Superior to St. Clair, but the old Jewish Center represented the best tradition of the modern Orthodox Conservatives of the late 1920's and early 30's. Here is where I attended Hebrew school four days a week after school, Sunday school, and participated in all of the recreational opportunities it offered. But synagogues need money to operate. This was something my family did not have an excess of! I always remember how my mother made us a part of that temple, with tremendous sacrifice of personal pride. She literally begged the director at that time, Mr. Moritz, to allow us to attend the Sunday school. In all probability, there were hundreds of people like ourselves who would have liked to enjoy the wonderful facilities of the temple, but she was one of the few who had the tenacity and determination to literally shame the temple into accepting us. When I look back, I realize it was a good investment for them because since attaining maturity, each of us has contributed culturally and financially to the Center. (This brings me to the essential quality of kindness that must be shown when doing a good deed; Mr. Moritz could easily have said "yes" to my mother without allowing her to debase herself so. All she wanted was to give her children the best Jewish education).

The Jewish Center was even more than a temple to each of us. It became an integral part of our personal lives. For Hal, my next oldest brother, it was a place to develop his basketball skill. He spent many hours there, shooting baskets and learning how to become the skilled ballplayer he became. Asher, the youngest, was the swimmer. I vividly remember teaching him the basics of swimming after throwing him into the pool. The psychology of learning to swim was something I did not know about. All I did know was that the best way to teach swimming was throw your pupil in the water, work the corners, and make him paddle. It worked in most cases, and I was a success as a teacher even in those days.

My sister, Pearl, also became a part of all this, participating in different ways. Pearl was two years younger than I, somewhat serious, and an intense person. This was a trait that all of us had inherited, and it showed itself from time to time. Girls are always better students—at least I thought so then, and Pearl probably learned more in Hebrew classes than any of us. She graduated both from Hebrew elementary and high school, while I only finished Hebrew elementary school. She also acquired a great love for tradition and an appreciation for the synagogue and what it represented. Pearl matured early and she, too, was left with wounds that never healed, because of the difficulties we encountered in growing up.

I was always athletic in some way, even as a young boy. I ran, swift as a deer, and I prided myself that no one on the street could run as fast as I did. There were many who challenged me, but I was unquestionably the winner, always. At least, that's the way I remember it. I did not fare as well as a fighter, but fight I did—at the drop of a hat. Now this is something that is difficult for me to interpret. I consider myself a mild person, yet when driven to anger—and this has always been an instantaneous response—I fight like a tiger in a cage. I didn't just have one fight, but perhaps fifty, or even more. These fights were not for supremacy, or for power, for I was a tall, thin kid while some of my opponents were broad, heavier, and bigger-boned. But fight I did, and many was the day that I came home with a bloodied face and nose! What I fought about is still a mystery, though at the time I felt it was necessary. It can be said that I learned how to use my hands well, and even though I suffered in the process of learning, there was much that could be said for this training. (In contrast, my son has never had a fist-fight with anyone in his whole life).

But sports were not to be my destiny, for Ma did not agree with the theory that a healthy body makes a healthy mind. She abhorred sports and there was many a time that she would destroy copies of the Sport Story Magazine that I was reading. This did not deter my ambition to become a track star; I made the team at Patrick Henry Junior High the first year I tried out. It was a memorable experience, but my athletic career was short-lived. I was forced to curtail athletics and go to work part-time after school. This meant a seven-period school day instead of the usual nine, and I was required to obtain a work permit. How I ever obtained a work permit at such an early age is still a mystery to me, and in all probability the man who issued it probably couldn't have cared less.

My mother cried when I told her that I had taken a job selling newspapers. In those days, paper hustlers were rough and tough, and she was worried about my contacts with the so-called lower elements of society. But there was no other choice, and I was happy to get the job. I had the "hot" corner under the bridge at 55th and Euclid, hustling sheets for two cents and pocketing one-half cent per paper as a commission. Some of you may remember the paper hustler on the corner, always shrieking out the headlines as he shoved a paper in your hand. That was me! I learned to move fast, selling my papers as good as the best. Fifty cents a day was my usual take, and that was a lot; mother accepted it quietly. Maybe the boys were rough and tough, but I didn't feel contaminated or affected in any way. In fact, it probably did me more good than harm.

On the weekends Pa took me to the old wholesale market

on Broadway, bordering Woodland. I am always asked by people who know me if my business was an inherited one. Not that there is any shame to this, for I would have been glad to take any business over when I started out, but this was not my good fortune. Of course, you cannot compare going to work with your father at twelve years old to the actual work habit, but if you knew anything about this kind of work, you would understand. One of the strange facets of my father's business was in the choice of specialties from which he made his living; it was certainly a part of the total produce business, but it would be impossible to select a more difficult aspect of the business: Watermelons. Watermelons were the Summertime Deal, going from early May to the middle of September. Next came the Wine Grape Deal, from October to mid-November. And then, as a finale, there was the two-week Wholesale Christmas Tree Deal.

These sorts of "deals" were the entry-level escapades for all of the merchants who were looking for a small business to start out in: It required little capital, and only a small shed to cover the merchandise. More and more thoughts flood my mind as I remember those bygone days; the past seems to come back to life.

The old wholesale market had its beginning in the heart of the downtown area. It began on East 12th and Woodland, and covered all of Woodland Avenue on both sides of the street until it reached Eagle and Bolivar. Broadway was also the same kind of street, with merchants housed in old buildings from East 18th to East 30th. It was not the kind of market we have now, for it was constituted of an unorganized group of buildings of every size and description, with some poor and some good storage facilities. Refrigeration had not yet entered the scene, and most of the warehouses had only the most primitive facilities. Loading and unloading areas were haphazard, and only in a few instances were there sufficient spaces for loading trucks.

There were many interesting names on the doors of those buildings, for the wholesale market represented the birth of independence for the small merchant. Only in America could one hope to put up a sign saying, "I am my own boss, in business to serve you, even though my name is Rini, Catalano, or Cohen." These were men that exemplified the greatness of America, for this was more than a dream. There were only a handful of merchants out of a possible total of two hundred who had more than a rudimentary education. Many of them still spoke with a distinct native accent from Italy, Greece, Russia, Poland, or who knows where. All of these men were hardened, determined fighters. Life was not easy for them, and if the business required opening up at midnight and working till late afternoon, so what? It was their own business, and who could ask for more than that.

The markets attracted many kinds of people, all of whom are a part of something that inherently makes them unique. For the men who owned those businesses, the development period was one in which they learned instinctively how to protect their interests. They learned how to talk to bankers, railroad men, brokers, and farmers, even if they had difficulty speaking good English. There was also the matter of money. It is hard for the average person to comprehend the amount of money that is transacted in the wholesale food business. Money was like water, and it trickled through your fingers. The sky was the limit for those merchants who engaged in speculation, for there were highs that could be attained that would make your head spin. By the same token, the lows were just as extreme, sometimes leaving a speculator without a dime. There were men, however, who opted to follow the normal patterns of business, hammering out a little each day; this allowed a man to make a living wage that brought some comforts to his life. These were the men who remained in the business until they died—none of them retired.

Watermelons, My Father's Dream

For my father, life was not that simple. He had too many other problems. Always undercapitalized, he had to search for a partner. In most cases, the partner would have the money, while my father would do all the work for half of the profits. This was a business that required each owner to use his mind as well as his body in order to generate earnings.

Why anyone would choose an item like watermelons as

a specialty is beyond my comprehension. Even today it is one of the most difficult produce items to handle. May was the month when they first began to ship, but if you know anything about watermelons, they didn't get really good until mid-June. (That still holds true). So for the first month you sold only to let people know that you were "in the deal," because most of the melons were not ripe-looking, had only a fair taste, and were over-priced. Trouble, did I say? Double trouble! Watermelons came in and were sent back for credit because they were pink, cracked, over-ripe, or broken. You name it, that's what happens with shipments of watermelons.

But my father believed in watermelons. He thought they were the up and coming thing. He insisted that people had to have them, and he would buy the first and last carloads religiously, regardless of price. It was not for the money he made, or attempted to make, but for his pride in receiving the first carload. How proud he was when it arrived! It was as if someone had given him the entire world on a platter. This was his only way to tell the world: I, Max Feren, am a man to be reckoned with—I am the Watermelon King!

He constantly experimented with watermelons, trying to learn from past performance which varieties would sell the best. Even though there have been many changes in watermelon varieties, the principles remain the same: Watermelons are either large or small, round or long, and differ only in color or striping. It was my father's belief that every good restauranteur should serve watermelon, featuring the long, green Tom Watson melon. (The Tom Watson was the leading slicing variety at that time; the Charleston Gray and other varieties have since replaced it).

Unfortunately, watermelons are a lot like people: they look beautiful outwardly, but when you get around to know them, they don't live up to your expectations. The Tom Watson watermelon represented to me, at least, the many things that could go wrong in a watermelon deal. Die-hards never learn, and my father was someone who insisted that he could not be in the watermelon business without a carload of those long melons. He seldom made any money on that variety, for he was constantly at the mercy of his customers because of the over-supply.

July 4th week has always been recognized as the week for watermelons. It is the peak watermelon period of the year. I remember one of the coldest July 4th weeks in our history—at least it proved to be that way financially. Pa was loaded to the hilt with fourteen train cars of melons, maybe a total of fifteen to twenty thousand units, and the weather turned exceptionally cold. Can you understand what affect that had on our morale? How about the winter we were going to face, for we were like the squirrel family, gathering all of our acorns in the summer to get us through the long winter.

It was a cold, miserable winter for us that year, and financially we never got even. This was not all that happened, for Pa was determined to make watermelons the kind of dessert fruit that people had to have. His faith in this fruit was unfathomable, even in the face of calamity. Never did a season go by that he did not invest in a storage facility that he hoped would enable him to store watermelons until Christmas. His beliefs were strong, and he backed them up financially with his investment, but the watermelons always disintegrated long before they were supposed to.

One year, he used paraffin wax to seal the watermelons' pores. Another time, he painted an entire carload with a strong paint, hoping that this would enable them to last. Then there was the year he painted the fruit with a heavy coating and stored them in the largest commercial storage plant in Ohio, the Federal Cold Storage Company. This might have been successful if the pipes in the storage plant had not leaked ammonia, dripping the poison liquid on the entire lot of watermelons. Pa was heartbroken each time he met with failure. And each failure brought financial disaster. He did not live in an age like ours, in which anything from any part of the world is available to us, any time of the year.

What have I learned from my father's exploits and my own? I've learned that the market is the face of the world; it mirrors man's basic nature in his fight for survival. On that battlefield we see all the hate, bitterness and jealousy that man is capable of. Even the language of the market is strong and forceful, replete with the use of four-letter words and profanity. There are no subtleties, nor is there ever any question what your competition is trying to do. But the one thing that makes the market unique is the world it represents. Here in this separate world the drama of life is unfolding before us.

The men that play on this stage are not any different than the banker or executive who is dressed impeccably in fine clothing; their goals are all the same, and the same antagonism and competition exists. The banker who would like to charge all that he could in interest, is not any different than the merchant who takes a merciless profit on any of the items he has purchased. The worker is the same misunderstood person, whether he works in a factory or in the market; his complaints and gripes are the same, and so are his ultimate goals. Given a chance to steal, many people will take advantage of it. On the other hand, those who are honest remain that way, in or out of the market.

All of this reiterates my philosophy that the world of the market is like an open book: our love and hate are hidden under the same cover. This is why the market has been so much a part of my life. It has given me every opportunity to express my feelings. I have never had any compunction about telling anyone I disliked him, or that he has mistreated me. There may have been some question about the use of terms I may have used to express myself, but in the true spirit of godliness, I only said the things I truly felt, in the manner I knew the individual I was speaking to would understand.

When all is said and done, this was the life I loved. This was the life I chose. The life of the market satisfied my deepest, heartfelt emotions. It was a place where I felt completely alive.

"Pushing It" In The Depression

The depression struck when I was 17 years old. When the depression hit us, it hit us hard. Things became tough financially and there were no jobs to be had. There was still an opportunity for me to Mohawk, but I was getting tired of walking six to eight miles a day to sell my "Mohawk" products. (Mohawking was selling items like aspirin, razor blades, jerky, shoe laces and other sundry items directly to the public going door to door to homes, or more typically to businesses, such as bars and saloons).

In the part of Euclid Avenue in front of the May Company, I saw a pushcart peddler selling fresh fruit everyday. He seemed to get a fair amount of action and after talking to the owner of the pushcart, he said, "This is a busy spot and I get lots of traffic, so I make out well here." I did not think to ask him how he got permission to use the spot or anything else about his business. I could see that it had potential and worked well for him.

I figured that I might be able to successfully do the same thing as that pushcart vendor, so I got a pushcart, picked up some different fruits and some vegetables, and I set up a stand at Fourth and Prospect, far enough away that it would not be a conflict with the pushcart man in front of the May Company on Euclid Avenue. It worked out well for a few days. It was an active spot I chose and I got a lot of action. I had it made—at least I thought I did.

I was standing there about noontime with a pushcart full of everything good, just waiting for the lunchtime crowd. I saw a person walking towards me and didn't give it another thought. He then walked over to me quietly and said, "Do you have a permit?"

I was stunned. "What kind of permit do I need, sir?" I asked.

"First of all," he said, "you need to have a license to sell food. Secondly, you need a permit from the May Company allowing you to use part of their property."

I was flustered, aggravated and I answered him curtly, "Does the pushcart peddler on Euclid Avenue have a permit?"

"I'm sure he does," answered the man, "but I'm talking to you right now. If you don't have a license or a permit I'm going to take you in."

"What about my pushcart and my fruit?" I asked.

"That is your problem. You are going to jail because you broke the law," he replied. There was no way to talk him out of this situation and he led me off to court. My pushcart was left behind, unattended.

The courtroom was full of people who had been charged with one thing or another. After an hour or two of waiting, my name was called and I came before the judge.

"What is your name, young man?" the judge asked.

I answered, "Maury Feren."

"You have been charged with violating law number three, selling food without a license and having no permit to use space belonging to another company. How do you plead?" the judge asked, and I had no answer. The situation had made me angry, desperate, and ready for a real fight. I knew nothing about how a court operated.

Finally, I said to the court, "I'll tell you my predicament. I am the sole provider for my family. There are no jobs out there of any kind. It is the only way I can make enough money to bring home for my family. The system does not offer help to anyone. All you want to do is to take away my source of income. It is not only unfair, it is a travesty. What do you want me to do? Let my family go hungry, or go out and steal? I'm only trying to survive."

The judge listened, even though I had shouted at him. "Young man," he said, "you have broken the law. Laws are made to protect people, not to hurt them. I should penalize you, but I am not going to do that today. However, if this occurs another time, you will go to jail. I won't let you go off so easily next time."

I recognized that I was being given another chance. Somehow, the judge had been moved by my outburst. He understood my dilemma. "Thank you, sir," I said. "I appreciate your understanding." When I returned to my pushcart and stand, all that was left was the empty cart. What did I expect?

A MOHAWKER LEARNS
ABOUT LEMON POOL

This is a story about lemons, not real lemons, but "Lemon Pool". I would bet that you never heard the term, nor would you know its meaning. Neither did I, but it was a lesson in life that I'll never forget.

In my early youth, I used to "Mohawk". That was a term used for someone who sold sundry items on the street, either wholesale or retail. I would purchase cards of aspirin, razor blades, meat jerky, shoelaces and other sundry items that I could resell at bars, cafés, restaurants and confectionary stores. These cards were purchased from a local company, State Novelty, located on West 6th Street in Cleveland, part of our "downtown," so to speak. There were many other Mohawkers like myself who sold the same products, starting from downtown and going from East to West on the major streets of the city.

I always preferred to work St. Clair Avenue, because there were at least one hundred bars and cafes on the street. This was so because it was at the heart of Cleveland's industrial manufacturing area. When the average blue-collar worker finished his shift, it was likely that he would stop at a bar to have a drink with his fellow workers. There were many places he could seek liquid refreshments. Even in depressed times, there were thousands of men working in this area. It was my beat to work from West 6th Street downtown, to the Fisher Body plant about 150th Street. Remember, I traveled by foot and with a backpack of goods to sell.

I was walking on or about 55th Street one day when a plain looking young guy stopped me, seeing my bag and said, "What's your name? What are you carrying in your bag?"

I replied, "I'm Maury Feren and I'm Mohawking, selling sundry items to bars and cafes around town."

"You look familiar," he said. "You from the 105th Street area?"

I answered, "I am. I live there."

"Do you know Joe Capp, Davey Weisman and his buddy Maxie Bloom?"

I wondered how he knew these guys. We were a long way from East 105th Street. I answered, "Sure I do, how do you know them?"

"I've been around," he said. "Those guys have known me a long time." That was his opener.

I thought it was strange. He didn't look as if he came from the East 105th Street area, but he knew something about each one of the guys he mentioned. It was noontime and I was tired. The day hadn't been going so well, so when he asked, "Do you play pool?" I replied, "No, I've never played, nor do I have any interest in learning."

His answer perked me up a bit. He said, "How would you like to make some easy money?"

"I don't play pool," I said, "so how could I do that?"

"Easy, man," he said. "I'm really a good player. Trust me! There is a guy in the poolroom across the street that thinks he is a champ, but I can take him with one hand behind my back. Do you have any money on you, Maury?"

By this time we had become more closely acquainted and I had begun to call him Joey. I said, "I have a little, but I'm not interested in learning anything involving pool."

His answer was a pat one: "Don't do anything yet; let me show you what I can do and then make your own decision."

I thought, "What could it hurt to see what he was talking about?" We entered the poolroom and he addressed one of the guys standing by the pool table and asked him if he wanted to play.

"Sure," the guy said, "for how much?"

"A quarter a game," Joey responded. I gave him the quarter and the game began. It was so easy for Joey; the balls just flew into the corners, as if they were magnetized. Four games later he had won every match just as easy as eating pie.

Then Joey became serious. "Do you have any extra money on you?" he queried. "It will be the easiest money you ever made."

I was a little uneasy about this and I hesitated for a moment. This looks like a sure thing, I thought. So I pulled out all the money I carried with me that day and gave it to Joey to bet.

Well, it isn't hard to figure out how it ended. Joey was good, but his opponent was even better this time around. In a few minutes, the game was over. So was all my money. What could I say? I knew immediately that it was a set-up. Sometime later when I told the story to a friend he said, "Do you know what the name of the game is that you played? It is known in the trade as 'Lemon Pool.'" It was more than a game; it was a life lesson.

SIZE MATTERS
Selling Cucumbers in the Market

My first job in the Northern Ohio Food Terminal found me working for the Thomas M. Rini Company in 1936. The Rini Company was the second largest commission house among 50 or 60 merchants in the industry at that time.

In the early years of produce marketing, there were many times that the farmers and the shippers would consign their product to a particular company who specialized in that produce crop. The term "commission" indicates how the transaction would be handled. The receiver of those products (crops) would sell them for the shipper or farmer. The seller could send in the total returns of that shipment and then deduct the commission. That charge would vary from 10 to 15%. The seller was morally bound to get the best price he could and to send back honest returns. It made sense to do that honestly because your reputation depended on it in the industry. However, there were many times when the market was flooded with product, so the returns were especially poor.

Today we do not think of cucumbers as an important vegetable. It is sort of a decorative vegetable and it is not used in proportion to its past history. Years ago, they would do pickling in barrels and jars. Cucumbers were used as an appetizer and as a basic ingredient, in addition to sweet and sour pickles.

Beginning in early spring, the Rini Company would receive four to five freight car shipments of cucumbers. There would be odd sizes, with the heaviest groupings in the big sizes; those would be sold to European ethnic communities, mainly the Polish people. The smaller sizes would be sold to fancy markets, while the medium sizes could go to the regular grocery stores. You have to remember that there were five hundred bushels of cucumbers in a carload! These shipments were mostly from South Carolina.

In contrast to today, there were many hucksters who knew where to sell those cucumbers, so there were potential buyers if the price was low enough. In the 1930's, hucksters would use their own trucks, rent a horse and wagon, or use a built up auto that could carry enough produce by using the roof and back end of the car.

There was a major problem in this situation, however. The hucksters were a separate breed of men; they were motivated differently than the average working man. If they felt that the price was too high on any produce item they wanted to buy, they would rather not work at all than limit their profit. In fact, these hucksters would rather play cards or go to the poolroom upstairs of the restaurant in preference to going out to huckster, unless they believed the price was really cheap. It created a dilemma because they filled a definite need for closing out the remaining last remnants of any carload of produce of certain produce crops.

Let me give you an idea of what would happen in terms of dollars. There are 500 bushels of cucumbers in a rail car load. I was in complete charge of that sale. Remember, 1000 retail merchants went through that market everyday. The food terminal was at that time responsible for 90% of all edible produce sold in the Cleveland area. That is how important it was. Today, the terminal represents about 30-35% of all the fresh edible food shipments in the Cleveland area.

I would sell 100 bushels of extra fancy cucumbers to the carriage trade, 110 cucumbers average per bushel at $2.25 a bushel. The next size up, approximately 90 count per bushel, I would sell about 150 bushels at $1.75 a bushel. I'm then left with about 250 bushels, and these are about 60 to 75-count bushels of big, giant cucumbers. I would, over time be able to pickup 50 or more sales to ethnic growers or the Polish trade at about $1.50 a bushel. I still have 200 bushels to go. You have to recognize that this is a perishable product with a three-day wholesale shelf life. I start to offer these cucumbers at $1.25 and am pushed to sell at $1.00 a bushel. I still have, even after this, 50 to 75 bushels yet to sell. My last move is to offer them at .75 a bushel—reluctantly, but they have to go.

Now all of this sounds quite easy, but it wasn't. The hucksters learned to stand by to get the best price. I had to fight to get the best price for the shipper. You also have to consider how much a dollar could buy in those years, in the 1930's. We were just coming out of the depression and things had just begun to look up. The hucksters of yesterday are no longer to be seen on the streets. It was a way of life at that time, but it disappeared along with the small family grocery store.

GETTING PRESSED
My Experience as a Wine Grape Merchant

Visualize this experience, back in the 1920's, 30's and early 40's: Saturday was generally the day the immigrants would come down to the market to purchase wine grapes. This was a family trip, and you would see the husband, wife and the children there to make the purchase. There were also only six wine grape merchants that offered these grapes for sale. The outdoor displays would be loaded with piles of boxed grapes, separated by variety. It takes twenty-five boxes well filled with grapes to produce fifty gallons of wine. If the grapes were a slack pack, it created a problem. You needed to be sure that the grape boxes you purchased were filled well because the pressed grapes would not fill the pressing barrel otherwise. It would also mean that you would have to make an extra trip for more grapes, probably from another lot. Oftentimes, there were merchants who could speak to the immigrant families in their native tongues. It was a battle of wits, as they negotiated price. Yet in the end there was little chance that the customer could beat the rap as there were a dozen dealers and they were all in cahoots with one another, setting one price in every unit stand! It turns out that the salesmen had the advantage to begin with.

Fundamentally, most of the merchants were honorable and fair, according to their standards. I was just a young man then, working as a part time wine grape salesman after hours during the late afternoon and on weekends—so I became part of the fix, willingly or not. It was not my best experience, but it is worth telling the story about the way it really was.

Money was scarce. If you could cut a few corners here or there, it meant some extra dollars for the dealer. There were "skinners", the dealers who showed heavily packed samples. When it came time to make the delivery, they would shake the boxes up, take out two or three pounds and repack the extra weight into other boxes, since the original boxes were open-faced and marked with the weight, everything was visible to the buyer. However, the delivery agents would unload the boxes fast as lightening, then away they would go. By the time the buyer arrived home, the boxes had begun to settle and he would see some of the empty spaces between the bunches of grapes. However, he had already paid for the grapes, so there was nothing he could do. (Of course, when he came back the next year, he was more wary. It was always a battle of wits, with the customers becoming smarter every year).

I worked for a combine of twelve merged merchants. The trade called them "the clique". I was hired because I had a solid reputation as a good talker and a reliable salesman. It was no easy task to try to persuade a foreign born person who barely understood what you said that you would give him fresh grapes from a new car lot that would be tightly packed and that they would be the variety he wanted and not a substitute.

There are two things of importance to know: It takes 25 full boxes to fill a 50-gallon barrel of wine. The barrel must be full to ferment properly. If you are short weighted, you have to return to buy enough grapes to fill the barrel. The similarity of certain grape varieties can fool you at times, but it is essential you know the varieties that serve you best and produce the wine you want.

For example, the Malaga grape is similar to the Muscat; however, it is harder, has less juice, leaves a wine odor and cost considerably less than the Muscat, which is considered the "jewel" of the home wine making industry. Often, the dealers would re-mark the boxes because of the outward similarity of the grapes. The dealer could pick up a dollar a box or more. Although this was not a common practice, it did take place. Consequently, the wine that was produced by the customer was a disappointment to them.

The Carignane and the Zinfandel have the same general appearance too. But the difference in taste, flavor and juice content was like day and night. The Zinfandel was rich and blood red when squeezed, while the Carignane was light red, with less juice and not easily detectable. If a customer was given a bum batch of Carignane with the impression he was getting Zinfandel, he would come back complaining either about the weight, the variety or the quality of the grapes he purchased. He would swear at the merchant who had fooled him and then walk into the same trap next door with a different dealer from the same clique.

Looking back, I can still remember this picture: A big, husky Hungarian man who came with his wife and children to buy grapes. His reddish brown mustache was thick and heavy, almost drooping down to his chin on both sides of his face. This was not an unusual appearance for a Hungarian man of that generation. His wife was dressed in a typical old country Hungarian manner: A black dress, no makeup, hard veined hands and the look that comes from a life of hard work.

"Muscats, I want," the man would say. "Last year, I get fooled. No more fooled. I want real Muscats, no Malaga." I did not need an explanation. I knew the story. He had been taken last year by another merchant. I don't speak Hungarian, so all I could say was, "Me give you good grapes, real muscato (Muscats). Me treat you right. Fill 'em up boxes, good price." It was a hard fight, so difficult for me to convince him I would be fair. The wife was even tougher to please. Although she spoke poor English, she still made me understand what she expected of me. Perseverance finally won out and I persuaded them that they could watch the boxes being loaded and even help the driver. This assured them of my honest intentions.

This was the drama for the wine grape merchant's dealings of yesterday. It was a battle for survival. The annual wine grape purchase was an important one for the home wine maker in those days. If you were an honest merchant, the competition would beat you. It was easy to say, "Why should I loose? This man can afford it better than I." That was the rationalization of the merchant. Were those the good old days? For those of us who remember, it should give us pause to think. There was always some kind of scam. Although this was a minor one, it still stands out in my memory of what it took to make a so-called living during the depression.

Potatoes—The Con Deal

Have you ever been conned? I have, so I must tell my story of how it happened. The second largest distributor of wholesale produce had hired me for my first good job in the food business, T. M. Rini, Inc. I was employed as a buyer as well as a salesman. This happened in 1940, and one of my jobs gave me the opportunity to buy local produce. The medium size truck that could carry five tons of weight had just begun to become available at that time; these were Ford and Chevrolet trucks with dual wheels and a stake body. This was a smaller truck than those used by larger haulers, but it allowed the smaller farmer or shipper to haul produce from longer distances. The new vehicles allowed a trucker to load one hundred fifty-pound bags and deliver them with no mechanical or weight problem. My friend, Dave Marein was a trucker who specialized in hauling potatoes. These were grown in Mantua, Middlefield, and Smithville in Ohio.

Freight cars arriving at Northern Ohio Food Terminal, 1930's.

It was a cold wintry day when Dave approached me and said, "I'm stuck with a good load of round white potatoes and I can give you a cheap price on them because the original customer reneged on the order." He assured me that they were good. I examined the open bags and saw that they were satisfactory and agreed to the purchase and the price. I was not experienced enough to recognize that though there was a canvas tarp over the potatoes, the sides of the stake-body truck were open, which left the potatoes exposed to the wind and the cold. I paid for the load of potatoes with a company check, never realizing that this load of potatoes had been frozen.

I unloaded the potatoes. The next day, I was shocked to

see a pool of water around the potato pile. They had begun to thaw and there was potato juice all over the floor. Frozen potatoes can't be salvaged. They became a total loss. I was so ashamed when I had to face my boss and tell him my story. He was understanding, only because I'm sure he may have had a similar experience in his produce career.

I talked to Dave Marein a few days later. I no longer considered him a friend, because I am sure he knew the potatoes were frozen. When I asked him about it, he said, "When I sold you the potatoes they were good. If you didn't handle them properly, it is not my problem." He refused to discuss it, nor would he make any adjustment. We never spoke again for years after that incident. When we finally did, he still insisted that I had mishandled the potatoes. I can only say, "Live and learn."

Early morning activity at the Northern Ohio Food Terminal.

A "Good Time" with Strawberries!

When the strawberry season comes around, it reminds me of my first contact with them. It was the 1930's and jobs were scarce, with the Depression fully underway. The only way for me to make any money was to go out and huckster. What is "huckstering?" I would buy a few crates of strawberries, have the wholesaler store them for me for that day and I would go out to try to sell them, house to house.

At first, I tried the neighborhood surrounding the market. It was a poor depressed area, mostly black, with terrible housing conditions—Orange Avenue in Cleveland, Ohio to be specific. So I walked down the street crying out, "Berries, beautiful berries, twenty-nine cents a quart!" I sold a few quarts here and there, then out of the blue, a heavy-set black lady stuck her head out of the window and called, "Boy, I'll trade you berries for a good time!"

Congestion and activity at the market, 7:00am

I was taken aback. I was only eighteen years old, just out of high school, and I had never found myself in that situation before. It was an eye opener! The hot sun beat down on my wooden crate of berries and they began to melt. I could feel my heart beating as I ran for my life. It was a moment I will always remember: I can still see that woman, with her head and half of her naked body sticking out of the window, and the berry juice running down my shirt. That was an experience I'll never forget!

But there is more to this story. We all have forgotten when strawberries in winter were almost a dream. In my wholesale produce days in the 1940's in mid-December, the first strawberries that were packed came from Homestead, Florida, shipped by Wishnazski, Nathan and Company. Those berries were packed in twenty-four pint cases and came by Railway Express. Our allotment was twenty-five crates. Transport from Florida took three days and receiving the strawberries was like welcoming an important personage. I want you to imagine opening up a crate of beautiful strawberries, glistening with moist freshness and shining in their brightness. It was almost like the sun had come out on the coldest day of the year. What a joyful experience that was!

Carving "I Love You" In Watermelons

I don't know of any love affair that matched the courtship of Bess and me. The year was 1936. We met through my best friend, Harry Zinner, and began to date. As time went by, Bess and I began to spend more and more time together and our romance flourished.

Bess worked at The Bloch Company, off of Superior Avenue. Her father was the foreman of the plant and they would drive together, morning and night. Even though we began to date seriously, I don't think either of us contemplated our future: We enjoyed being together and didn't look farther than that.

My father was a wholesale watermelon dealer located in the Northern Ohio Food Terminal at 40th Street, off Woodland Avenue. Since he could not afford a regular hired driver, he would wait till noon for me to finish my job at Rini's, and then I would drive the truck and take over the deliveries. My two brothers, both much younger, could pitch watermelons, but they couldn't drive. I finished working around 5 o'clock, hopped in the back of the truck with my brothers, and my father drove home. That was the end of a twelve-hour day that had begun at 4am!

As we drove home—at least half of the time—Bess and her father would cross paths with us even though she lived on East 118th and Kinsman, and I lived in the Glenville area off of East 105th and Superior Avenue. I'll never know for sure if that coincidence was planned or not! But picture this: I would be sitting in the back of the stake-body truck, my shirt off, filthy from railroad coal dust. (The soot came from unloading watermelons from open freight cars). When Bess saw my father's truck coming, she would wave to me—and that became the best part of my day! She waved even though I was blackened, my hair tousled and totally unkempt. That wave of her hand was the beginning of our future.

As fate had its role to play, Bess had an uncle who peddled produce every day. Every once in a while, he would stop by my father's watermelon stand and purchase a few watermelons for his route. One day, in one of my artistic moments, I carved Bess's name on a watermelon and asked Uncle Brick to deliver it to her as a favor to me. Bess and I were eighteen years old and our relationship was beginning to move along. Soon I was brave enough to carve "Bess I love you" on a watermelon! Thus began a long courtship. Carving love notes on watermelons became a regular occurrence over the next few years.

Unfortunately, Uncle Brick had a heart attack and died in my place of business. I tried to give him artificial respiration, but it was not enough. He died before the ambulance from St. Vincent Hospital arrived. At that time, CPR hadn't been invented and the only method of resuscitation available was artificial respiration. I realized that at least a thousand people a day passed through the market and that I could be of assistance with my basic first aid knowledge, learned at the YMCA. Over the years I set up a program so that injured people could be given first aid at my place of business; it became so important that I purchased two oxygen tanks to help emergency cases. Success is always limited in heart attacks, but I did manage to help many people who would have died otherwise. I figure I helped at least a third of them.

Bess's and my road to marriage was marked with many lapses: We would be "on" for a while, and then "off." There was no particular reason for that; it was just the way it went. The fact was our love was so strong there was no way we could stay apart for very long. We would often attend the same weddings and dances, and would end up together again by the end of the evening. Then it all came together.

When we were twenty-three years old, we made the decision to get married. The love we had for each other never waned in sixty-seven years. We enjoyed a marriage made in Heaven and the Fates were with us.

My Brother Hal

A Basketball Story

Oftentimes life hits you with some interesting shots. Why do I use the word "shots"? You'll find out as I tell the story. My brother, Hal, who was four years younger than I, was a terrific all around athlete. He played basketball in junior high and did well even though he was much shorter than anyone else on the team.

But he had heart. He moved like a demon possessed him, fast as lightening. No one could stop him from getting to the basket and he had a good shooting percentage, no matter whether he was in the thick of the action or on the free-throw line. He was the star of the team. It was a show just watching him cut through his opponents on his way to the basket.

But then, in 1930, it happened. For some reason or other, he had a physical examination—I don't remember how or why it came about. The diagnosis was not good, but mercifully we didn't understand much about it at that time. The doctor called it a "leaking heart." What does that mean? We were to find out somewhere along the way. In the meantime, Hal was forbidden to participate in sports for a year. That was a stopper. He must have gone stir crazy.

One day Hal fell and broke his arm. I put him on a streetcar going down 105th Street and took him to Mt. Sinai Hospital. We had no family doctor in those days. If we had a problem, we would go to the nearest hospital—if we could pay for the services. After his arm healed he resumed normal activities.

When he was nineteen years old, after graduation, Hal took a job for the Mongrief Furnace Company. His job entailed traveling to small towns to sell furnace inspections; he was part of a team that would inspect your furnace and usually find something to fix. Michigan was the first state he went to. I never found out much about his job, but you can be sure it was no picnic.

Because he was single when war was declared, Hal volunteered for the Air Corps, hoping to train as a pilot. He was sent to Texas along with Julie Foxman, another

Clevelander. Julie made the cut, but Hal did not because his medical records showed that he had a deviated septum, a condition that limits your breathing. An unrestricted airflow was essential for flying. Hal was very disappointed. The army shipped him off to London, England. He never gave up trying to become a pilot and finally, as the war claimed many casualties, the Air Corps relented and shipped him back to the USA for training. Julie was an instructor there. Hal married Myrna Levine during this period. He became a Warrant Officer and never went overseas.

After the war, Hal became a partner in the M.B. Feren Co. and was an integral part of the business for many years. When he hit forty years old he had a heart attack, probably a result of what the doctor had called a "leaking heart"—it must have been the determining factor. Ironically, Dr. Bronfman, a heart surgeon at the Cleveland Clinic, met with Hal, Sonny, and me. At that time the heart bypass operation was in its infancy. Dr. Bronfman, who had performed a small number of these procedures under the supervision of Dr. Crile, wanted Hal to undergo a heart bypass. Hal's own doctor believed he could help Hal just as well with medication. Sonny and I stood by, listening to everything the doctors said, however the decision was for Hal and Myrna to make.

Who knows if the bypass would have been successful? We'll never know. Hal passed away at forty-four years of age, so young with so much to live for: three children and a wife. They missed out on so much because of his early death. They missed the best years of his life.

MY WARTIME MEMOIRS
1943 - 45

"Pre-Pearl Harbor father!" What did that mean in 1942 when we were already involved in the war? That is how I was classified, and for a short time I believed, along with hundreds of other men in the same classification that I would not be drafted because I was married and had a family. Obviously it didn't matter.

So what did happen? Lets take a look back and re-examine the past. Who was Maury Feren in January 1943 when he left for basic training? I had been working more or less since I was thirteen, a product of an Orthodox Jewish home. This was not modem orthodoxy, as we know it today; it was different, yet there were many similarities. I'm spending time writing about orthodoxy, not because of my religiosity, but because it was and still is a part of who I am.

If we look closely at my past history, you'll find there was a great deal there that was a reflection of the times. I'm sure that as a family man—husband and father of a daughter who was the pride of my life—and an owner of a business, I believed that I knew it all. Little did I know how wrong I was.

The world I knew was bound up in particular ways. There were my friends, all Jewish of course, with similar values and a comparable cultural background. Religiously, I would say I was the one who had the most religious education and was the most observant. Everyone was of one sect at that time. There were no classifications. If you were Reform, it meant your religious practices were way out of the norm. Dietary laws for me were part of my understanding: There was no question about it, we didn't eat out, in restaurants or wherever. If we did, it would be in a kosher restaurant. When we went night clubbing with other couples, I would order a toasted cheese sandwich and a drink, and pass up the regular menu, even if it was a price-fixed menu. Up until the time I left for the army at age twenty-eight, this was a way of life. It was not a problem.

Before marriage, I would walk to Bess's home for courtship

at major holidays, Rosh Hashana, Yom Kippur, Passover two days, Shavuoth, etc. Six miles there, six miles back, even if it was past midnight when I left her house. It was not a problem. I never thought about it. Even then, my friends thought it was strange, but it never made any difference. This was a way of life. There are two things to remember: We did not observe Shabbat; Saturday was always a work day. We never thought about that either. So what you can gather from this is that in my environment, at least at home and in my community, I lived with Jews and observed in a great sense what I would term a "Jewish life," at least for that time.

The market: Here is where another entire dimension of my life took place. This was a raw life, literally a jungle. Knowing how to survive in this jungle took its toll. Everyone, mostly immigrant families and first generation Americans like myself, were fighting for economic security and recognition as Americans. It was no longer enough to be just Jewish. I wanted to be an integrated American, someone who was recognized as a successful part of the scene. The more successful, I believed was the easiest way to become recognized in those terms.

Who were the people I met? What role did they play in shaping my character? There were Italians, tough Italians, lots of them and they never let go of their toughness. It was their way to power. There were Europeans—Germans, Poles, Slavs—a few Arabs and a few Waspy-type Americans. However, the base was European Caucasians. And blacks. Yes, there were Negroes who worked in the market, blue collar, of course, if you could call it that. But that isn't the crux of the story. The point that I would like to make is the limitations there were in exposure to other people and other cultures.

BASIC TRAINING

Moving into the world of the army was almost like culture shock. It was also another life. Let's take a closer look at what went on. First of all, there was the shock of leaving home and my family. The initial shock was over, but the pain of parting remained, a permanent part of the two-year enlistment.

Maury, 28 years old, proud of his Army khakis; his
sister-in-law, Phyllis Keller stands behind him.

January 3rd, 1943, I left for Columbus where I took the train to Cincinnati, on my way to Spartanburg, South Carolina. Spartanburg, South Carolina, where was that? Must be some secluded country spot in the middle of nowhere. It was. But that did not matter, the place was unimportant. All of the basic training camps were in some dismal part of the country. Besides, they were all the same. They were built the same, barracks, recreation buildings, and the PX where you could buy food and luxury items, plus some basic items like toothpaste, shaving cream, etc. (The PX charged bargain prices, because I think my pay for the month was something like $100 or $125. That was because I was married and a father. Single men received around $75 or thereabouts).

Now take a look at my background. I would say I was generally athletic, not gifted, but a good example of a strong physical man. I played a little baseball when I was younger, fairly good, at least I thought I was, and I was an excellent runner. All of these attributes were of not much value in my world of business. But they did have certain advantages in the army. There were some other aspects that go into the development of this subject. My beginnings in the workplace were hard and tedious. From the time I was thirteen until I graduated at sixteen and a half years of age, I worked at least ten to twenty hours a week at various jobs, selling newspapers on the corner of Euclid and 55th, Saturdays at Uncle Louis ten to twelve hours, and teaching swimming a few hours a week. So work was not a problem. After graduation the work week began to extend to fifty to sixty hours or more. I don't even remember or count the time I put in working. When I started my business, I put in even longer hours. It didn't matter. I was finally working for myself, twenty-eight years old, fiery, strong, and ready to face the business world big time—and then the army hit me like a ton of bricks!

So here we have this guy, a workaholic in general terms, but I didn't think so, because I was doing something for myself. I was on my way to success, financially at least and I had a family, with our son, Alan, on the way.

Basic training begins. It's hiking, running, walking and calisthenics. Early morning rising, say about 7am, a half-hour for breakfast and reveille. That was terrific. I had been getting up for thirteen years at 3-4am! Lunchtime I think we had an hour or something close to that and we could sit down to eat. That was even better. I had never sat down to eat lunch. It was always a stand-up procedure: a sandwich gulped down and then back to the job. The best part of the day. We finished at 5pm, an eight-hour day. Who could think like that? That was a picnic compared to my previous work!

I had a problem, a major one. I was not tired after the day's training. Lonely, yes. The training became intense at times for me in terms of the mechanical requirements. I'll come to that shortly. But I did well in everything else. I could creep and crawl with the best of them. Calisthenics were the easiest thing for me. In physical competition on the simulated battlefield I came out fifteenth out of one thousand men. At that time, I considered myself an older person, twenty-eight years old, with most men in their late teens and early twenties. So I was older in that respect. When I look back, I can laugh at myself. But it's one thing to be athletic, it's another to be able to cope with the people, the instructors (the cadre) and the officers. That was the tough part.

Our cadre trainer, a guy named LeBlanc, was my idol. He moved like an Apollo figure and he could go through the routine like a masterful machine. I envied him. Besides, I wanted to be able to do that, so I could remain in the USA. They kept reminding us that after our seventeen-week basic training, we were going to go overseas, so we better learn to do it right. Over and over, you heard that refrain. It began to sound like a song that never left your head. But in the army, there are always rumors. Rumors keep you alive. They went like this: "We are leaving for the Pacific immediately; you'll never get a chance to go home first, no leave time. We are going over to Europe. We are going to retrain in another camp. All pre-Pearl Harbor fathers will not go overseas. Pre-Pearl Harbor fathers will be sent home in a few weeks." And on and on. Of course none of this was true. But this is what you lived on. It kept you going. There was hope. What else was there?

This is when we get to the heart of the army training. You

are looking at one angry guy, taken away from his family, leaving a business he had fought for and a personality that had never really taken orders well. Now I was in the thick of it. Angry. I think I was always angry. Ask me why? I can't tell you that. I don't know. Fighting. I guess I got into fights because, maybe, I was angry. I didn't like to be pushed around. I don't think I ever looked for a fight. They just happened, but it was never a singular occurrence. There were reasons. Every fight had a story and a reason. Who am I to judge my own responses?

ANTI-SEMITISM AT HOME AND ABROAD

There was plenty of anti-Semitism in the market, which I had just left. It was mostly from the immigrant Italians. They were the worst. "Morta Cristo," Christ killer, they would say when something occurred they didn't like. It did not take me long to figure out that the best way to quell those occurrences was to fight it out. There were quite a few of those fights in the market. Maybe many more than I remember. But they happened.

However, this was a new page for me. Now I was going to do something different. I was going to show them what a good Jew could really do. He would become the best soldier in the division. He would befriend everyone he could and do anything to maintain friendship and understanding. That was my goal. I read everything I could about anti-Semitism, trying to understand it so I could explain it to any of my critics if it should happen. It did not take long before I was accosted. "Hey, Jew boy, where are the rest of you? Staying home, raking in the dough, screwing our wives and girl friends. What few of you are in the army die in the rear someplace doing routine office jobs. What the hell are you doing here? How did you happen to become an infantryman? Your kind don't even belong here."

Remember, I was not dealing with highly educated or sophisticated men. There were men here from every part of the country. The South, the North, Appalachia, Kentucky, California, Utah, Wyoming. You name it. They came from some places I had never heard of. The name "Jew" was synonymous with hate and misunderstanding. Try as I might, I made no headway trying to explain who I was and why there was no difference between us. They could not understand that. There was no way I could reach most of the men I met. Even though we were living through the trauma of separation and a strange life, we could not come together or bond in any way at all. It was a sad result. I had learned something about myself that I had never realized up until this time: I was Jewish and that did make me into a separate person. Although I was an American by my standards, I would always be a Jew in the eyes of those men who were intolerant of anyone who was not of their faith. It was disheartening and I was disappointed. I did try, time and time again. I did have a few verbal disagreements and I don't think I actually had any fistfights. But that was basic training. I knew I had to behave, or else. Or else maybe K.P. for a month; no leave time for town; stuff like that. You don't have to be brainy to figure that out. Besides, my real battle was with myself. I had lots to cope with. The loneliness never eased up. It was always there. And I was having difficulty with my rifle. That is, putting it back together after it was fired.

Let me tell you that story. Everything is going along well. One or two weeks have gone by. I can see myself out on the battlefield, pack on my back, shouldering arms, and marching off to the beat of a band and loud drums. Marching of course into the unknown. Flags are waving and people are clapping and music is everywhere. Who would have thought of the living hell I was yet to go through on the battlefield a few months later? Third week, rifle range. "Men, you will be firing an M1 Rifle. This rifle will never leave your side. It will be your mother, your father, your priest, your guide, and your third arm. You will carry it, treasure it, clean it, shine it and it will and always must be in perfect operating condition. Each day that you shoot it on the rifle range, it must be cleaned perfectly. For those of you who do not meet the inspection requirements, there will be no visits to town. You won't get to town until you can take apart your rifle and put it together again, perfectly clean."

Maury Feren knows in his heart, this will never happen.

I'll never get to town, because I know what is going to happen. The rifle will be my nemesis, and that was an understatement. It took me hours to discover why this rifle was so hard to put together. How can you put a rifle together if you put some of the pieces in backward? Why did they fit in backward and how do you get those pieces out once they are stuck there, because they were put in the wrong places? What a dilemma. I kept thinking if I am forced to stay here until I can put this rifle together, it just might not ever happen, unless someone helps me.

Who would be that someone? I don't know who finally came to the rescue, but he was truly a godsend. The next day on the rifle range was not as bad. I had a general idea of how to put the rifle together. Although I struggled twice as long as my friends and acquaintances, I did manage to put the rifle together. Putting a rifle together is one story, cleaning it another. "Spit and Shine." That is a common term in the army. I had yet to learn what it really meant. I would find out soon enough.

INSPECTION TIME, FOLLOWED BY K.P. DUTY

It happened more or less out of the blue. I had been inspected for clothing, for saluting, for bed-making, for cleaning our barracks, for standing at attention and for reveille. I truly was sick of inspections and the officers who inspected us. In fact, I was up to my neck in inspections. I thought they were idiotic and a waste of time and energy. I looked disdainfully on while the inspecting officer did his job. I knew that I was trying to be a good soldier, and if I tried I would not have any problems. I followed orders as they were given, good or bad, never answering back, but honestly trying to do a good job. My goal was to be the best soldier I could be. I also wanted the men in my outfit to recognize me as the best soldier who also was the best representative of his own people. That was a mental standard I set. I never deviated from that course. The tricks and turns the road took in my days in the army were not the result of my deviation from my goals, but were a result of the different routes the trail took.

It was not too much of a surprise to be confronted one bright afternoon after a day on the rifle range. "Inspection of your rifles, men,'" the sergeant called out. "Lieutenant Blah Blah Blah is here to inspect them. Attention! Shoulder arms. At ease, men." So in walks this fine looking looey, facing each man. As he walks up to me, he says, "Soldier, present arms for inspection." What a silly way to inspect. You go through a lot of unnecessary military commands, open and break open your rifle and the lieutenant looks in to check and see if it is clean. It is the open part that needs to shine and sparkle; any dot or semblance of a dark spot and that means your rifle isn't clean, at least by the standards of the army.

I came to attention. "Has your rifle been cleaned, soldier?"

"Yes sir," I respond.

"Do you call this rifle clean, soldier?"

"Yes sir," I reply in a weak voice. "I cleaned it for two hours. I believe it is clean."

"You call this clean?" he said in an exaggerated tone of negation. "It is not exactly my idea of a cleaned rifle."

By this time I had had my fill of all those inspectors, those false, embarrassing officers who only wanted to catch you off guard and incriminate you in some way for some minor infraction to show you who was in command. I lost my temper. That was easy for me, a common practice in my past life I used to do it all the time. But now was not the right time to lose it the way I did. I found that out, only too soon. My reply was spontaneous and affirmative. No question about that.

"You are not clean," I said. "This rifle is certainly clean."

Well, there was no immediate reply for a moment. Then a loud shout came out of this so-called even-tempered Lieutenant.

"K.P. for a week. You'll really find out what being clean is when you hit the kitchen all week."

I did, and there were no visits to town that week as well.

It was a tough week. I got through it and I only agonized more about my bad luck in being in the army at this time. I truly didn't know how good I had it for the moment. What lay ahead would make this place look like heaven.

MORE ABOUT ANTI-SEMITISM

Jewish soldiers were a rarity in my basic training outfit. I don't believe there were many of us. If there were, I did not know them, nor did they identify themselves as Jews. I did. I made my religion a part of me. I was an American soldier who was Jewish. I was proud of that and no one had better question it! I spent a great deal of time explaining Judaism and what it was, if there were listeners. Foolishly, I believed that people would like to know: If they found out what being a Jew meant, they would overcome the anti-Semitism they had been taught. My successes, if any, were rare. I don't really believe I made any progress. I may have gained respect, but I'm not sure of that either. I had an occasional confrontation. "Jew boy, where are the rest of you? At home, making the dough, getting the dames."

It was the same theme, over and over. No one seemed to care that there were Jews at the front, in the fighting lines, doing their part. All they wanted to do was stir up antagonism. Didn't they know that we were only two percent of the total population of the USA? They didn't want to know that. They only believed what they already knew: Jews were crooked, shrewd; we had all the money; we controlled the banks; and many of my fellow soldiers believed we had caused the war. Trying to explain any negative aspects of their theories was a waste of time. I tried and tried to be philosophical. It never paid off. Fighting was one way I could gain respect, but you can't fight the world. I quickly learned that. But that did not stop me from trying.

What do I remember most about my basic training? My desire and hope to be a good soldier; to fit into my company; do my work and to be one of the guys, a regular guy, one that could be counted on. I think I did that. I honestly believe I was successful on that score. I marched with the best of them. I was also a good marksman. I had high scores for shooting targets on the rifle range. I received the Good Conduct Medal. Laugh about that one. Don't laugh. That is the only thing that singles you out when you are a private in the army: your medals, your insignia, your war ribbons, where-you've-been ribbons, etc. It's your identifying story. When you go out wearing your ribbons and your medals, it tells a story. Your Good Conduct Medal means you've met certain requirements. Some men never got it. Others may have worked longer and harder to get it. It was the badge of acceptance. There was the Rifle Shooting Medal as well and some other basic ones, too. I was proud of that medal. I was a soldier now.

IRV

On the way, while all this was going on, I met Irv Berkson. What can I tell you about Irv? He was as different from me as anyone could be. He came from a different world and acted as if he was still a part of it. Six feet tall, one hundred seventy-five pounds or thereabout, good classic features—nondescript as a Jew, but fairly representative as a handsome man. He was well built, and let's say arrogant and lazy. Irv did not want to be a soldier from the word go. He let everyone know that. At our first encounter, I opened with a "Hi, stranger!" He replied in a somewhat negative manner that he wasn't too interested in making my acquaintance. We met a couple of times and he was a little more responsive. Where we clashed was what brought us together. It went like this: Irv is trying to find someone to replace him on a ten-mile hike with backpack. I hear him approach someone and offer twenty-five dollars to replace him. "Twenty-five dollars," he says. "I'll give you twenty-five right now. All you have to do is to call out "Yea" when they call out the name Berkson. They won't know the difference and you'll have the twenty-five dollars."

We are not talking peanuts here. Twenty-five dollars at that time was a third of a month's pay for a single man. What a shame for our people, I thought. "Irv," I said, "you are a Jew. You represent all of us. What you do and say reflects on every Jewish soldier these men will meet." Irv was quiet.

He listened. I don't know what he was thinking, but it was a start. Our friendship bloomed slowly, of course. Irv didn't understand where I was coming from, but he must have been listening. He stayed with me. Then it was K.P. time for him, for one reason or another. I don't remember that part. Again, he pulled the same thing, offering twenty-five dollars and getting away with it.

Irv Berkson became a life-long friend

Irv was the only guy in camp, a grown man, whose mother came down to see him. Everyone knew he was the rich kid on the block. He made no effort ever to try to explain that in any other way. Irv was actually pretty close in age to myself. He had lost a girlfriend whom he had spent a great deal of time loving. But at some point they broke up and he was carrying a broken heart within him when he was drafted. As the only boy in the family, his sisters always made a big fuss over him. He was the cat's meow in his own house and he carried that with him into the army.

THE FOOD PROBLEM

At that time I was struggling with the food in the army. At irregular intervals Bess sent me weekly rations of foods that I might eat, and always a hard salami. Packages never came on time, but would all hit at once, two or three combined packages would arrive. At that point, Irv and I would divvy up the perishables, and one time we buried the salami. Unfortunately, we forgot where we buried our cache and it was lost forever! It's one of those stories that we always talked about when we got together. Irv did finally put those Chicago habits behind him and began to act like a good soldier. We talked about that change many times when we got together. I don't know whether I was the impetus for sure, but he did realize that he needed to make a change and he did. As a finale to that part of the story, in the forty to forty-five years of our friendship, Irv went through life the same way—he was always given special attention! Somehow he managed to get his way and be a constant figure of attention. Both his first and second wives played along with him. Even in between wives, as a bachelor in his Gold Coast apartment, Irv and his pink Cadillac roadster remained a part of that same pattern. That was Irv's style. It never changed. How he fared in combat, I never found out. But he did make it, wound-free, and he was a combat infantryman, so he must have seen a lot.

I spent many happy occasions with Irv. From the first time that we met, until his dying moments, Irv was one of my idols. Maybe because he seemed to sail through life. Maybe it was his flair, maybe it was all cover-up. If it was, he sure played the game for a long time. Irv deserves more than a passing moment. He made my life so much easier in the army, because he listened. He knew how I felt about Bess and the children. He knew who I was, because in the army, when you are a private, that's all you have, memories of what you once were.

As a soldier, all of your individuality is taken from you. You are not required to think for yourself. You are taught to follow, unquestioning. That's what all the discipline and commands try to emphasize. You must react at once: follow, follow, don't ask, don't question. I guess it works, because the army has always functioned this way. But putting me into a situation like that was quite different. I'd always been a thinker and had just begun to take on leadership qualities. My business required that. I had hoped that I could become a 2nd Lieutenant by going to Officer Training School. I had the necessary IQ and I believed I had the ability, but everything was moving so fast, I never got the opportunity. It was basic training and out to combat. They needed men more than anything else in June of '44. I found myself in combat fourteen days after D-Day.

FOOD

Irv and I spent a great deal of our spare time together. We traveled to Columbia, S. C. on one of our visits and that's where I ate my first beefsteak "out". Up to that point, I was fighting my way through the food. What did that mean? Well, I did not eat any of the beef or pork dishes they served family style in the dining hall. Neither chicken, nor fish. Remember, this was all new to me. I had never eaten strange foods out of the house. We had kept kosher in and out of the house, outside of a toasted cheese sandwich from time to time. What was the big deal?

What did I eat? Picture this: A big dining room, hundreds of men eating at one time. The foods consisted of lots of mashed potatoes, gravies, meats, fried chicken, pork, etc. I thrived on the cooked green beans, if they had no bacon; turnips, parsnips, rutabagas, cauliflower or Brussels sprouts. There were never any salads. Then there was S.O.S. for breakfast. They called it "Shit on Shingle," and it tasted that way. Still, a guy had to eat something. The PX helped a great deal and I did have the money. That was not a worry. As an interesting point, Phyllis and Jack Keller, my sister-in-law and brother-in-law, were also stationed in the same army camp and I did get some help from them. It was nice to see them, anytime I could. And if I could eat some of the food Phyllis prepared, it helped me get through the day. Best of all, I feasted when Bess sent me the packages from home. That was a trick in itself. Any kind of meat was on ration, and who knows what she had to do to get me those hard salamis—they were some treat—and all those other goodies as well. The salamis always came covered with mold, and I peeled the mold off, trimmed it and gobbled it down, often in one sitting.

I hope you can understand the dilemma I was facing. I understood there was no sin in eating "tref" if there was nothing else available, but the difficulty was in adjusting to it. I never managed to eat any of the meat or poultry meals in the seventeen-week period I was in camp. I just couldn't put it together, but that wasn't the story with Irv. He was able to eat and enjoy everything. Maybe that was why I liked him so much. He seemed to take everything in stride. Was it true? I'll never know. That was his way of coping.

Here is a typical Irv story. He called me post-war. "I'm coming to Cleveland," he said. "Get a couple of nice rooms for my wife and me in a good hotel. I'm coming up for the football game and will be staying over Saturday and Sunday." At that time, his wife's family had a big piece of the original Cleveland Ram's team. I believe his father-in-law was a trucking magnate. Irv got into town, saw the rooms and turned them down. "Get me the best suite you have available," he advised the hotel manager. That was Irv all the way. He had flair, and a positive approach and nothing but the best would suit him. That's the way he always lived, even with his second wife, Edith.

But Irv was not all bluster. We owed him a lot. Coming through Chicago on our first trip to the coast, we meet Irv between planes. Our children, Alan and Shelley, were with us and he treated us to a fabulous meal in one of Chicago's great restaurants. It was the first of many such visits. But the memory of that meal remains with us. It was one of the best I remember. A funny thing that this comes up now. When we went to visit Irv in Chicago, we never had any meal that wasn't top notch. It had to be the best around or Irv wouldn't be there. In one of Chicago's great hotels, we enjoyed a wonderful dinner in the Edgewater Hotel dining room at the peak of its elegance. Picture a gorgeous room with incandescent chandeliers that covered the entire grand dining area. This place was lit up with the brightest lighting you would see anywhere. It was the epitome of dining elegance and I only got there with Bess because of Irv. He wanted to show us the way he lived, and he did. Another time it was the Pump Room in the famous Ambassador East Hotel. This is where half-naked Nubian men dressed in turbans and gorgeous colored uniforms served us in a torch-lit room.

I think the funniest story that had happened to us when we first visited Irv in Chicago was when we were getting off the railway train in midtown. We picked up a taxi right off the train and asked to be taken to the Palmer House. This taxi driver drove us around for half an hour. We paid him an exorbitant fee and put it out of our mind. When we walked out of the hotel the next morning, we looked around and lo and behold, the railway station was within walking distance, not more than a half block away! Farmers in a big city. It happens all the time. Interestingly, flying was not as common in the late 40's or 1950 as it is today. Bess was reluctant to fly, so we chose to go by train. It took a little persuasion, but we did fly back in a comfortable plane. Shows you how things can change overnight.

Irv always made it a point to entertain us in the best places whenever we came to visit. I remember one visit where he entertained us at the Standard Club, a Jewish in-town business club. Posh. Of course, why wouldn't it be? That was Irv's style. But that never interfered with our relationship. The contrast in personalities and life style made our friendship even more interesting. I could always count on Irv to give me a subtle insight, sardonic at times, into my predicament or his. Family difficulties were always a good place to start, and Irv had his share of them: an ex-wife; sisters who had their own problems; a new son; a new wife; plus personal problems. I guess I had my share as well, not as complicated, but maybe I thought so at the time. I know now that there are worse things than that.

THE ARMY AGAIN

Back to the army days and on track once again. As I related previously,eating the army food was really a problem. Believe me, it was a battle, but that would be the easiest part of this two-year trip. When we went overseas and into combat the problem intensified. K-rations covered that well. You received three meals a day in a box that contained a two to three ounce container of chopped ham and eggs, one of pork in a suet—all grease—and one of cheese. I did well for quite some time with the cheese, until they decided it needed more protein and added bacon bits into the cheese. So now I not only had ham and pork to contend with, I had bacon. I had been trading my meat tins for cheese until that wore out, too. Finally, there was no other way: I had to go the route. I took the first step—hungry, cold and with no choices left, I opened the tin of pork smothered in suet. I had no place to warm it and it felt like I was biting into a slippery piece of something. I can tell you it didn't go down well.

The C-rations were served when we were in transit or on reserve call, or when conditions were easier. These were regular size cans of pork frankfurters and beans, a beef meal of some kind, and another that I don't remember. After a ration of K-rations, anything else was heaven! Can you blame me for looking everyday for my package from home? Unfortunately, on the front line the packages might come in two's and three's, and if you're a combat soldier the first thing you learn is that you can only carry so much: You have your mess kit, canteen, field kit for first aide, your basic toothbrush and comb, the belt that you attach these things to, and your field pack. It doesn't take you long to understand the things you have to discard. Oftentimes it is trinkets from home, a camera or a pair of binoculars or a P-38 Pistol you've confiscated from a German soldier. What do you take, and what do you leave? Hunger is a big factor in your choice. There are also crackers in the K-ration, some high protein chocolate, and cigarettes, and it all fits into a package not much bigger than a Cracker Jack box. So there were times when I left much good stuff behind.

ALAN ARRIVES

I was still at Camp Croft and things were happening at home; I was not there, of course, to help with the family, or make any decisions. So what we had was a young mother, Bess, who was faced with a number of dilemmas. Her first was how to get me home for the birth of Alan. That's a job for the bureaucrats, but she solved it, contacting the Army and the Red Cross.

Here is how I remember it. I had been in basic training for a few months. I knew Alan was due sometime in April or May. When Bess finally delivered, on April 15th, I was able to get a few days leave during basic training. It was a quick, powerful visit. When I say powerful, let me put it in another context.

Bess and I could not bear to be parting, but it had to be.

The two or three days flew by. We hung on to each other, but we knew I had to return. It was a terrible time for both of us. It was like a sword hanging over us. I could not handle it well, nor could Bess, but I did leave and the "Bris" took place a few days after. Of course, I was not there, and Bess handled that by herself. She could probably tell you in her own words how difficult it was.

It was also odd and it felt strange to see all of my buddies, guys I grew up with. I was the only one who was drafted. Sid, Harry, Ed K. and the others all were on the verge, but I hit the jackpot. (Not one of my close friends from 105th Street was drafted.)

My loneliness didn't improve because the visit was too short, but what else was there to do? I was in the army's net and subject to what they wanted. A quick note: I traveled by railway car coming and going once again. I just reminded myself of leaving the Terminal Station in Cleveland by rail, to Columbus. That was a tearful send-off as well. From Columbus we traveled all the way to Spartanburg, S.C. What a trip that was. The whole world, at least my world, was moving in another direction.

I was no longer my own person. From now on I would be a product of the army. They were going to mold me into what they thought I should be. How wrong they were. I never did integrate totally into the army culture. I understood why it was necessary, but my ego system didn't allow it. I had been too thoroughly individualistic for so many years, it was hard to change that dynamic.

As I look back, I try to understand who I was then. The actuality of it remains with me. I did what was required of me, but I had no buddies, no one except Irv that I bonded with, and I lived on the fringe of the group I was in. I was never shunned, and was always included in what ever took place in the army barracks, but it was never a social approach and I never remember having any personal friends. There was plenty of time for that because we were free after 5 PM. The fact was that my energy level was so high, I never felt tired. I was in a play situation as far as honest work was concerned. After 5 pm I could run, go to town, read and do whatever I wanted. What I was doing was just filling time. I don't remember going to town much, but that was the thing to do. There were a hundred thousand soldiers in Camp Croft, at least it seemed that way when I went to town. All you could see wherever you went were loads of GI's walking from one side of the street to the other. You knew that the bars were full, because they always had a line-up outside. As far as girls, they must have been few and far between. I never got a chance to find out, in any case, because I really wasn't looking. I was out of the market. Besides, I was suffering from homesickness. This was all new for me. Fifty thousand soldiers were all I could see around me and I really didn't think I had more than one friend I could turn to. I'm still trying to put that together in my mind. Who was this guy I'm writing about and how did he cope with all of these changes?

ON THE HOME FRONT

Bess had her own problems while I was away. Before I left, we were living on 116th and Benham, off Union. However, there were some new regulations in rent control because of the war and inflation. With no new housing being built, every piece of real estate housing was valuable. Prices were frozen as well. So if you had a place to live, you were lucky.

Bess wasn't so lucky—and she was alone to deal with the problem. So here we have the set-up: The landlord decided that he needed our rooms for his daughter and her sick husband. Legally, he could evict Bess and the two children. He called his shot, and bang! Bess was ordered out. Tough luck. But that was the law. He was within his legal rights.

Fortunately, there was Morris Morgenstern, a lawyer representing the poor and the downtrodden who needed legal assistance. A picture of Bess and the two kids hit the front page of the newspaper, telling the story in detail. But that didn't solve the problem. She still was evicted and there was no place to go except downtown to the Cedar Road Apartments, or the 93rd Woodland Apartments. Both of those were basic government-built apartments in the poorest neighborhoods of the city.

I got a call from Bess. "Maury, I've been evicted. What shall I do? I can't find an apartment. I'd like to buy a house. I see that as the best solution."

I replied, "Bess, I don't want a house. I don't know if I'm going to live or die. If you buy a house and I'm gone, what then?"

That was a tough conversation. Buying a house was the last thing I wanted to do. We had a few bucks in the bank and Bess was going to blow it all on a house. I was angry and expressed it that way. Poor Bess. All she was trying to do was to find a place to live. I really couldn't understand that. I had my own problems and I felt they took precedence. Right or wrong, it never happened. Bess did finally find rooms, but it wasn't easy and she went through hell to get it together. Yet we do owe Morris Morgenstem, the lawyer, a great deal because of his efforts in trying to help. He was a dedicated, devoted lawyer who gave it his all.

Probably the most interesting aspect of this entire story is how two people who are separated by time and space can differ in how they visualize and try to cope with the same problem. It was different for each one of us. Fortunately, in the end it was Bess's practical approach to solving this problem that enabled us to survive. If she hadn't taken charge, I would have come home to find my family sleeping and living with my in-laws. Saved, only by the grace of God and the persistence of Bess. Take a little note here and remember this about Bess: She was tenacious and persistent. She'd never let go until the job was finished. Once you had seen her in action, you would remember what I said. No matter how long or how far—no matter what—Bess finished any job she undertook.

We turn now to a few months later and I am scheduled to go overseas. Bess met me at Fort Dix and we spent a couple of days at Aunt Dora's. We then replayed the whole scene of parting once again. It was a difficult time. I can still feel the pain of separation. We both knew what lay ahead. It was a time for clinging. Bess was in a bad way, because she was nursing at that time. She had to carry a breast pump with her to relieve herself for the couple of days she was gone. I was impressed that she was able to manage it.

In the meantime, we got to know Uncle Harry a little better. Unfortunately, he was so involved with the policies of the government, Zionism, Socialism, etc., that he failed to recognize the seriousness of my situation. The situation looked dire and grim, but Uncle Harry felt confident and buoyant in his approach to it all. "Bring back a few German tanks," he said. What did he know about guns, wars and all else? His was a political world. As a point of interest, he suggested that Bess and I attend a Zionist lecture one of the nights we were there. It didn't seem strange to him, because his life was built around those ideas. Can you believe that? Do you think I would care about a lecture twenty-four hours before I left for overseas? My last few hours with Bess, who had come alone by train to spend those last few days with me? That's just what I did.

Uncle Harry was truly an intellectual, well versed in Russian history, the Socialist movement and Zionism, and he had a tremendous literary background of Yiddish and American literature and culture. However, he was not a practicing orthodox religious person. He was far into liberalism, in any form it took. Aunt Dora followed similar lines of thought, but was also on the other side of the spectrum. She was more in tune with contemporary life and was able to bring some balance into this picture. She did manage to give Bess some stability after I had shipped out, and Bess got to see Charles de Gaulle, the great French general, who was given a ticker tape parade in Manhattan the day after I shipped out.

It was good for Bess and me to have that time together. As short as it was, it still gave us something to hang on to. We had those memories to give us strength when the going got rough on both ends.

TO EUROPE ON THE QUEEN MARY

I'm on the Queen Mary, England's classic luxury liner,

made into the world's largest troop ship. How many soldiers are there on the ship? I don't know and can't even begin to fathom how many there were on that ship. This ship could sail under steam faster than 75-80% of all the ships at sea. Navigation was treacherous at that time and everyone was concerned about being torpedoed by a sub. It had happened many times. There wasn't much room to move around. You had your bunk, with fifty to one hundred other men in the same area.

Meals were sloshed around in a mess kit, and I don't even remember what they served. It didn't matter. We all were worried about what was going to happen next. Boredom set in for the seven to eight day voyage, with little to do except play cards; though that was not my thing, there must have been hundreds of card and crap games going on over the long haul.

We were ready to disembark. After seven or eight days on the ship, we landed in Southampton. Land at last. Fresh air and sunshine and a place where you can breathe. It was great just to get off the ship, having been confined to this one spot for days without end. I don't remember the food or what I ate. All I do remember was the closeted bunks, where we were tightly packed together. Now that was over and the fear of subs and torpedoes had diminished. What was in store for us now?

I did forget to mention that I had been trained to be an anti-tank 57-millimeter gunner. That meant that I was part of an eight-man crew that would set up this smaller artillery piece that was used only to knock out tanks. It could be a little weak on that score, but it could be effective if you got close enough. Each person on the squad had a designated position and would perform his job in precision in order to facilitate action and speed. You would also interact as an infantry rifleman. So basically you could be classified as an infantryman. We were also trained to use the bazooka. This was a giant tubular gun that had enough power to attack a tank and cripple it. It was to be carried on your shoulder and it would take two men to operate it, but it was only effective up close.

Now it was time to find out what my new outfit would be. We were set up in a field camp somewhere in the countryside, someplace in England. We lived in tents and we were sent out on hikes and into the fields performing as we were trained to do as infantry soldiers. After the first day, I was transferred to another group, only this time I was attached to a machine gun outfit. As we marched into the field for inspection, a general came up to each soldier more or less to personalize his visit, with emphasis on courage and all that. When he came to me, he said, "Soldier, are you ready? Do you have anything you want to say? How are things going?" "Sir," I said, "I have been trained as a 57-millimeter anti-tank gunner. I don't know anything about a machine gun. I've never shot one, nor have I ever held on in my hand." "Don't worry," he said, "you'll soon learn." Then he walked over to the next soldier.

This wasn't funny. Shooting a machine gun was not an overnight learning process. It took weeks of training. I ran haphazardly from one sergeant to another beseeching them to get me out of the outfit and even into an infantry group, to no avail. Since you had to go through army regulations to talk to an officer, it was impossible to get to a lieutenant. My cries for help were unheard, and I was stuck. But the army was not through messing things up. Two days later, I was placed in an infantry division. Don't ask me how or why. It had nothing to do with my complaints. All of this was happening while the fighting was going on at Oklahoma Beach, during the landing at Normandy. It was about June 10th.

TO FRANCE

I must talk about my trip from Southampton to Cherbourg in a huge ship. Hundreds of soldiers were put into the hold on the bottom of the ship. There was hardly room to move around, all of us crowded into that solid mass of humanity, loaded with packs, rifles and gear. The air was stifling and we were all packed so closely together, you could feel and smell the breath of the men around you. There wasn't a man there who wasn't frightened at the thought of what we were headed for. There was no news of the front and what was happening around us. All we knew was that the Allies had landed. The rest of the news was hearsay. We only knew that now we were headed for battle.

I don't know or remember how many hours we spent in the hold of that ship. I do remember it seemed forever. When we finally got to see the light of day, we were put in small landing boats that seemed to skim through the water, and for the first time we saw the debris and havoc of the landing at Cherbourg. It was a sight to see: as far as your eye could look, there were machine guns, tanks, artillery weapons, jeeps and every kind of military gear you ever dreamed of, scattered all over the beach. There were pieces of steel, twisted and torn and in every kind of shape you could imagine. Think of what each of those men thought as they stepped out on the beach. "What if?" is all that any of them could think of —and that is exactly what I thought. What was it like where were heading? This was it! There were to be no more practice runs. It didn't matter what I had trained to become. Now I was an infantryman and I was going into battle. You can be sure I was saying my prayers regularly without stop. They say there is no atheist in a foxhole; if I ever had doubts about a God being there, I didn't even begin to question it. I wore my "mezuzah" around my neck through the entire war. (A mezuzah contains the major prayer: "Thou shall love the Lord thy God with all thy heart. May the Lord bless you and keep you." It must be written by hand for authenticity). It was my only connection to the world I once knew. It was my passport to come home.

We landed and prepared to march into wherever we were heading. We were put on open trucks and were driven to someplace in France. All was quiet around us. The roads were dusty and there were trucks going back and forth in both directions. A few tanks en route, many jeeps and plenty of activity. The 2nd Infantry Division, 5th Division of the Third Army, was on the move. The Red Diamond (our insignia) was ready. A few hours later, after waving to an occasional group of French bystanders, we arrived at what would be our final destination before entering combat.

There were occasional sounds of shells bursting in the air

somewhere not too far from where we stood. It was an eerie feeling. This was real. Tomorrow would tell the tale. "Dig your foxholes, men!" the Captain yelled out. "You better dig them deep enough, because if you don't, it'll be your ass, not mine. I'm not here to protect you. That's your job."

Nobody needed a push or shove before we started digging. It was no easy task, but I'm sure no one even thought about that part of it. The sounds of artillery loomed in the distance. We could hear the boom. Those sounds kept on coming.

Night fell and we had already eaten our K-rations. We lay there in the foxholes, shivering, praying and thinking. What would tomorrow bring? Then a call came out of the blue. "The Jewish chaplain is available for anyone who is of the Jewish faith. You can meet him in the Headquarters area." About twelve or fifteen of us went to meet the chaplain. I remember little about him. His name was Chaplain Dickers. He later went on to long-term service in the army, finishing his career somewhere in the Far East.

The prayer service he led was basic, simply given, and more secular in nature than I had been accustomed to, but who cared at that point? It was the closest to God that I could get. I wasn't looking for anything else. Was it reassuring? I'm sure it was. Soldiers on the battlefield don't question the existence of a Supreme Being. It's the only hope they have for survival. Without that hope, there is failure and death. I've seen it work that way too many times: Once a soldier gives up hope, his chance of survival goes down at least fifty percent. You have to believe that you are going to come out alive. If you believe you are doomed, the chances are it will turn out that way.

Back to our foxholes we went. It was dark and almost pitch black. The only sounds we heard were the muffled thuds of the artillery that kept pounding away every few minutes. Then we heard an announcement by someone; I don't know who that person was and never found out: "Are there any men out there who are acquainted with first aid procedures, or have some experience of any kind in basic medical treatment?"

No one answered. It is easy to understand why. No soldier in his right mind ever volunteers for anything, even if he knows the subject. That is one thing you learn early in the game. But my luck was no better this time than when I was drafted. I was Number 13 then. This time I was Number 3. "Feren, come to the front along with…" and he named a number of other men. Time stopped for a moment. They removed all my ammunition and rifle immediately. I was then given a different helmet, with a big Red Cross insignia on it. This insignia covered the entire front and back so that it could be easily seen. I was also given a medical field kit that I slung across my shoulders.

I BECOME A MEDIC
AND SEE MY FIRST ACTION

"You are now a First Aid Medic," the Captain said. You will be attached to Company C under the supervision of Captain Greenberg and the Lieutenant." It was already late night, but I was put on a truck along with a few other men, and off we went—not too far, but the shelling seemed louder as we moved forward. I was a front line medic. Nothing would change that. This is where it all began in earnest.

Early AM, we were called into action. I found out later we were fighting in the hedgerows of St. Lo, about twenty or twenty-five miles inland from Cherbourg. We were in the thick of it. At first I walked erect, thinking I would be able to move faster. But the shelling and rifle shots began to whiz by in every direction. I didn't know at first whether to bend, duck or creep and crawl. Then my first cry for help came up. "Medic! Medic!" a soldier cried out. "Help me, I've been hit!" I don't know what I did. Initially, I froze. The actuality was that I had opened my kit and examined all of the items in it. I didn't think that much about it, because I didn't know that I would have to use it that soon. I remember bullets flying through the air and the boughs of a tree blinding me as I tried to go through. I got down on my knees and then I moved forward on my belly as I pushed toward this GI.

Fortunately, it was a minor wound on his leg and I

bandaged him up. Since I had the little morphine syringes, I thought I would try one on him. I told him I was going to give him a shot with a needle to relieve him of his pain. That was my first encounter with wounds and one that reminded me how inadequate I was to give that kind of help. I felt like I had failed, because I knew that there might have been more that I could have done, or I could have been much more proficient than I was. I learned much that first day of combat. This was not going to be a good choice of a career. My chances of survival diminished a great deal after that first day. I knew that this was not the best job I could have had. Attached to the infantry company, the medic was literally helpless. With no gun and only his wits to save him, the best he could hope for was to avoid the enemy in anyway he could possibly manage. The chances for survival were in the hands of God. Artillery shells and M-star shells came from everywhere, with no rhyme or reason. Oftentimes there was rifle fire coming from two different directions. It was frightening to hear the whiz of bullets going by in the air so close you thought that they were aimed right at you.

My first days under fire were like a staged drama. There was constant artillery and loud explosions everywhere I turned. The landscape itself was brutal, because we fought on small farms, separated by hedgerows that were four to six feet high and a yard or more wide. There was much to do, because the sound of the word "Medic, medic!" reverberated in my ears constantly. Some of the wounds were small, shrapnel and light bullet wounds that either went through an arm or a leg, or perhaps a soldier had a superficial cut caused by a bullet.

On one occasion, I remember an artillery attack that demolished an entire company. For those that remained, it seemed that they had all taken a hit with shrapnel. It covered their arms and legs, embedded either seriously or in smaller pieces on different parts of their bodies. It was a memory I shall never forget, because I took care of so many men that I ran out of bandages and morphine. There were men who were badly hit who kept moaning and crying for help. It took hours to get them all back to the hospital field tent. But somehow we managed it.

The thought comes to me now: How helpless we felt carrying a man in a litter, four men holding the soldier up, and shells bursting in the air, some close, others with just the sound of them. It was a frightening experience. There was one good thing that came out of all this. I was no longer called "Maury." My new name was "Doc." I'll never forget that. Being a Doc with foot soldiers gave you a special classification. You were no longer regarded as just one of the guys. There was a certain prestige that went with it. Everyone looked to Doc for anything that pertained to good health. (We are not talking about diet, because a foot soldier would eat anything he could put his hands on—it didn't matter how old it was or what it looked like. If it looked edible, he'd eat it). The Doc was more than just a guy you wanted beside you if you got hit. He could give you pills like sulfadiazine, or a shot of morphine, and of course everyone assumed he had some medical training. Alas, that was not true. I often wondered about how much the Lieutenant knew back in the field hospital. Captain Greenberg was a full-fledged doctor. The Lieutenant was a dentist by schooling. I never had the chance to find out.

Yes, they were both Jewish, but I was the only Jew in my Headquarters company of thirty-two men, besides those two officers. The company that I was attached to as a medic had no Jews in it beside me. Can you imagine the resentment these men felt, thinking that they were fighting for a cause that included Jews, but there were no Jews on the front lines? There was no way that I could explain this to them rationally, as hard as I tried. Interestingly, even the Chaplain's assistant attacked me on that premise. Here was an educated man of the cloth who would not allow me to explain what was happening. The reality was that there were many Jewish men fighting in every part of the army, some in the rear areas. We were doing our part, but only two percent of the population of the USA was Jewish, so it would be difficult to find them, except from areas that were highly populated, such as New York, Pennsylvania, California, etc. It all depended on where you came from. In my particular area, I was one of the few of all of my friends and acquaintances who was drafted. I would have to say I was the only one, with the exception of Al Lieberman, who lived next door to me. My other friends, who lived in different parts of Cleveland, managed to escape the draft.

There were other men who brought up the lack of Jews on the front line, but it was always same story: The Jews have all the money, they escaped the draft, they control the banks, the film industry and on and on. It was a constant fight that I never won. Initially, I had hoped I could reason with some of these critics, but it never worked out, I never found out what the guys in my outfit thought about me. I felt as if I was accepted and part of the group, but I never bonded with any one person in my thirty-two-man outfit. My two friends were from Headquarters Company. One was Jerry Goldberg in the Pioneer Company and the other was Nate Eisenberg in the Anti-Tank Company, specializing in breaking down mines. Both of those guys played an intimate role in my army life overseas. Unfortunately, I could only get to see them when we were in reserve, or when there was a rest period. Life was pretty rough on the front lines and before long it would take its toll on me.

The first signs of battle fatigue took place sometime in July, after a month of fighting. You have to understand how battles are fought. A company or two moves in and begins pounding away with artillery and infantry support; the push goes on and you dig foxholes and stay there until it is time to go forward. All this time the din of battle and constant thump of explosions land all over the front, wherever that is. You feel as if your head will come off each time one of the shells land. The noise becomes so rhythmic; you lie there waiting for each shell to explode at regular intervals. It is a continual BANG! BANG! BANG! Never-ending.

After three or four days of this, if you are not surrounded, you are sent back as a company and put into a reserve area. Here you can pull your thoughts together and sleep in another foxhole, but there is hot food and the possibility of some amenities. These are the good times. There were other times where I never got to change my socks and lived in the same clothes for a month. Shaving was done in a helmet with water; cold water only in most cases on the field and as far as washing goes, most times we just washed our faces and exposed extremities. Cleanliness was not as important as survival.

It was the survival technique that would keep me alive. Again, I refer to my versatility. I was always able to scrape up extra food from somewhere. Because I spoke French, I got out into the countryside and brought back eggs, bread, and occasionally some smoked meat. That was a rare situation. In combat, there were no food choices. You carried your three K-Rations for the day and that was your answer for food. I always shared my food with whomever I was attached to during the fighting. I did understand this. My friends were always willing to accept food from me. This included my food packages from home and other little tidbits I would gather up. I always carried extra food of some kind. Of course, it would not always be to my taste, but it got me by. However, it did not work in reverse. I doubt if any of my buddies shared anything with me. I don't think that is strange, now that I think of it. You learn that to survive you must come first.

I learned a great deal about life in the army. My initial hope for socialism, where everyone would share alike in a Utopian world, was shattered after my experiences both in basic training and on the battlefield. I learned that there are people who will always try to escape from doing their share; their only interest is to take care of themselves. As far as sharing, that was only an idea. I also learned that in a society where money was not a measure of success, the only recognition that one could get was to be in a position of power. The officers and the elite group that made the decisions were the people in power. They lived their separate lives and took care of themselves first. They were the power. The only difference between power in that kind of society is that if you were not in the in-group in the army, there wasn't much that you could do to get ahead.

If you didn't know anybody, you were just another nobody filling in the holes. In the capitalist system, it's the guys with the money that have the power. Here on the battlefield, life was an equalizer. I saw all my ideology fall away and I was left with only dreams of a society that hoped to equalize the way of life for everyone. It was disturbing to discover that I had been fighting a losing battle in ideology. I had begun to recognize the deficiencies in the system. In theory, socialism would work well. However, the practical aspects of it required higher personal obligations than ordinary human beings could offer. It was the beginning of a more realistic, practical approach to the realities of living.

A BOUT OF BATTLE FATIGUE
AND A DAY OF REST

Fighting conditions became worse as we went along and there were many times that we were bogged down. It was early in the first month of battle that I had my first bout with battle fatigue. What is the definition of battle fatigue? There are a lot of new interpretations; however, what actually happens is that your mind refuses to accept everything that is happening to it. It just bogs down and admits defeat, whatever that means. In my case, I knew that my mind had just given up because of the constant pounding, the sound of the shells, the explosions that kept coming through the air and the constant fury of the battles that were being fought around me and on top of me. It seemed as if I had no strength to fight back. I did not want to accept that, because I believed I was a stronger person. I wasn't. I had to ask to give up. However, I felt a sense of responsibility. I didn't want to leave the fighting. I owed it to myself and the fact that I was a soldier. I needed to be there. It may be difficult to understand my reasoning, but even if it wasn't rational, it made sense to me.

I went to the commanding officer, who was my captain, and told him how I felt. I said, "I'm totally out of whack at this moment. I don't think I can stand another day of battle. But I know I will feel better if you just send me back to the field hospital for a day or two. I'm sure I'll be back." I don't know if Captain Greenberg believed me, or how he felt. All I do remember is that I was sent back to the field hospital for rest.

I received no pills, no special medical attention, nor did anyone question me as to why I was there. I do remember that I lay out on the grass in the beautiful sunshine. The sky was perfectly blue and all I could see for miles around was the blue of the sky and the sun shining brightly overhead. It was such a good feeling to be alive at that moment. It may be that I never treasured life so much as I did during that one day of rest.

But the signs of war and battle were not that far away. There were muffled sounds of shells exploding, and every once in a while a Mustang P-51 would appear out of the blue and zoom away, going faster than the speed of light. It was an awesome sight whenever they appeared and I was taken aback with their speed and maneuvering qualities. They also gave me more assurance and hope for an early end to the war. But this was still in the earliest stages of the war and my thoughts were only dreams. Yet, this was one of my most memorable days in the army.

Did I recuperate in a day? I really don't know. I was back at the front the next day, took my place in the company and continued on. Did I suffer from my negative approach? Who knows? I doubt it. All I do remember is that I went back and tried to do my job. No one said anything to me. I received no negation, nor any words of encouragement. This was a job. Everyone else was trying to stay alive. That was their most important concern, taking care of themselves.

I never sat down and tried to analyze why I made that choice. I did see many men who had battle fatigue. I watched them react and never thought too much about it in my initial meetings with it. I also watched soldiers who pretended that they had battle fatigue and who offered every good reason they could bring up to be sent back. But the officers were not that naive. You really had to be in bad shape before they would ship you out. During our periods of rest, and while in reserve, I would work in the dispensary, assisting with minor cuts and frozen feet, or anything that GI's would complain of. The rules were tough, and Captain Greenberg would not try to stretch them. Oftentimes I felt he was too hard on the men he interviewed and sent back. He rarely relented.

Now that I think of it, I wonder why he never said anything more to me about my choices. He may have understood my motivation, but he may have figured he had nothing to lose if I failed to come back.

When I did come back to actual combat, it was just as it had been before. There were continuous advances with the company I was attached to. Did I have more stamina and more desire when I returned? I truly don't know. I was aware of the danger I was in and fought constantly to get out of my outfit. It just didn't work that way. Despite all my maneuvers, it just never came to pass.

My first thought was to get to a company commander and insist on more training. I would emphasize that I had no medical background and that it was unfair to the men. "This is a cross you must bear," the officer replied. I tried this at two or three different levels, but no one would listen. It was a futile task. These officers kept insisting that I would get training at the next rest period, whenever that would be. It never happened. There was no one to train me.

We had already lost half of our original company. All of the new replacements were training haphazardly in the States. It may have been that some of them were in the same predicament as I, not knowing anything. This always struck me as odd. The army worked in funny ways. In many instances, there was no rhyme or reason why they chose to do certain things, or why they selected certain men for special jobs. In many cases, it made no sense. I could have done well in the Quartermaster Corps, since I had a food warehouse background. Instead I was sent to the infantry and then the medics because of necessity. I could never understand their reasoning. Did it work? I still don't know. I will never find out where I helped and where I failed to help. It was never an easy choice, whatever I did. All I could hope for was the opportunity to make a choice. I made many of them.

One of the strangest experiences, of the many I had, was my meeting with two Clevelanders who landed in the same outfit as I did. Traveling in Cerise Forest, I came across an old acquaintance, Federico. Here was a guy who had been a peddler, who used to buy fruit and vegetables in the Food Terminal. Now he had landed in the same Division as me, attached to another company, but a part of the Red Diamond 5th Division, 2nd Infantry.

I mentioned Nate Eisenberg in the early part of this story. Picture this: Nate had been a buddy of our entire group before the war. Because of his marital status, age, or what have you, he was drafted two years before I got there. Oddly, he was attached to Headquarters Company as an anti-tank mine expert; actually, that was also a part of the training the 57-millimeter squad was supposed to receive. As it turned out, we never got that training in our basic schooling.

You can hardly guess how cold a reception I got when I hit the front lines and met Nate. He had been gone two years, spending a year and a half in Iceland. He was very angry and expressed his anger, noting that not one of us had ever marked his going away, nor did we ever send him one letter. I wouldn't even think of faulting him, because all of those men were angry and justifiably so. What did they care about "pre-Pearl Harbor fathers" and all that jazz? They had already served two years before I even got there. Feel sorry for me? No way. They didn't care. It took weeks before Nate and I could get it together as friends, but then we became good friends, because of who we were: First, we came from the same area; we were also Jewish; and we had had a close relationship before the war.

One day, I suggested to Nate that I would love to get out of the Medical Corps. Things were so rough, I told him, that I didn't believe I would ever get out alive. Our losses of medics continued to mount. "How long do you think I can go on like this?" I asked. Nate came up with a good idea. He mentioned that there hadn't been many mines to destroy. In fact, there had only been a few. He said, "I think I can help. We have a Jewish lieutenant and he is a good guy. He is in charge of our outfit. I'll talk to him and see if there is any possibility to get you transferred. I believe you have a good chance to get in, if he agrees." Boy, what a break that would be, I thought. Hope it can work out.

Well, you know the story. I never got out of the Medics. It just wasn't in the cards. It was just my luck that every time the door opened, another one closed. As Nate had promised, he talked to the Lieutenant and he said he would try to get me transferred. I was elated. The next day the mine team went out to de-fuse some mines a few miles away. It happened just like in the movies. While the Lieutenant was telling his men what to do, someone stepped on a mine where the Lieutenant was standing. He lost his leg and was taken to the hospital to get treatment. Of course, I never knew how that ended. But that was the end of my hopes of being part of the mine team.

There was another opportunity that had some possibilities when I thought about it. I might use my basic French skills and become part of the reconnaissance team. This outfit, composed of a select few, would move out and scout the forward movement before the regular troops moved in. They seemed to be quite successful because they were sent out any number of times with no casualties. They operated in a Jeep with two to four members of a team going out separately. I became acquainted with the officer in charge and suggested that I might be helpful interpreting. He listened, never giving me any answer, so I don't know for sure what he would have done. Let me satisfy your curiosity by finishing the story in a couple of brief sentences. Not too long after I spoke to this officer, the team left for reconnaissance in some part of France, early in the campaign. They never came back, which meant that they were either taken captive, or were destroyed by enemy fire. I never found out. Another good tip gone bad. It goes to show you, if the odds are not there, you'll never beat the rap!

THE LIBERATED COUNTRYSIDE

While all of this was going on, there was a diminishing aspect to the bitter fighting we had experienced in the first two months. We had already been moving steadily into the Normandy area. These were wide-open spaces, with a few small villages scattered between them. Things were happening so fast, the infantry began to move in trucks and tanks. You'd find GIs hanging on the sides of tanks as the trucks came rumbling in. The noise could be deafening, and in each village the soldiers were showered with flowers—and kisses were even thrown to the soldiers as the trucks went by.

In the interim, I took advantage of the freedom I had gained. (Discipline was different on the front lines; few stern measures were taken by the officers for soldiers not toeing the line exactly). I would wander out into the countryside by myself during these rest periods, talking to the French people I met. I even developed some personal friendships around the Loire Valley and in Chartres, where I met a French schoolteacher and his family. I did keep in touch with them for many years after the war. I also managed to send them packages of food post-war, when food was still scarce.

By now, everyone knew there were collaborators during the war. Women as well as men played the game, catering to the victors. Now the tables were turned and there was a price to pay for those who collaborated. For the women, it was one of the most demeaning things that could happen to them. I stood by in one little village where a number of men and women from the town were cutting off the hair of the women who had sold out to the enemy. It was an awesome sight. There was yelling and screaming. I tried to find out exactly what had occurred, but all I learned was that they were collaborators.

During this whole period I began to make strides in my speech. Speaking French was so essential wherever I went alone, because few Frenchmen knew English. Oftentimes, my tongue would become tired and sore from the constant effort to make myself understood. It was a challenge, but I managed to do fairly well with it.

My attempts at the French language went back to my first entry into France, riding on a truck with a bunch of soldiers. As we went by one little village, a Canadian on the truck struck up a friendship with some people we met, because he spoke French. Some of the words sounded as if I had heard them before, and I remembered that I had studied French in the eighth and nineth grade. I was determined not to be left out. I wanted to know what made these people tick. What was it that singled them out and made them different? Were they really different? This was my reason for working so hard to try to understand them: It was a chance to find out whether people in another country were different. If they were, what was the reason for that difference? I never stopped thinking about that wherever I went.

There is no telling how many places I went by myself or how much I saw. I was always moving around during rest periods, never staying in the same place as my company. I was a loner. Yet no one seemed to care and I guess I didn't mind it myself. It was an interesting time. Besides that, the burdens of the war had begun to ease off. We were on our way to Metz. Of course, I didn't know at that time what a hell that place would be.

THE STRUGGLE FOR METZ

Metz was in the Alsace-Lorraine area, bordering Germany. Here was an area with a long stretch of armed towers that were on top of a hill. There was no way to attack these hills without sacrificing hundreds, maybe thousands of men. This area had changed hands five or six times over the years. First German, then French, then German, then French again. It was a real hellhole. There was every kind of defensive armaments that they used to protect themselves. All you could see were holes from which artillery would shoot down upon you. It was solid cement, who knows how thick. The more we attacked, the more men we lost. It was the most decisive battle for survival for our outfit. The casualties were horrible. It became so bad that I insisted we could not go out as medics to take care of the wounded, because we had had so many casualties.

The firepower was awesome. We made no headway, locked in and unable to move for six weeks. Here is where the horrors of war became synonymous with my mind and body as part of a whole. Oftentimes I lay in my foxhole waiting for the shells to explode, one after the other, rhythmically like a clock ringing bells. My ears ached, my body cried out for an end, but to no avail. The shells kept coming.

I remember one occasion when we were stationed on top of a hill and we were ordered to move because of the firepower. I never got up, rolling all the way down the hill on my stomach and back, rolling and turning myself until I came to the bottom of the hill, taking refuge in some kind of space. I could hear and feel my heart go thump, thump, thump, and it was as if I could feel my heart jumping up and down. You call that frightened? I would not hesitate to say yes. This was not a unique experience, because there were other times that were quite similar.

I can remember lying in a foxhole all day with the interminable sounds of shells bursting around me all day long. These are memories that never leave you. However, there are some experiences that are stranger than fiction. Picture this: I was alone in a forest, separated from my company for no reason whatsoever. Maybe they were close by. I can't remember. As I was walking, I walked right into a German soldier. Can you believe that? He was as frightened and surprised as I was. He faced me, took a turn about and ran like hell. I did the same. It all happened in a flash and it was over. I couldn't describe his face. All I could see was his uniform and I knew he was a German soldier. Such is the life of a soldier. He never knows what is coming next. When I look back, I always wonder what that soldier was thinking. It sure was a strange experience. On the other hand, he may have seen the highly marked Red Cross helmet, which is so obvious up close. (Even from afar it is very pronounced). Who knows? He may have wanted to be respectful of the markings. But I doubt it.

I have mentioned to you that the name "Doc" stuck to me all through my combat experience. It is easy to understand why, if you've ever been on the front lines. If the medic is there, you have an 80% chance of survival, if he can get you to the field hospital in a certain amount of time. Everyone recognized that fact. It brought a quiet respect with it.

I GO WITH THE CAPTAIN

So here is the picture: We were out in the fields somewhere in Germany. There was a lot of brush and trees, little hills, some open ground and a great deal of cover if it was needed. This was a small company operation and there were two groups of men: A dozen men or more in each group, with a captain in charge of one section and a lieutenant in the other, with one medic. That was me. So the captain says, "I'm going to take the medic." Remember, I had no weapon. All I could do is administer first aid. The lieutenant said, "It would be better if I took him because we are moving into a more difficult area." They stop to discuss it for a few moments, but there is no choice. The captain got his preference, because he had the seniority.

We made our move, under the captain's direction, scouting the area going in an entirely different direction from the lieutenant. We traveled for half an hour or more and met no opposition at all. However, the lieutenant found himself in another situation. He was attacked along with his men, ambushed, and almost all of his group were hit with small arms and suffered major casualties. It was a strange time. No one knows the whys and wherefores of why those things happened that way. It was just one more time when fate intervened and there was no way that anyone could explain it.

METZ

Now the battlefield moved to Metz. We were still trying to get to those well-fortified emplacements. They were built to a thickness of ten to twenty feet; they seemed to be impregnable. There was a terrible loss of life in attacking those fortresses of stone and iron. They were protected so well, we seemed to make no progress at all in attacking them.

While all this fighting was going on, we were on the line for a solid month or more, with no rest whatsoever. The tension and the stress were unimaginable. The loss of lives and the wounded soldiers who appeared each day were a critical factor in how we felt as medics. Even though we wore the Red Cross helmet and carried the Red Cross flag when we went out on the field, we lost medics. Either they were wounded, hit by shrapnel, or just died. It was a terrible period. Everyone knew that the odds for survival were minimal. We thought a lot about it. At least I did.

So picture this situation: You are looking out at a large field area that extends for half a mile or more. In order to get out to this field where there is crossfire and shells coming in all the time, you have to go over a high railroad track embankment. It is at least ten to twelve feet high. Each time I went out carrying the flag, there was shooting and I ran back for cover, frightened out of my wits. I was determined not to go back. This was not the first time that I questioned the ability of the officer in charge to lead, but this was a more serious gesture.

"Captain," I said, "it is impossible to work here by day. Every time one of us goes out over the tracks, they try to shoot us down, and they succeed in some cases. Doesn't it make more sense to work at night, so that we don't have the loss of life we've had in our medic squad?"

The Captain looked at me with astonishment. "Are you telling me that you won't go back out on the field?"

"Captain," I replied, "all I ask of you is that you go out yourself and see if what I am telling you has merit. All I'm saying is that they are shooting us down unmercifully and the crossfire makes it even more dangerous."

The Captain listened. Again, I don't know why. Actually, what I had done was insubordination in battle, subject to who knows what. But he didn't take it that way. He decided to check it out. He was wearing the Red Cross helmet, carrying the Red Cross flag. He climbed up to the top of the railway embankment, went over it—and then an array of bullets went right through the flag! Needless to say, he flew over those tracks, came back to our safe area and never said one word. All he did add was that there would be no more daytime operations. That was another one of those situations where I used poor judgment that turned out well. It could have turned out the other way just as easily.

"I'LL SHOW YOU WHAT A DIRTY JEW CAN DO!"

I haven't written much about the antagonism I faced from time to time from ignorant soldiers who were definitely anti-

Semitic. My first encounter was early in one of my earliest experiences going to the front. We were all on a truck, maybe fifteen men or so, and a soldier jostled me severely when the truck went over a bump. I realized that it was an accident and just let it pass. In the meantime, the soldier was not so quiet about it. He may have been bruised, or his hatred for Jews came out, so he attacked me verbally. "You dirty Jew, who do you think you are, jumping on me like that?" I didn't respond angrily at first, but he was insistent. As I said earlier, I was an angry man. In this case, I was even more angry.

I had done nothing to this soldier and he was looking for a fight, or to taunt me with his verbal abuse. He kept on raving. There really wasn't a lot of room and the truck kept moving, but I didn't let that stop me. "I'll show you what a dirty Jew can do," I told him. Bang! Bang! Bang! Bang! Before you know it, this guy was down. I hit him hard a few times, plus the truck motion helped to throw him off balance. He didn't know what hit him. He never said another word when he got up. Everyone on the truck kept quiet. I was aroused, ready to take them all on. Not one of them said a word. It was the first of many such experiences. Was I too sensitive? I don't think so. Could I have handled it differently? I would not have wanted to. This was a distinct case of hatred for Jews. I found out from all my experiences that talking and trying to explain why you were entitled to equality and understanding was not the way to go. Might is right. And I followed through with that thinking any number of times in the army. Never again would anyone call me a dirty Jew and get away with it. There were a few who played that game, but it never worked out for them.

I do want you to think of me as I was. I was at the peak of my physicality, highly trained for endurance, having endured the rigors of battle, death, and all that goes with it. I had put too much into my soldiering career to be pushed aside. My fighting (street fighting) experience had already given me a base for any encounters that I would face any time in the future. There was another aspect to this, which may or may not be psychological. I was an angry man. I am sure that I have mentioned this in my previous writing, but if I haven't, this is an interminable fact. I could go through any ordinary experience, but faced with bitter antagonism, or recognizing deep antagonism, triggers something within me. It is such a powerful force; I've never really had control of it. As we moved into other areas during those difficult times, it may have been the combination of stress and anger that triggered my responses. However, I have always recognized that they were there. You will get a more vivid picture of this as it developed into more serious circumstances.

FROZEN FEET, A SERIOUS PROBLEM

The fighting goes on in Normandy and the battles seem endless. We are in a better position than we were early in the campaign, but we are still continuing to enter battle after battle. There may have been some respite from time to time, but all of us are battle weary. The weather has changed and we are into solid cold winter weather. The GIs are reporting in to sick call at every rest day complaining about frozen feet. This was really true and a serious problem that all of us had to face: cold weather, light snow, and you wore high shoes and the same socks day after day. Some men never took off their shoes and wore them for days on end without changing them. Interestingly, we slept in foxholes in the cold, but no one got sick. All of us were concentrating on just staying alive, and were not concerned with the ordinary uncomfortable situations we faced. But frozen feet were real.

Captain Greenberg and the Lieutenant had so many cases to see that I helped evaluate them. However, when I disagreed with the officers on who should get to go to the hospital, I ran into some personal difficulties with the officers. "Captain," I said, "these men are in serious trouble. Look at the swelling and the frost condition these feet are in. You can't send them back to the front without treatment." But their job was different than mine. Manpower was short. It was essential to keep every man in the lines for as long as he could stand. They refused to listen to me and took their own decision as the right thing to do. I was unhappy, distressed, because of the injustice I saw. But I was helpless and unable to fight back with any effectiveness. It was not the last time I would see this take place, but whenever it occurred I would do my best to be of help. Oddly, there were also many occasions when we would perform medical service on captured German soldiers. It was ironic, but the reality was that it was the human thing to do.

WOUNDED IN ACTION

When I think back, I wonder what really happened. How did I walk into an ambush with shrapnel falling on me at Etampes, France—a little village before we got to Metz? Etampes is only a name. I doubt if the village was more than a block in length, squared off in four different directions. All I do remember is a beautiful road flanked by big trees. It was a lovely setting, but in minutes it turned into a disaster. There was a flurry of explosions and in the process, I felt a burning in my chest and a number of other places. When I looked, I saw I had been hit by shrapnel. I was rushed to the field hospital and then to the main hospital a few miles away.

When the nurse saw me, she took my blood pressure, went into a panic and called the doctor. After a bit, my pressure went down. I knew it was high, but for me that was not unusual. (I remembered that back home I always took my blood pressure tests on Sunday. When the insurance man arrived with the doctor, I would have been lying down for a half hour. That was the only way I knew to take those tests; otherwise, I might have been rejected).

But this time I was not so anxious to go back to the front. I knew more what was in store for me. I kept telling the doctor and nurses that I didn't feel good. I used every excuse I could to keep myself in the hospital. But they did not listen to me. They kept me in the hospital for three days total. By nightfall of the third day, I was back in the Medic Corp where I had begun, with no exceptions for the shrapnel wounds I had acquired. Although they were minor, I wanted to use this as an excuse to move on. It never happened. The cards were not falling my way. They never did. Strangely enough, I can hardly remember the pain and the shock of that shrapnel wound. The mind sometimes can hide a great deal. As a matter of truthfulness, it was a superficial wound. The doctor recognized it as such. And he probably made many harder decisions than that one.

I never considered myself to be especially brave, but for some odd reason, I always wanted to be in front. I was always in front, behind the officer in charge. Rarely did I move in the back lines. I remember a night attack that took place under the moonlight. A full moon. Do you know how dark it can be with no lights out in the fields, with nothing to guide you but the stars? I'm not a star man, so I left it to others to show the way. This was a company movement that took place in darkness. The light was just strong enough to get some idea of where we were going. We were also going to cross a river in small boats. Again, my front line antics brought me to the first boat, where I took the oars and headed downstream toward our objective. It was only after the objective had been reached that I realized that I would have met the fighting head on. Fortunately we moved out with no opposition. From all of this you should be getting some idea of the workings of my mind. It was a yes/no mind. Some days I would be very positive, at other times I would do some negative things that put me at risk. But this was my nature. I followed no straight path. There would always be a time for me to deviate from the norm. It was part of the unpredictable nature of the man. I could no more explain this than talk about it.

The war had taken its toll on everyone. The fighting had gone on so long, everyone was fatigued, worn out mentally and physically. We had been on the line for a month or more. Initially, when the war was going well for us, there was a policy that GI's who had been in combat would get a three-day rest pass in Paris. Paris had been liberated. What a city it was! GI's talked about it, raved about it, and thought only about the possibility. Paris, city of wild women, song and dance, and it was just around the comer. Actually, we were less than thirty to sixty miles away. It could have been the greatest three days ever. Alas, that was not to be. All leaves were canceled. Even though our company was in line for a rest period, Paris was out. The tide of battle had changed.

Instead, we were to get three days in the village of Pont-a-Mousson. Where was this little town and what was in it?

To begin with, there was a place to shower, a chance to get clean clothes, and a chance to get some different food. Maybe even a place to buy food. There were a couple of bars in town. There was wine, of course. But after that, what was there?

So here is this worn-out soldier coming into the village with no thought of anything but rest. But after one day of rest, what then? Something got into me. First of all, I wasn't going to spend my days of rest in a bar, sitting there downing beer or wine with my buddies. Secondly, I had no buddies. That was a reality. And I was not one to sit around. There was absolutely nothing to see. There was no place to go, either. But France's second largest city was sixty miles away. Nancy. It was a thought. And then the thought turned into action.

A CLOSE CALL IN NANCY

It was not long before I was on the road, hitchhiking on my way to Nancy, wearing my Red Diamond emblem on my shoulder for identification. Think about this. I was no longer in my company area. I hitched a ride with the artillery company battalion who had a lightning insignia on their sleeve. Just my way of telling you I was out of my area, subject to I don't know what. I wasn't actually fighting, so I really did not disobey orders. I was in a so-called rest area, so it may be I was not off limits. On the other hand, in a war situation, I might be classified as AWOL. Whatever way it might go, I was on my way. Not thinking correctly might be one way of putting it.

So I jumped on a jeep with a bunch of guys and an officer. "Where are you going?" I asked.

"To Nancy," they said. So I was on my way. Remember that Nancy was a city that had just been liberated. It was once a great manufacturing center. Now it was in the primary stages of reopening its gates and renewing itself both in the ways of its past, and in a new direction.

I walked through the center of town and since it was the noon hour, all the stores were closed. Actually, they close for two hours. I had hoped to purchase some gifts for Bess and the kids, but I had to wait for a later hour to do that. While I was walking, I saw a contingent of freedom fighters, dressed in rugged freedom fighter gear, guerrilla style, with berets and guns, marching in single file through the square. There was a call to arms, and a French officer was giving each of these men a rifle and supplies that would attach them to the French Army. It was an interesting ceremony, without much pomp, but you knew you were watching an important historic moment in the lives of those men. They were no longer fighting alone against the enemy; now they would be a part of the French Army. Besides, once again, the French Army would be back in the field, a vital part of the strategic fighting forces. It was an exciting display of patriotism. Even without the flags flying, those men looked like the real thing. I'll tell you more about them later as we go on with my story.

Nancy, what was there to see, now that I was there? There were hundreds of men from the artillery division moving around, lots of tanks and jeeps. The Red Diamond insignia stuck out like a sore thumb. At least I thought so.

So looking back, what strikes my mind that I remember so well? France was known for its houses of ill repute. When I had read Balzac and Maupassant, I always found references to such places. Never mind that prostitutes worked there. It was hard to explain my thinking, but the reality was that I was curious.

I walked into the brothel, part of a red light district, mid-day, and there I saw the Madame serving drinks, and at least fifty men moving around in different parts of the rooms. There were no women visible when I walked in, but there were fifty or more guys ahead of me—that is, if I had been interested in that part of the action. As I indicated, I did want to see: The rooms had brocaded walls, ornate furniture, beautiful drapes and the drinks were well fortified.

I got to talk to one of the soldiers who seemed to be somewhat interesting and we just struck it off well, initially. He did happen to mention an important point that I may have overlooked or hadn't thought about.

"Do you know," he said, "this place is off limits during the day?"

"Well," I said, "so why are you here?"

"They generally don't bother the guys, so the guys come around, kill a little time and have some fun. And this isn't the only place to go. Just across the street there is another spot that will make this one look ordinary."

So off we go, heading across the street. You have the same scene: Lots of GI's, maybe more than fifty, the Madame, and a few girls roaming around. Basically, not too much different, but a little more elaborate setting. Well, think of this: You have a line-up of fifty or more guys, black and white. So you take it from there. How could you like to be Number fifty or sixty, even if you were in the market for action? That is for that day only, how about the past action?

Putting all that aside, there was something that did come out of this. I didn't read it in books, but I did see it in France. It was an eye opener. But I can't stop there. The climax is yet to come. It wasn't more than five or ten minutes after we arrived that someone yelled out "Raid! The MPs are coming!" Do you know what that meant? Anyone caught would be put in jail, and in my case, sixty miles away from my outfit—who knows what that would come to? I was not frightened. I was numb for a moment, but it didn't take me long to figure out what to do. I ran out of the back room as fast as I could, hit a big walled fence, climbed over it like it was two feet high, even though it was way higher than that, and ran like hell, not knowing what direction to take.

I was safe. But that was the end of my trekking for that day. Nancy? I had had it. Whatever I left behind in that town, it was over, never to be seen again. I hitched a ride back to Pont-a-Mousson and got there in time for chow. Was it worth it? I can't say I'd do it again, but when the call for adventure comes, I guess I'm the first one there. This was not the only episode of this kind to happen to me. There were others. Some were not as exciting; others tried to live up to that pitch and oftentimes beat the rap. For the most part I kept up my visits in the French countryside. I continued to speak to everyone I could who would speak to me in French, and I continued my travels by myself.

RHEIMS

This brings me to my next story. The city of Rheims is noted for its champagne. The entire Rheims area is designated as the only area in France that can be called "Champagne." Rheims was a liberated city. When we marched in, most of the area we saw was in ruins, devastated by bombing. In order to enter the city, we had to cross over the river, because the main bridge leading to the city was demolished. Can you picture this? A thousand soldiers descended into the valley of the river where the Engineer Corps had set up a temporary bridge. We head up the hill, tired, weary, bleary-eyed, carrying our packs. As we reach the top of the hill, each soldier is handed a bottle of champagne! Giving a soldier a bottle of anything would make him jump up and down. You can imagine the excitement of a thousand men and a thousand bottles of champagne. It was a thrilling moment. The crowds standing by cheered, French flags were flying, and there were flowers at certain spots. It was a rousing welcome.

However, my life wasn't based on a bottle of wine. I wanted to see the city, meet some French people and find out what was happening around me. It wasn't long before I hustled dinner in a French family's home. They were nice enough to offer to feed me a true French chicken dinner. As I remember, it was quite good, but I can't think of how it was prepared. As I looked around the city, I was amazed to see entire warehouses of wine that were stored in cellars, with the walls blown away, easily available for anyone to take. But I didn't see any looting, at least at the time I was there.

THE COLLABORATOR

Then I had my biggest surprise. I was walking down the main drag, with houses on both sides of me. Not more than fifty yards away I saw a group of French guerrilla fighters holding a man, leading him out of a house. They were wearing the guerrilla shoes, jackets and the beret, and they really looked serious about what they were doing. This was not a relaxed group of men. All of a sudden, I saw a guerrila fighter take his pistol out of his holster, aim it at the man they were holding between them, and Bang! Bang! Bang! It was over. He was dead, shot right through his head. I was startled. I froze up immediately. I didn't know what to think.

When my senses were clear, I walked over to another group of men and asked them what that was all about. They were not the least bit surprised. One of them answered immediately. "Collaborator," he said. "That's what we are going to do to all of those people who collaborated with the Germans."

I know he meant it, because I was only fifty yards away or less when it happened. Those freedom fighters had walked into that house and dragged the victim out. After they shot him, they left his body where it fell, never turning their head to look back. All you saw was this man lying there, and they marched out like soldiers. It's a sight I shall never forget. This happened so quickly; it was over before I knew it.

From there, I wandered around town doing a few things that I truly don't remember. I will always remember Rheims, not for its champagne, but for that brutal moment when those so-called freedom fighters took justice in their own hands. That scene is just as vivid now as the day it happened. It is a memory that will be with me forever. I had seen death many, many times—but not in this same manner.

As you know, I always loved books. Books kept me alive when I could stand no more pain mentally. Pocket books were always available somewhere and I always carried books in my pack to keep me company when we were waiting for combat, in rest periods, or any time things slowed down. I have no idea how many books I read, what they were about, or what they were.

One day I know I was carrying a book of poetry that I ordinarily would not have read, and I met a pleasant young soldier who seemed interested in the same subject. Shelley, Byron, Keats, Browning and poets of that period were always my favorites and my interest in them had not diminished. We talked, and over a short period of time we built up a friendship. This may have been a rest period. However, we went into combat a few days later. Life moves rapidly in those kinds of situations. Our friendship was not long lived, since this soldier died in the next battle that took place. I don't know his name, can't remember where he was from, what he really looked like, but I do remember the relationship. It was a sad ending.

A PERSONAL FAILURE?

There were many sad endings that took place. This was only of them. Another time, the Captain came to me and told me a story about a very young Jewish soldier in whom he tried to instill confidence. This soldier kept insisting he wanted to leave the outfit, to try to go back to some other kind of work. The Captain continued to explain to him that there was no way other than the one he was taking. The Captain thought that I might be able to advise that soldier, or just guide him to a better understanding of the situation. When I spoke to the soldier, I knew there was a major problem in the offing. All I saw was a very frightened man who was so terrified, all he could say was, 'I don't want to die. I know I will die if I go out to fight." He whimpered and literally cried out for help. It was a terrible interview. I didn't know what to say, except to try to comfort him, to alleviate his fears, yet give him a realistic appraisal of the situation. I never made much headway. Our only meshing quality was our Jewish identity. I could not reach him any other way.

I have mentioned the positive qualities of a combat soldier somewhere in this story. You cannot go into combat thinking that you are going to be wounded or die. If you do, you are beat before you start. You have to believe that all of the bullets and shells around you are for someone else, not aimed at you, because you are someone special. God or some Supreme Being would be watching over you, futile as it might seem at some moments of terrible combat.

That soldier was a prime example of that same lack of confidence. He was hit the first day he was fighting, killed by a mortar shell and it was over. But it wasn't over for me. It was a personal failure. I felt that I had failed to do something that might have helped. I had recognized his youth and the lack of courage that he had shown. I knew that there was no way that he could escape his fate. He had given up before he started. But why should I feel guilty? I was stuck in the same hole that soldier had been in: I could not move or be transferred myself, so why did I feel guilty? I never understood that, but that feeling of helplessness remained with me for a long time. I don't know what the Captain felt, because I never discussed it with him. But why should he be distressed? He was fighting his own war.

HEIDELBERG

Heidelberg, Germany, and Maury does it again. Does what? The same thing that he has been doing all through this story: He goes off on a sight-seeing trip. Why do I skip to Heidelberg? We still were fighting in France, but this story popped up in my mind and I want to get it in before I lose it.

This was the Big Push. We wanted to move across the Rhine. We did, and we were on our way to Berlin—not my outfit, but the 3rd Army. But a big battle was to come. Here is the picture: Thousands of vehicles, tanks, trucks, artillery units and armored tanks are ready to go. Here we are in a gigantic staging area, somewhere near Heidelberg. We are not talking company, nor subdivision, but the entire 5th Division. I think it was made up of 15,000 men. Armies move slowly until they get going. It takes maybe two or three days to get all those troops together.

Of course, I got restless. Well, I think to myself, these guys are still playing around, so why don't I just take off for a couple of hours to see the town. I knew that Heidelberg was famous for its castles, the University, and also a famous river. So off I went, heading for the main part of the city. I met a few civilians, managing to get some directions, and finally wound up along the river, right next to Heidelberg University. What a pretty sight. I sold some of my hoarded cigarettes and chocolate for some fantastic amount of money.

I did get to make the acquaintance of a pleasant civilian who spoke fairly good English. Although I was basically hostile to his comments, I listened and made no rebuttal. It was a strange conversation. I sat beside the river for a while, who knows how long that was. Then it dawned on me that I ought to head back to my outfit. I did, and as I returned to the staging area there was a big surprise awaiting me. The Division was moving out. Everything was moving, the tanks, the trucks, the artillery units and the infantry. Where was my outfit? I knew where I had left it, but where was it now?

Can you imagine how I felt? I was lost, really lost. Fifteen thousand men and vehicles on the move. Where was this little thirty-two man company? I walked and I asked, "Headquarters Company? Do you know where they are? What part of this area are they in?" I walked and walked for at least an hour. There was no way to identify it. Everything looked the same. This was all part of the 5th Division, 2nd Infantry. But where were the Medics, a part of Headquarters Company?

Then I really began to get worried. This was no longer a joke. I was separated from my outfit and the Division was on the move: The real thing, right into combat. I began to think that I would never find them and I was trying to figure out what I could say to any officers who might stop me. It was a frantic hour or two. Then my luck changed. I had walked right into my Medic outfit. It was a miracle! I don't know how it happened, but it did. And I didn't question the why and wherefore. It was another story like many of them that ended happily. No one had missed me, nor did anyone question me. I continued on just as if I had been there all the time. The Big Push did take place, but that is another story for another time.

COLLECTING POSTCARDS

There are also many idiosyncrasies in war. Soldiers do many things that they would not think of ordinarily. Everyone who has read stories of war will remember situations where the soldiers would ransack the houses they passed through. If they bivouacked in a house, there would be nothing left for the owner that was worthwhile. It was actual pillaging. This was not uncommon. Everyone did it. In some cases they would try to carry "objets d'art." In others, they would just pick up trinkets. It was no secret that many soldiers would hit a home and just go through the drawers of the bureaus for anything of value. It was a strange phenomenon. Most of the time, what was left in the homes was junk.

In my case, I always picked up postcards. Picture postcards were synonymous with European customs. I found the most interesting cards everywhere I went. I always filled the back of the card out with stories of where I might be (censored, of course) and some idea of what I was doing. Pearl Kabb, my sister, saved all of hers and she had a stack of them somewhere; there are some good stories stashed away! I wrote almost every day, using army speed mail, as well as those postcards. But the mail only allowed for a small amount of information. Bess also had a stack of them as well.

JERRY FROM BROOKLYN

Well, we are settled in a little town in Germany, someplace I can't even remember. The name is secondary. Here is where my friend Jerry comes into the picture. Jerry was a young guy from Brooklyn, N.Y. Quiet, friendly and generally never bothering anyone. He was a fairly good-sized man, about twenty or twenty- one years old, and looked capable of handling himself. Because he was Jewish, Jerry was constantly berated in his company, which was the Pioneers. They worked on bridges, repairs, and general things. Each time I talked to Jerry he would tell me how they treated him. I was angry about that. "Jerry," I said, "don't let them do that to you. When someone razzes you, stand up to him. You are big enough to handle most anyone your size. I'm not asking you to hit the big guys. Start with the smaller ones and they'll know you mean business and you won't be pushed around." But Jerry wasn't that kind of a guy. He was a mild-mannered man and he didn't want to fight anyone. Too bad for him, because he went on being pushed around.

Anyway, in this scene, we were walking down a street in this little German village and minding our own business. Along came this freaky southern guy right behind us. He started to nag us, called out names such as "rag peddler," "hunky dory," and anything else he could think of to rile us up. I asked him in a quiet way to leave us alone. The Pioneer

Unit was a special team and they carry pistols instead of rifles. This guy had two of them, one on each side, sticking out of their holsters—and he wore them like he was Mr. Wild West himself. It was almost like a Western movie.

Well, the ragging continued. I told him again: "Leave us alone. We are not bothering you."

He replies, "What are you afraid of, the officers that are housed on both sides of the street?"

By this time I had finished talking. I was hot. "I'm not afraid of you, the officers, or anyone. Let's get into that open field on the next street and see who is afraid of what."

We did just that. Jerry was my second. This guy removes his pistols and holster and starts dancing around me. "Dance,'" I said. "You aren't going to dance long. We'll see who is the rag peddler."

I gave him a lesson in boxing that he might never forget. When I got through with him, he was battered up pretty good. I understand he went to the first aid area for treatment. I never heard another word about it, but I do know this: The guy never bothered Jerry any more. The others slowed up on ragging Jerry too, after that, but I couldn't fight every battle for him. He was in a separate unit. Anyway, it is a good story.

THE CASTLE

Back to Metz, which was still on the borderline of France, the Alsace-Lorraine area. We were in reserve and there was something like three hundred or more men in a big beautiful castle. Let's look around and take a picture, and this is what you'll see.

We were stationed in gorgeous rooms—big spacious areas, brocaded walls, beautiful chandeliers, and gorgeous furniture of French design. There was artwork of every kind: statues of porcelain, and paintings on the wall. This was a beautiful castle, a little old, but the pieces of art were breathtaking. We were there about two or three days. Outside the castle there were fruit trees, a beautiful garden, and all kinds of flowers that were still in bloom. The kitchen looked a little run down, but outside of that, the place really looked good. The owners must have left in a hurry, because all of the original furniture and art were still on the walls and in the cabinets. No jewelry, that I am sure, because the soldiers would have found it at once.

So the officer in charge issued an order, something like this: "I expect no one to touch anything in this castle. It is private property..." And so on. Who was he kidding? The first day, the officers strip the walls, take the art pieces, and ship them off home. How they managed this, I don't know. It wasn't a few moments after the GI's saw this happen that everyone got into the act, including myself.

I picked up a couple of expensive pieces of porcelain and stuck them in my pack. That was my only take, because I had no more room. I also managed to ship them back home, so there must have been some way that we could do this legitimately—that is, according to our standards of what was right. I don't have to tell you, this castle was stripped to the bare walls. I don't know how many pieces were originally left there, but whatever was there was soon gone. That is what happens when an army moves in.

Think of how big that castle must have been. Even though we slept on the floor, over three hundred men were barracked in this one place. So whenever I think of Metz and all the tough fighting that took place there, I remember the wonderful castle we were housed in for those few short days.

Don't think that we ate castle food because we were stationed there. We still got our C-Rations and the usual food we always ate. But it was one of the easiest spots to rest our bones during the entire war. I wonder what I would think of this castle if I would go back to see it now. I'm sure I'd see it through different eyes. Yet for that time, it was a great experience. Better yet, we still have those two pieces of porcelain in our cabinet. I also know that they may be two of the most exquisite pieces that we own, besides the fact that they are also the most expensive. It's a funny thing—even in wartime, materialism steps in.

METZ AND BEYOND

Metz was finally overcome at a tremendous cost of life. I don't know the actual count, but it was one of the costliest battles of the war, with the exception of The Bulge. That is another story we'll get to soon. I do know that soldiers from every part of the line would curse Patton for his willingness to send soldiers out to fight, knowing that their chances were nil. There was a continuous parade of manpower that continued to attempt to climb those walls and knock out the armaments. This went on for six weeks, so you know that this was a major stopping point for Patton's 3rd Army. But we finally got through and we were on our way to Germany. First stop, Saarlautern. We were beginning to move closer. At least we thought so, as we moved through two or three small villages in the next few days.

FRATERNIZATION

Germany. This was another story. Here is one of the strange parts of soldiering that you only read in books. When you think of victor and vanquished, you think of master and slave. It doesn't work that way. There we were, moved into a little village in Germany, housed in some homes, in some tents, and in constant contact with the German civilians. Who are they, the civilians? These are old men and women who could not fight, and younger housewives. There was a human factor that came into the picture at this point.

Germany had been at war since 1939. Those young women had been without men—their men—for three, four, five years. The GI's were nice. They brought food and cigarettes and chocolate for the pretty girls, and for their children. We sometimes would be in a town for five or six days, waiting to go back in to fight. Relationships built up. The GI's found the frauleins quite responsive. There was some fraternization, some sexual activity, and it was all done in the spirit of the times. It was wartime. There were no rules. There was human nature.

Of course, there were orders from headquarters that forbade any fraternization. Who would listen to that, if the rules were not enforced by punishment of some kind? The officers had more important things to worry about, so it went unnoticed. There was more and more fraternization as the days went on. And the gifts of food, cigarettes and chocolate bars were standard forms of trade.

What does all this have to do with me? I was the star of all of these negotiations. I was the key figure. Why was I important? Easy answer. I had the sulfa pills. It was said, and I imagine it was true, that sulfa was a wonder drug. It could prevent venereal diseases and infection if you took one pill before contact and one after contact. Well, I had the sulfa pills. I was "Doc." I opened the door. So if you wanted to be protected, once again I was the key man. I gave out sulfa pills like they were a dime a dozen, and of course I was everyone's friend for that time.

Probably the thing that puts all of this on another setting was the inconsistency of the thinking of all those people who were getting together. They were friend and foe, but they came together because of their own need for a relationship, the physical and natural inclination of woman and man. It is hard to believe this, yet France was the home of love and everything physical. The French women were pretty, responsive and our allies. On the other hand, the German women were neither as pretty, nor were they our allies. They were our enemy.

As it turned out, there was more sexual activity in Germany wherever we went, than in France. It was one of the enigmas of the war. I was never able to figure out the answer. The funny thing about all of this is that I had read about all of these happenings in books. Now it was happening before my very eyes. This did not go on only in one area. It occurred time after time whenever the soldiers stopped for more than two or three days. It is also remarkable what a little food and chocolate plus cigarettes can do for relationships.

It makes one wonder about the strength of hunger and the sex drive, which are the driving forces of life. It was December 1944. The weather was cold, but we were not fighting. We had worked our way up to Luxembourg, to a little village called Lorenzweiler. What a small village that was. What a respite as well. I know I was battle-weary and my head ached for some way to escape all that I had done and seen. It was a low period emotionally for me. I was depressed and aching to get to anyone who could put me into any kind of normalcy, even for an hour.

A MEMORABLE FRIENDSHIP

I walked through the village by myself, trying to find some solace in the surroundings. It was a beautiful area and I remember the trees and the well-kept homes quite well. The weather was fairly mild for December and there were still spots of green visible. Tourists called Luxembourg "Little Switzerland," and the name has remained even to this day.

As I walked along one of the side streets I saw a fairly attractive woman washing her windows. Why do I say "fairly attractive"—she looked like a beauty to me! I had been out in combat for a month or more, so anybody had to look good. I mean *real* good.

I called out to her, "Parlez-vous francais, madame?"

"Oui," she replied,"je parle francais, parce-que c 'est la langue du peuple ici."

I then spoke to her in a very sensitive manner, in French, of course. (Isn't it funny? I used to correspond with the family but now I've forgotten their names). I reached out to her in an emotional state.

"I have been in a living hell," I said. "All I would like to do is to sit down in an ordinary home so that I can once again feel that there is some normalcy in the world. I will not bother you. I won't ask you for wine or beer. I will not bother you in any way that will be offensive to you. My only wish is to try to regain some sense of the personal identity I once had. It would be a great favor for you to do this, but I am really in desperate straits. If you could help me, I would be most grateful. Who knows? Tomorrow we may be once again going back into combat. This is a rest period and we are awaiting new orders." This was really a plea for help. Maybe she felt my pain or maybe she wanted to do something for her country, because Luxembourg was liberated. She invited me in.

I sat down in her living room, took off my shoes at her request and began a normal conversation. "My husband will be home in a few hours. Would you like a glass of wine and some cheese?" She was most hospitable, and I spent an hour or so talking to her and getting my bearings. When her husband came home, he was quite friendly as well. He was quite ordinary looking as I remember, and he spoke very little. However, they suggested that I come for dinner the following day.

That was truly the best thing that could have happened to me at that point. The entire outfit was on edge. We had heard something about the Big Push that was to take place, or that was already in progress. We were waiting. The call could come in an hour, in a day, or maybe more. We waited every day for news of a pullout. We did not know at that time that the Battle of the Bulge was already in progress.

What a relief it was for me to have someplace to go to during my off hours. Combat soldiers don't drill or do any thing of any consequence. All they do is wait. "The call is coming," the officers would say. "Don't stray too far from headquarters.'" Well, there was no place to stray. The entire village was not more than two or three city blocks. Big it wasn't, so there was no other place to go. So I found myself returning each day to talk to this woman, whoever she was. Our relationship was built on her ethnicity and my American culture. I told her about my family and my hopes of returning home. I talked about the loneliness of soldiering and how difficult it was to see friends whom you had learned to love go down before your eyes. I talked of the wounded and the dead and the hardships I had endured. I am sure that I did most of the talking, but she listened. I did manage to eat another dinner, a few days later. And then we got the call. "We are moving out this evening," the Captain said. "Get your gear ready to go and be ready to move out at 18 hours. No exceptions. Everyone be in place when the clock strikes." It was over. I never got the chance to say goodbye.

Those people were so friendly, so decent and so nice, I would never forget them. They were like an oasis in the desert. Their friendship nourished and sustained me, particularly that woman. I can't remember what she looked like, nor could I describe her in any way. All I do know, it was a haven for me during those five or six days we were on alert. When the war was over, I made it a point to send them packages of food. I also corresponded with the family for many years. I also treasured those letters and you may find copies of these letters from Lorenzweiler, Luxembourg, written in French.

These are the kind of experiences that break you down. You are left with memories that are sweet and good, yet you are helpless in the wake of a war machine that does not allow for sweetness, or even bitterness. You can only be involved in the one thing that matters—the direction of the war.

THE BATTLE OF THE BULGE

It was Christmas and we were entering the most embittered combat experience that we were to have. Metz was the worst, but The Bulge would be a close second. We moved out. Light snow began to fall. I remember that part well. I don't know how cold it was, but I remember the snow. It was all over the place. We slept in foxholes that were hard as rocks to dig, and everyone had to dig his own. There was no one to dig it for you. The deeper you dug it, the safer you were. We learned that early in the game.

Then the medical toll began to take its place in the fighting men. There were lots of frozen feet, and when we hit an area where the men could be checked, there were more tough decisions. The Medical Officers knew that the men were needed and they were tough on letting the men go back to the hospital.

One day, I rebelled and criticized the Captain for his decision to keep different men on the line, when I thought they deserved some attention at the field hospital. The Captain said nothing, nor did he argue about it. I am of the opinion that he still maintained what he considered a fair stance, in spite of what I said. It's also a funny thing that he never pushed the insubordination process on me, since I was so critical. But things are different in actual combat. Most of the rules of familiarity are broken when men are faced with so many other challenges. He recognized that and probably felt I was distraught because of all the tragedy that was going on around us. And remember, Captain Greenberg was a fairly nice guy. I had very little to do with him on a personal level. Although we came together on a closer level when I became his jeep driver near the end of the war, I never achieved any personal closeness. (This was probably due to officer and soldier separateness. The war was starting to taper down when I was driving a jeep, so I think that we were moving closer to normal officer/enlisted men regulations).

We hit the front lines, coming in on the flank of the main fighting. This did not lessen the tension, nor minimize the power of the German army. This was the last big push of the German fighting force. The power that they exhibited at that major battle will go down in history as the biggest display of manpower of a talented war machine. I have no idea of how many men were fighting and how many fronts there were. All I can think of is the days under fire and the constant fear of dying. The artillery and mortar fire seemed to be endless. It went on for days. We never thought it would end.

Artillery fire has something special about it that you never forget. There is a certain whiz that seems to come from nowhere. It has a sound that alerts you to the massive explosion that is going to take place in the next few seconds. The trouble is that you never know where it is heading or where it is going to land. You always think it is going to land on you. Sometimes it did come very close, close enough to try to decide whether you should get out of your foxhole or stay in. It is a scary, eerie feeling. And you never forget the whiz. It remains with me to this day. The closest thing that I can think of that reminds me of that whizzing sound is when two trains pass each other going in different directions; there is a similarity there that I can put together. The individual happenings that occurred at The Bulge are all massed together into one big package. Everything is blurred, coming together only as an endless time of days of fighting, with no end in sight.

There was one situation, sometime in March, when the Battle of the Bulge was over, that all my fears came into play. I always wondered what I would do if I was called upon to go out under fire to help someone when the chips were really down. It's odd to think about it, now that it's no longer in my mind as a choice. I do know I had high standards for myself as a soldier. I also believed that I did have a responsibility to carry out my part of the bargain as a medic. I also was not a fool, nor would I go into a situation knowingly that I thought would be foolhardy.

But you don't know those things beforehand. I remember when I stayed hidden one day when there was a terrible battle going on. My mind refused to let me go. Right or wrong, this was my own decision. I will accept any thought you may have on its negative effect or whatever you think. It is easy to criticize when you are not there to see and feel the intensity of what is going on around you.

THE BRONZE STAR

However, in this one case that I am writing about, I never stopped to think of what might occur. We were in the thick of it. A major battle was in progress. Bullets were flying through the air; bombs were exploding nearby. The cry went out, "Medic! I am hit. Help me!" One hundred yards away or more, a soldier lay on a slightly inclined hill, with two of his comrades beside him. I crept and crawled and kept myself as low as I could as I tried to get to the three men. There were bullets coming from somewhere. I never tried to find out where they were heading. I stayed on track until I finally got to this solider.

Unfortunately, his two buddies were dead, and I crawled over them to get to this guy. I bandaged his wound and gave him a morphine shot. All this took place under fire. Then I told him that I could not carry him alone and that I needed his help to get him back to safer ground. It was some job. I dragged him at one point, but I got him back. I'll never forget the feeling I had climbing over those two dead soldiers. It was a scene that will remain with me forever. I don't know who the soldier was, nor did I ever learn his name, nor what happened to him after he went back to the hospital.

I was not aware that my captain sent in an account of my bravery to the Army, officially nominating me for a Bronze Star Award. It passed and I received it some time later in the year. It was a surprise to me, because I did not know that he had recommended it. There was another unknown element to it that I was truly pleased about. I should say not pleased, but overwhelmed with pride. I was being recognized for something I did, because I was who I was. I had not hustled anyone for this recognition. I was being honored for something I earned, something I was doing almost every day of my fighting, and I was not accountable to anyone but myself.

This was the highest achievement I could hope for as a soldier. I would never be an officer, but I had earned respect for what I had accomplished. This medal affords me the greatest satisfaction I have achieved in anything I have done, outside of my family, in my entire life. I am proudest of those years as a medic, because I know that the work I was doing was saving some lives. I was helping men get back to the hospital, which gave them an 80% chance of survival. I was the instrument. I could take credit internally. I believed that what I was doing had great worth. I also will never find out why I made that choice that day, or whether I would do it again, given the same circumstances.

ANOTHER BIGOT

Things were not always great in terms of relationships, even on the front line of combat. There was one particular time that I recall that disturbs me even to this very day. The sergeant in charge of our medical group was an ordinary kind of guy. I really don't remember having much contact with him, or any personal connection. I still don't understand what brought on this incident. If I had had any argument with this man, I would be able to understand it. As far as I knew, I was just another medic in the group. At least that is what I thought.

This is what happened. It comes back to me as clear as day: We are in actual combat, and instead of K-rations, for some reason or other, we are fed at a field mess kitchen. I don't remember exactly where this occurred. So I get up to the sergeant, who was serving, and he approaches me this way, imitating a foreign Jew.

"Vot vould you lick, a piss of this, and a piss of that?"

Well, to say I was angry, that would be the least of it. I was so mad, I dropped my mess kit on the floor, grabbed him by the throat and this is exactly what I said to him. "Do you hear me talk now? How do I talk? Do you hear any accent such as you imitated? If you ever talk like that again to me, I'll close your windpipe so you'll never be able to talk again."

The guy was frozen in his tracks. He couldn't say anything at all for a few minutes, but he just looked at me. He never uttered a word after that. Again, here was a sergeant in charge of men and he pulls that kind of stuff. Hard to figure out.

Actually, no one said anything to me after the incident. There were no officers present, so it just went by the other men. I know that the other men recognized how angry I was. As I indicated, I had no personal relationships other than the standard ones, so life went on just as before. Nothing changed. We were all trying to stay alive. That is what soldiers worry about most.

YOUNG LIBERATED POLISH JEWS JOIN OUR GROUP TEMPORARILY

Just about this time we began to run into Polish refugees of Jewish origin who were liberated somewhere along the way. Again, names and places are a blur, but I can remember their youthful faces. These guys were quite young, eighteen, or in that range. Two or three of them attached themselves to our company. Dressed in striped prison camp uniforms, they stuck out like sore thumbs. As time went on, they acquired khaki pants and field jackets. They were warm, friendly men and they would do anything that any of the soldiers wanted. They knew little English, but they knew enough to get by. If we wanted eggs, or anything from the countryside, they would go out and scavenge food. They always came back with something or other. The soldiers used them for "gofers." Even though they were foreigners, everyone took to them. They hung around, glad to get food and some kind of shelter during this period. We were somewhere around Essen, Germany, at that time. They spoke German naturally, so they had easy access to all of the civilians.

It was a sad day for all of us, including me, when the officer in charge of the outfit told them they could no longer stay with us. It was quite a painful goodbye. I had established a personal relationship with one of the young men. Foolishly, I had said to him that I hoped to be able to get him back to the States. There were tears in both of our eyes when we parted. But in my heart, I knew that neither of those men would have any difficulty in survival techniques. They had been through so much; this would only be another trial for them.

American soldiers anywhere, on any front, opened up their hearts wherever they were. This would only be a question of bureaucracy. I am certain they were able to take care of themselves and that they would find their way somewhere. Unfortunately, I would never know where, nor what happened to them. This was not a unique experience, because if you talk to other men who served all over Europe, you would hear of similar incidents.

DANIEL, REFUGEE FROM GREECE

My friend Daniel Cohen, another refugee, who was from Salonica, Greece, attached himself to our company. He was of the same breed, and even though he spoke no English, he was able to manage. He could do anything—forage for food, bring back eggs, chicken, meat or what have you. He spoke French, Greek, Hebrew, Yiddish, and possibly German. This guy was all over the place. He even hustled girls for some of the guys. Again, food and cigarettes and chocolate were some of the easiest barters for the women in most areas. Daniel was a champ at making contact.

Daniel and I had a common bond. He was a Greek Jew.

Believe this or not, he spoke French to communicate. He was a loving, kind person. Can you imagine my feelings as he identified himself with that classic Yiddish song, "Belz, Mein Shtetele Belz"? This is a mournful plaintive song that bemoans the loss of this beautiful village, and has all the memories of home, family and peace. It still remains a classic piece in our musical heritage. Daniel remained a friend even post-war. We corresponded for many years. At a later time, after the war, Daniel sent a package to me to New York City. He did not realize that New York was five hundred miles away! Somehow the package got to me. I don't remember the process, but I did get it. A few years later, we visited Daniel and his family in Israel, but that is another story.

Daniel was an enigma to most. He was a little man, but he moved like a fire. He was all over the place, ready to do anything. He discarded his prison garb almost the first week and was clothed in a GI uniform and boots. The sorriest part of his story was how he got to where we were in Germany. He had lost everything he owned. He had also no knowledge of anyone in his entire family. As far as he knew, they had all died in the last camp where he was detained. All of these refugees had a great talent for survival. They were able to survive only through their own diligence and their ability to meet every situation with some form of finesse. Daniel had that capacity and he used it well.

Unfortunately, when we finally got to see him in Israel after many years of separation, he had lost that piece of himself that had separated him from the ordinary. He was now the father of two or three children, and all of the drama of yesteryear had disappeared. Daniel was now one of us, and those characteristics that singled him out had been lost in the melee. Israel was also in a struggle for survival, particularly at that time. Daniel had served in the Israeli army, seen combat, and had suffered some kind of after-effect. It did not seem to me, or Bess, that he was in a normal state.

However, Daniel was a storybook hero. I admired him and loved him for who he was during those days in the army. He brought me friendship and returned my affection. It served both of us well. He will always remain with me as a glorious memory of hope and determination. Daniel disappeared along with some of the other refugees when he was forced to leave. It was a harbinger of what was to come. Liberation of a German army occupation camp was the last thing on my mind. It was something I had never expected, but it was in the cards and would play an important part in the future.

MAIL CALL

There were times when mail did not come in for weeks or more. Other times, it came in double doses. I wrote almost every day, either on postcards I had confiscated (I should say "looted") or V-Mail.

Packages from home were always a high point. When mail call did come up, I'd wait patiently to see whether I had a package coming. Most of the time, it took weeks to get to me, because of troop movements. At other times, I would get two packages at a time; this complicated things, because I could only carry so much. There were always salami in the package. Most often they arrived full of mold. I would scrape off the mold and devour the rest. But with two packages full of goodies, I found I had to dispose of much of what I had received. Bess was a good shipper and I got plenty of packages, helping to carry me through, particularly after a long siege of K-rations. What a delight it was to open up those boxes. I don't want to remember how lonely it was and how I longed for home. I guess everybody who was stuck like I was felt the same way. It was all we could think of.

THE POINT SYSTEM

During one of these crises there was a hidden agenda. There was a system of points that the army was to use in order to release soldiers at the end of the war. It was a long way off, but the point system created a certain amount of negativity. Let me explain. The captain and the lieutenant were single. That meant no points for a wife, or for children. I came up with something like forty points, plus points for my wife and children. Points were given for overseas duty, for both battle stars, and for medals. The officers and some men were teed off because I was to receive the benefit of points from my family. They resented that, because they felt that they had to serve longer terms and had to spend more time in battle to equalize the situation. It was a sore point for both the officers and the men I was in contact with. It may sound strange to an outsider, but when you are in this kind of situation, every point counts.

85 POINTS = DISCHARGE

It was this factor that got me out of the army earlier than I had anticipated. I got out in November 1945, because I had two Bronze Stars, five points each; my family; time overseas, five points; Purple Heart and five battle stars for major battles. I needed a total of eighty-five points. This combination worked in my favor and saved me a month or two more in service. I remember how happy I was to know that I was to get out at the time I did. I was given some kind of option to wait be transported. I chose to leave and took the train myself!

You can imagine the joy I felt as I got off the train at the Terminal Tower and walked up the ramp carrying all of my belongings in a duffel bag. At the top of the landing, Bess was waiting for me. What a wonderful day that was! It was a day that lasted forever in my mind. I can still feel the joy that surged through me as I was finally able to feel Bess near me, to touch her, to hold her and just to be there. I don't know who else was present.

THE YOM KIPPUR LETTER

One of the strangest things that would happen to me, occurred somewhere in France on Yom Kippur. We were in reserve, meaning we had just come off the line of fire. However, that also meant that we had to be ready to move out at a moment's notice. Reserve was something that we all relished. It was a time to put yourself together and even though you knew that you would soon be back fighting, you would savor every moment of freedom you were given.

We had just completed a disastrous campaign, trying to break through the Metz fortifications. We had suffered a great many losses, and morale was pretty low. We were in a nearby area, not too far from the actual fighting in the Alsace-Lorraine area. Metz is the door to that historic spot, whose nationality has changed many times over the last hundred years, from French to German, then returning to France and then occupied by the Germans in World War II.

I don't remember how I knew it was the holiday, but I remember the incident well. I was resting, lying on the ground above the foxhole I had dug. It was broad daylight. We could hear the sound of guns somewhere in the distance, but nothing came close to us. At least that is the way it seemed at the time. I knew that I did not have to fast, that the law of fasting did not pertain to this circumstance. However, years of training gave me no alternative and I decided to take a shot at it. I knew it was foolish of me, but I thought maybe I could do it.

It was my practice to write home almost any chance I got. It was in these situations when we were in reserve that I did much of my writing. It was a beautiful day and I had discarded much of my uniform and was soaking up the sun in one form or another. "Never take your helmet off. It's the best protector you have." That was something that we had been taught forever. But soldiers don't take these things to heart.

Since this was a sort of free area, the cook had set up a coffee pot and some cookies in the far end of the camp, approximately two hundred yards away. It was about noon and I recognized that I had lost my energy level. I said to myself, "You are a fool, you know. There is no reason for you to fast. It is not required, particularly in a situation like this. Why would you do that? If you should be called to move out, your energy would be gone and you would not be able to function."

The reasoning was good and I decided to give up my fast. A few seconds later, I put my writing stuff aside, left my jacket and my helmet next to it, and headed to a big old barn a few hundred yards away, where a coffee pot had been set up. I should have had sense enough to at least wear my helmet. When I finally reached the coffee, I poured out a cup into my mess kit and headed back to my foxhole. As I returned to my foxhole, I heard the sound of a mortar shell whizzing through the air. There is an unmistakable whiz that mortars make; it is probably the most distinguishable of all the weaponry that is used. I didn't have to wait more than a few seconds before it landed right next to my foxhole, destroying my jacket and my helmet, cutting the letter into tiny pieces.

So there you have it, a clear case of religious non-observance, if you can call it that. But the result was fabulous! All that I lost was my clothes. The fortunes of war; that is what they call it.

Although we were expecting more of the same, nothing else happened. That was the only shot that came through! You don't wonder about the whys and wherefores, but you do take the good ones when they happen. I often wondered about that stroke of fate, but the only thing I make out of it is you don't tempt fate. That same day, I sent Bess the fragments of the letter I was writing, with an explanation. Unfortunately, explanations don't do too well, especially when you are far away and you receive fragmented letters. Bess was quite concerned when she received it, and it took a number of letters of explanation before she was satisfied. But it only goes to prove one thing: There is no right or wrong when you are in a situation like this. Your fate is in the hands of something bigger than all of this and I was saved to continue on for many more years.

There are always periods of highs and lows on the battlefield. It is no different from everyday living, but the stakes are higher. During my army career my physical level may have been at its highest level of activity and strength. I am sure that I would not have been able to do as much as I did and survive the physical ordeal that was required. It was not only a matter of strength, but also the ability to fight in wet, damp cold weather, lying in cold clothes in a foxhole and eating sporadically, with only an occasional meal that was filling enough to remember. It was an ordeal, but the truth is, I did well with it, except for the mental anguish. That is where I had the most difficulty.

Strangely enough, I was generally in front of the company, moving with the best of them, wherever the action was. As you may have seen in the movies, the new fighting line was made up of men walking in single file instead of clusters, so that if a shell hit or there were a number of explosions, the separation would be helpful to some in the front and some in the rear. Generally we would be eight or ten yards apart as we marched or made our way through the terrain.

On this particular day, I felt weak and dragged out. I gradually lost my front position, as I remember, and slowly moved my way to the rear. I thought nothing of it, except that I knew that my energy had dissipated. I didn't stop to figure out why, and never found the reason for it. It just happened that way. Sometime during the day, we were attacked by a barrage of artillery shelling that came out of nowhere. It happened so fast, no one had any time to think or to do anything but try to get out of the way. The shells landed mostly on the front part of the company and all of the men who were in that area suffered severe casualties and some of them were killed instantly. Trying to explain that part of it leaves you again with that same thought: How did it happen that way? Your answer will be as good as mine.

A NEAR RIOT

You know already that I never followed a pattern of conformity in my army career, so the following story will not be any great surprise to you. I was in the last stages of the war. We were somewhere in Essen, Germany, and most of the bitter fighting was over. There were still pockets of resistance and we did get our share of the fighting. I was in a little better situation, because I had become a jeep driver for the medical officers. I was not on the actual line of battle.

For some reason or other, I was told to drive our officers to a prison camp a few miles away. It was not an actual prison, but a building set aside to hold the prisoners temporarily. There were U. S. soldiers guarding the building and everything was well controlled. A number of German prisoners seemed to be moving around and were allowed to have a certain amount of freedom of movement. The jeep at that time was a symbol of American style. Any foreign vehicle would be just as impressive to us as the jeep was to the Germans.

A number of German prisoners surrounded the vehicle while I was standing by. They kept looking at it. One of them came over to me, speaking in broken English, inquiring about its parts and operation. I was not receptive, nor did I intend to be. Because I had so much hate for them at that particular time, I could hardly hold myself back from expressing it. Then a couple of them walked over to the vehicle and talked to their comrade in German. When the next group of them came over, I was overcome with passion. I screamed at them in a Yiddish kind of German about how despicable they were. I could not control my emotions, because we had just finished liberating a group of seventy-five female Holocaust survivors who had been on a march to a prison camp. The horrors I had seen burned within me. I could not control myself. I shouted and screamed obscenities at them.

"You are murderers, baby killers, women killers," I shouted. "You have taken lives mercilessly, with no regard to innocence or justice, only because they were Jews. I am a Jew," I shouted. "Look at me and see whether you want to kill me, too."

The Germans became angry and began to yell back at me. It was almost a minor sort of riot, but the guards calmed things down and I climbed back in my jeep. In the process, the officers heard the shouting and came running to find out what had happened. When they asked me, I pretended to know nothing. I just said that the prisoners had become unruly for some unknown reason and I had had some words with them, but I didn't know what the problem was. They looked at me rather funny, because they suspected that I had been the culprit. I probably looked guilty. They questioned me further, and sort of reprimanded me for causing the problem. They knew that I had done something, but they couldn't put their finger on it. Actually, it was not the first time that I had created a problem, nor would it be the last.

ACQUISITIONS

Again, going back to basics. What were the basics of army life? You have to remember that we lived in a period when your money had no value. Possessions such as food, cameras, pistols (German only), rifles, daggers, swords and German insignia had great value. They were worth more than money. They represented prestige of some kind or another. Not in the truest sense, but in a way that gave it great significance. Being a free lance person, on my own, I had more opportunities than most to obtain some of these commodities. As a jeep driver at the time, I had more access to acquire these things and I was afforded more opportunities. Let me add that I probably had confiscated at least six or eight cameras, one pair of binoculars and a Luger pistol. Every one of these items had special value. You must also remember that you could only take what you could carry. As valuable as each one of these items might be, I could only carry one of each. Three pieces would be quite limiting.

However, that was not the only problem. I did have certain relationships I wanted to maintain. Although I built no personal friendships, I recognized the value of those objects used as tools for maintaining relationships. In each case, I used them as gifts. As a point of interest, each one of the cameras I took from live German soldiers who were going to give themselves up, had considerable value. At that time, German cameras were the best in the world and I had one of the best which I used for my Holocaust pictures. With this camera you looked through a wide lens from the top and then took the picture. If you look at my army pictures, you'll see how well the camera performed. The camera was terrific, because I knew nothing about taking pictures. Where did I get film? Film was as scarce as food and there was no film available, except for Maury Feren. I'll tell you more about that as we move along.

So picture this: The war was over. That is, most German soldiers recognized this fact and began to turn themselves in to the Americans. I was in my jeep, waiting for my officers to come back out of a building where they were doing some atrocity reports that we had been assigned to. As I was sitting in my vehicle, along came two German soldiers who were ready to give themselves up. One of them was an officer. I got out of the jeep.

The first thing I say is, "Give me your binoculars and your pistol."

He replies, "Officer. I want to surrender to an officer."

I answer, "Pistol, binoculars. You must give them to me."

The other soldier hands me his rifle, but the officer still insists, "Officer. I want to surrender to an officer only. I know I'm in trouble, but I insist."

"You must turn over your pistol and binoculars to me," I state firmly.

He finally does, reluctantly of course. I take him back to the jeep and await the return of the officers. He recognized immediately that the Captain was an officer and tried to complain to him about the loss of his pistol and binoculars. He did make some headway, because he was quite noisy about it. When the Captain asked me what he wanted, I said something about a pistol and binoculars someone had probably taken from him on the road. I knew that if I turned over these items, I would never get them back. I had already stashed them someplace in the jeep, hoping they wouldn't do a search or catch on that I had been the culprit.

I did get away with it. Interestingly, I gave both items away, more for a relationship than for anything else. I do remember giving the pistol to Sergeant Peterson. What the results were is inconsequential. That was my style. I did come home with an Italian rifle, a couple of swords with Nazi insignia, a dagger, some flags, some buckles that were inscribed "Gott Mit Uns," and a lovely pair of opera glasses, designed in pearl, with beautiful inlaid material.

There is a great deal more to this story than what comes out of this on paper. If you could see the picture as it really happened, you would appreciate it more. I can still see the frustration of this officer having to surrender to a mere PFC. If he had known I was only a medic, he would have been demoralized even more. He stood there almost frantic in his determination to surrender to an officer. It was a battle of wills. I was insistent that he turn over his arms and his binoculars. That was the important issue for me. I wasn't concerned that he would turn on me. The items were what were important. These were not the first Germans who were surrendering, because they came in from every direction once they found out the war had ended, but it was my first actual personal contact. I did obtain cameras in a prisoner line-up, but that is another story. The other thing that even makes this so important is that there was more intrinsic value in these wartime treasures than their monetary value. No self-respecting soldier would sell one of these items for money. It was a wartime memento, to be kept for posterity. Why did I give up the pistol? I hated guns and what they represented. I was the most grateful man on earth that I never had to use a gun. That was the only good thing that happened to me in the army as a medic: I didn't have to use a gun.

Back to the issue of film for cameras. Earlier in the war, coming out of Metz into German territory, right into Saarlautern, we discovered a Kodak warehouse. I picked up somewhere in the neighborhood of one hundred rolls of film. Now there was no way I could carry one hundred boxes of camera film, so I decided to try this ploy: I went to the Red Cross station and spoke to one of the men in charge. I said to him, "I'll give you one hundred rolls of film if you'll do the following. I'll take ten rolls now for myself. If I come back, I'll expect you to give me another ten, when the war is over, whenever that will be." I wasn't too concerned about where either of us would be, but I did want some assurance. "You'll have to promise me that you'll not sell any of these, but pass them out free."

Wasn't that a stretch of imagination? How could anyone pass up selling the film? I never expected that to happen, but it did! My faith in human beings' honesty was realized. Sometime after the war had ended, this same person gave me five rolls of film. I never questioned him on what he had done with the rest of it. There was nothing I could have done with them in any case, so it was just as well things worked out the way they did.

What bothered me most at that time was that an American company, Kodak, was in cahoots with Germany. How little did I understand about world trade and global opportunities! (It is not much different from what is happening now, with so many international endeavors and alliances that penalize our country and its workers).

A CLOSE CALL

Wrong way Corrigan. Well, we should say "Wrong-Way Maury."

As I mentioned earlier, I was made a jeep driver after my shrapnel injury at Etampes, France. So this was almost post-war, sort of like the war was almost over, but not quite in some locations. The intensity of the battles had lessened, but there was still sporadic fighting going on.

So I was driving the Captain some place that he planned to go to. The precautionary measures were not as prevalent, and the jeep was open, with no protection whatsoever. Remember this was a medical vehicle, with a big Red Cross on it—not much of a source of protection if an artillery shell comes through, because artillery fire comes from so far away, it cannot distinguish whom it will hit.

I was driving quite casually, enjoying the ride, so to speak, and not taking much note of what was happening around me or where we were headed. Some of you may be aware of my lack of directional sense, and others may not. Let me add that this was not the first time I headed in the wrong direction. However, in this case, it almost turned deadly. Somewhere out of the blue, I heard shots fired. I should have said, we heard shots coming from somewhere. We didn't stop to look. I was headed right for the enemy lines! It was almost impossible to believe. Here I was, almost on top of the enemy fire and I had driven there by myself.

I turned that vehicle around so fast, I believe it almost tipped. Even worse than that, I stepped on the gas pedal, pressed it to the floor and skidded away at fifty or more miles per hour. Driving as fast as I could, scared out of my pants, the first thing I ran into was a railroad crossing. It was not smoothed out and I hit it going full speed, sixty to seventy miles an hour. Remember, this was one of the early jeeps, and that was like flying!

But that isn't all that happened. When I hit that railroad crossing, my vehicle went up into the air about ten feet high. At least it felt that way. I do remember that part of it well. As I was coming down, I could see the horrified faces of the onlookers, who must have said, "Those crazy Americans!" I wasn't crazy; I was just trying to escape with my life. Fortunately there was no damage done to either of us, or the vehicle. I'm not sure what the Captain told me, but I'm thinking it was a serious reprimand.

ATROCITY CRIME SEARCH

We were at the end of the war and things had begun to relax in one way or another, so it wasn't as severe a reprimand as it might have been. When the war ended, I continued to drive. Our raison d'etre, or reason for existence, began to change as we became involved in the Atrocity Crime Search. This job was given to certain people in Headquarters Company and the Medical Corps was assigned to this particular job.

Again, we come into the Holocaust story, but this is one I will not write much about. It was too painful to relive. It still is difficult to recount those experiences. The memories and the people remain with you forever. The dead faces and the bodies that were so foul their odors remain with you forever and continue to remind you of what you saw. We liberated seventy-five Jewish women at Eggenfelden, Germany, once a part of Sudetenland, originally a part of Czechoslovakia. It is located sixty miles from Prague and was a part of Pilsen County. Everyone in Europe can recognize the area by this description. On one trip we dug up bodies for miles around us. The victims had been murdered by German officers while on a forced march to a concentration camp nearby. Those who were unable to continue walking were shot, piled in heaps along the side of the road, along with their belongings and their mess kits. Think of that odorous scene and you can get some idea of what horrors those people lived through.

The story in its entirety can be found in the 5th Division History Book, with some pictures. Michael Feren, my grandson, has the original history showing all of the geographic areas the Division had fought in and where and when we fought. There is a story in there about Chaplain Dickers, the Jewish chaplain who took charge of the entire operation, trying to revitalize those people who still had enough life in them to be saved.

It was a sad, sad sight. How those women survived is a story by itself. One of the questions I never wanted to ask about nor think about is the women's appearance. There were some who were so emaciated you did not believe they were alive. Others looked fair and a few looked good. It was not until many years later, when I read *Sophie's Choice* by William Styron, that I allowed myself to think about what I had seen. There was a mass funeral in Eggenfelden that week, with each body placed in a separate coffin. The entire town was forced to come out for this mass burial. Again, there are pictures of all of these happenings in the 5th Division Journal as well as the magazine *Photo Journal* put out by the Jewish War Veterans of America.

If you should ever get to Washington, D.C., it might be a good idea to stop to visit the Jewish War Veterans Museum. There is a separate Holocaust room. While you are there you will find pictures of the events just as they happened. I had taken fifty pictures of this tragedy myself. Fortunately, I had a terrific camera and the pictures came out well and remained clear over many years. I sent them to the Jerusalem Holocaust Museum, Yad Ha Shem. Some ten years later, I discovered another group of photographs and shipped them off to the Holocaust Museum in Washington, D.C. There still may be one or two or more that remain in my picture file.

This is not all there is to the story. It covers a lifetime of experiences. How can you bring back the friendship and caring you want to bring to these suffering people? Can you help with food? Does servicing them with Jewish prayers and books become helpful? What about the personal relationships you make with certain people? Where are they now? Who were they? Where did they go? Wouldn't it be wonderful to find out? What happened to them post-war, after the original freedom fighters left? What a story that would make.

There are many individual people I met with whom I had a personal relationship. Those relationships were quite deep and still remain with me to this very day. Their names are lost to me forever, but who they were and their response to life was meaningful to anyone they came in contact with. I was not the only one who made contact with these survivors. There were other soldiers, regardless of who they were, who brought food, gifts of sweets, cigarettes or anything that would be of value to these suffering remnants of the tragedy. Americans have a capacity for sympathy and reaching out in any situation where people are besieged by any kind of problem. This became even more evident in this particular situation, since only the chaplain and a handful of the soldiers involved were Jewish.

You must also take into account the restrictions that we as soldiers faced. The U.S. Army required that friendly relationships with the Germans were absolutely restricted. Even though these restrictions did not include the survivors, it did limit the possibilities. You must take into consideration that there was a desperate need for the survivors to be made to feel human once again. Any bit of love that would help bring that about would go far to help change their thinking. Unfortunately, we were not around long enough to make any real progress.

It was only a short time after we completed the atrocity search that I recognized a total change in the relationships of the officers and myself. During the actual war, I could approach either the Lieutenant or the Captain on an equal basis. I did do this regularly and it was considered normal practice, at least by my own thinking. In fact, it was never discussed.

PARIS

Paris! That is the city! I had written a little about the possibility of going to Paris for a three-day pass if you had been in combat for a certain amount of days. You should also recall that when Battle of the Bulge took place, all leaves were canceled. I was sure that now the war in Europe is over, I was going home through Paris. I had a twenty-four-hour pass. I was free for an entire day!

Jerry Goldberg and I left camp together and when we got to the city, we separated. Why? Easy to understand: Jerry was single. I was, of course, married. We had separate interests.

The first thing I had to do was sell my store of cigarettes. I had been saving my cigarette rations for months, until I had at least forty or fifty packs on hand in my backpack. Cigarettes were about the most valuable thing you could have in Paris, besides real money. I stood on a street comer and offered them to anyone who would buy them at whatever rate I had chosen. I don't remember how much I received for them, but I do know I came out with a large amount of money. It might be worthwhile to mention that a woman was obtainable for a couple of packs—maybe a bit more, but not much. I never checked the market, but it was a common rumor among the GIs. In fact, in Germany, it worked even better, with some guys implying that they were able to hit it off for one pack of cigarettes and maybe some additional chocolates.

Next thing I knew I was walking on the Champs Elysees, head in the air, looking all around me, tramping in the gardens, soaking up the sun, and if you look at the army pictures I have, you'll see me asking directions of the gendarme on the Boulevard. So where to go next? To a department store somewhere on the avenue to buy gifts for Bess, Shelley and Alan. I bought jewelry and some trinkets for the kids and once again I was on my way, wandering around—remember, by myself.

Paris was exciting. Always was and still is. I knew I was hungry, so I walked to a French cafe, ordered a glass of wine and some kind of meat for lunch. Of course, it was delicious. Why wouldn't it be? Anything would taste good after army food. But I'm sure it was better than the ordinary. The Folies Bergere, that was next on my list, but that was a nighttime frolic, so I had to fill in the daytime hours first. I walked into a museum that I stumbled on. I don't know what the name of it was, but I was in and out in a short time.

And the women! They sure looked good to me. Even though they hadn't eaten that well for a few years, they still managed to be quite attractive. I was also a little starved as well, so that made them look even better. But French women have a way about them. Anyone who goes to Paris can pick it out. It's some special quality they seem to have that singles them out. Now, I could have asked anyone of them to be a tour guide for me—on a strictly platonic basis. I know you'd love to hear me tell you I did just that. The truth of the matter is I didn't, and I never thought about it until now. So I continued on alone.

I did strike up an acquaintance with some French men asking for directions, or where to eat. It was a fascinating city. Everything looked interesting. I hit another cafe, had another glass of wine with something else to eat and sat and watched the people go by from my spot outside. It was a pleasant day and the sun was shining. Paris could never have looked better. I walked through the Boulevard, looked into the windows, and enjoyed walking along the Seine, watching the boats go by. What a dirty river, I thought, but by comparison today, it probably was much cleaner than it is now. From there I wanted to find a restaurant for a good meal, because it was dinner time and I had begun to feel hungry again. I had a fabulous meal somewhere. What it was or where it was is secondary. I got advice from someone I spoke to walking by, and it was as good as he said.

The Folies Bergere was next. Spectacular, of course. Even more so, because of the times, the place and what it represented. There isn't much that you could say about the Folies that you don't already know. It was a wonderful show, even more wonderful because of its daring approach of that time. They were way ahead of everyone else in the entertainment field. They seemed to know in what direction we were heading and they were leading the way.

Paris will always remain as the highlight of everything I did in France, that is, outside of the war. Those twenty-four hours were filled with all kinds of experiences and much pleasure. I was free of all encumbrances. I had no army restrictions and almost two years of army subjugation were behind me. When you think on those terms, everything else dims in the background. I found my way back to camp headquarters without any problem. That day was filled with indelible impressions. It wasn't the single activities that I did, but just the sum of the total. It was all there, interesting things, excitement, all kinds of people and so much to see.

The world looked brighter that day than anytime in the last two years. The war was over and I would be going home soon, if only for a few days or maybe a couple of weeks. Paris was indelibly stamped in my memory forever. It would always be the dream city of the future for me. It was a day I shall always remember. Unfortunately, the vision of France as a great liberating city disappeared over the years and the French nation as a whole had begun to express their nationalistic views in the world. They were no longer a subdued nation and once again Jews had become targeted in small ways.

END OF THE WAR IN EUROPE

Here we were. The war was over, and there was lots of time on our hands. There wasn't much for us to do, so the officers at Staff at Headquarters Company set up a marching and drill program. This truly turned the men off. They were quite bitter about it. They had suffered through months and years of war, some more than others. Now they were going to hit us with those chickenshit drills? We thought it was ridiculous, but the tide had changed. We were beginning to move back into the regular army status. Officers and men were to remain separate. There was lots of talk of when we would be going home. Who would be the first to go? Was the eighty-five-point requirement going to be the determining factor? Again, I began to feel the heat of being a "pre-Pearl Harbor family father." My two children gave me extra points and even though I had fought only a year, that fact would give me a big edge on guys who had fought longer, or those who had been in Iceland for a year. It was a sore spot for them and many people, including my Captain and Lieutenant, who bitched about It because they were both single.

Sometime in my past experiences, I was driving my

Medical Officers through a highly dangerous area. We had encountered enemy fire, but we did come out unharmed. It was not a pleasant experience. In fact, we were all scared shitless. I had forgotten about it entirely until I heard both the Captain and the Lieutenant discussing the possibility that each of them would send in a form for the other pertaining to the event. I was quite upset when I overheard the conversation and I expressed my discontent openly. "Captain Greenberg," I said, "I was in the jeep with you. I was the driver as well. If you both are entitled to medals, what about me? I'm entitled to one just as much as you are."

They both became angry and upset with me, but I would not let it go. First of all, I didn't know my release status. A medal gave you five points. I knew I was somewhat short of the eighty-five, so I was literally fighting for extra points and a way to get out of the army sooner. It was a losing battle. I never got the points. I don't know if they got their medals either. It doesn't matter now, anyway. But the temperature had changed. There was no more talk of being released and going home. All of the rumors that were flying around were about going to Japan to finish the fighting there. We were doomed to continue fighting in another part of the world. There was going to be a short period when we could go home for a week or so and then we would be sent out to fight in Japan. Points or no points, that was in the cards. It seemed to be a dismal situation. There would be no end to this war. It was to go on forever.

We were released and informed that we would have a week of leave and then we would be on our way to Japan. It was early summer as I remember, and Bess and I set off for Cedar Point alone to spend those few days together. It was a traumatic time. We were clinging to one another, knowing that every minute was precious.

As we lay on the beach soaking up the sun, everything seemed beautiful. The sky was blue and the lake was calm and restful. We watched the tiny ripples of the waves as they came in and it was a blissful time. Yet there was an air of sadness and finality about it. We knew what lay ahead, but we could not face the reality of it. The threat of going to Japan was ever in our minds. We could not get it past us. It kept on returning no matter what we did.

I was also quite honest with Bess. I wanted her to be realistic and to recognize the dangers I believed existed in this new threat to our lives. It was hard to tell her, but I had to let her know what was involved. "Bess," I said, "there is no way that anyone can escape these possibilities. This is a war of artillery power and strength. If I continue to work on the battlefield, there is no telling what can happen. It is a way of life that can only lead to some form of tragedy. The odds are too great."

Too brutal, you might say. That is true. But if you think of the reality of it, there was no other way. To live on false hopes, that would be foolish. The war takes its toll of manpower. Those who escape are lucky. Luck plays the major role in whatever you do. How many times would I be lucky? I was beginning to feel as if my luck had run out. I had escaped too many times. So when anyone ever questions the justification of the nuclear bomb, all you have to do is ask any soldier who had been in the Pacific War Zone or who was scheduled to be shipped out.

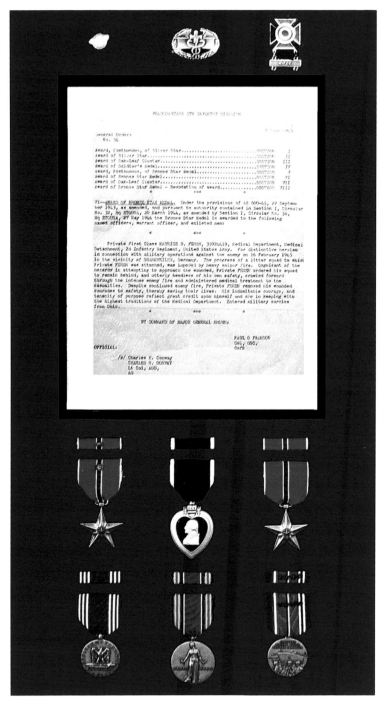

My Army medals are the most precious awards I
have ever received. They are treasured. This includes
the original copy of the orders for my Bronze Star.

Nov. 21, 1944

DEAR FRIEND,

HERE'S a paragraph that I wrote after one of the toughist spots I'd been in, which should give you a good idea of how I feel about all this, and something I think every one at home should know.

THE PAPERS + MAGAZINES glorify the heroes of this war. But who can tell the story of the wounded man who has done his best, and payed the price for his efforts. While the battle rages, he must lay there helpless, unable to move, hoping and praying that help will come before its too late. And when it does come, each minute seems like an eternity, the agonizing pain of being moved, the shells landing closer + closer. Fear, pain + shock surround him. Yet he smiles when you bandage him, and regardless of how hard and trying the trip back is, with each sudden jerk, like a knife, and each step we take is only a blurred dull pain, he never complains. Gratefully he acnowledges the proffered cigarette, or a drink of water, and when we are finally safe from danger, he thanks you humbly and says "Gee, I'm sorry I was so much trouble to you." Can one forget those things? Will it ever be possible for him to tell you the thousands things he thought of as he waited in a living hell, and death stared him in the face. These are stories that are never told, but that happen to someone somewhere in No Man's Land. If you'd ever walk through it, you'd understand why it's called that, and especially so in the black of the night. I know of nothing that is more terrifying than that, when your own footsteps, and the crackle of the twigs you step in are noises that are magnified to the utmost, and the shriek of the cold wind, like the sound of a shell whistling through the air at you, and the shadows of the trees loom as enemy soldiers staring at you with a pointed gun. Then a sudden burst of light covers the sky, an enemy flare, and down you go, with your heart beating wildly, hoping you haven't been seen. I suppose I could go on and on, but all this answers nothing, and I wonder what it means to the rest of the world. I tell this to you, for I know that you too can feel all of this. Yours Sincerely

Maurie

This letter was written to one of my best friends, Russell Swiler, during the height of battle. Mr. Swiler saved my warehouse space for me until I returned from the war. I am grateful for his caring.

Jerry Goldberg (left) and Maury

Jerry Goldberg my best buddy

Jerry and Maury
somewhere in Germany

Maury with Phyllis and Jack
Keller, brother-in-law and sister-
in-law, Spartansburg, S.C.,
basic training

Maury and Sargeant Peterson

Nate Eisenberg and Maury,
somewhere in France

Maury and Medic buddy

Maury and Nate Eisenberg
somewhere in France

Maury at Norther Ohio Food Terminal, Thanksgiving 1955.

The Banana Trade (Yes, We Have No Bananas)
How I Got an Italian Godfather

Probably not many of you can remember when all kinds of foods were rationed during the post war years, 1946–1950. It was also a time when some of the fresh fruits and vegetables were in short supply. They were in such demand at the time, it was almost an impossibility to purchase them at the legal prices set by the government. Bananas were at the top of the list of fruit shortages. This is one of those stories that took place at that time.

It is easy to look back and say, "It is wrong to support a black market." Let me tell the story and see if together we can justify that decision.

I was released from the army in October 1945, having served my country as a Combat Medic in the Infantry for two years in World War II. I reopened my business after closing it down completely while I was gone. Therefore, I found myself without a regular source of a banana supplier. Since I was a "complete service" wholesaler of produce, bananas were an essential part of my business.

There were three major banana wholesalers that I had access to. Each week, one wholesaler allocated three boxes, the other five boxes and the third, five boxes. These were all sold at the legitimate set government price. I needed at least 100 boxes of bananas to fill my orders each week, however, it was a dilemma: wherever I turned for more suppliers, I was told there were no bananas to be had.

Interestingly, the Northern Ohio Food Terminal has loading docks that face the front of each owner's unit. The dock runs from 37th Orange Ave. to 40th Street with 55 merchants, all at truck level. This would allow even the furthest unit that was being loaded to be served by a four-wheel truck or a pallet.

It was obvious when you looked at the pallets of bananas being trucked from one end of the dock to another that there were many bananas being sold. My problem was how to buy them. I made up my mind to take the next step.

I approached the first supplier in his banana ripening room and said, "Mark, I am willing to do whatever is necessary to obtain a few more boxes of bananas. I need them badly to maintain my regular customers who depend on me."

He replied, "I'm insulted, do you think I would stoop so low and black market my fruit? Get out before I really get mad!" I didn't expect an answer that rough, since I recognized some of the recipients of the loads of bananas on pallets that were being delivered on the dock.

I tried another new wholesaler who offered me one box of bananas at the regulated price with each 50 lb. bag of loose beets.

"That is crazy," I said. "I have to pay you $8.00 for every box of bananas with a bag of beets."

"It's all at a regulated, OPA price," he said. "It is legal.

A daily display at the market, 1955
Sonny (left), Hal (center), and Maury

Auction at the market. Freight carloads of oranges and apples
auctioned off by lots - 1950's.

Maury's Produce Gang, circa 1960 Harry Levine (head turned), Hal Feren (on truck), Ben Fertel, Morry Margolis (suit & hat), Joe Chernet, Riva Keller, Jack Bonchek, Maury (in suit), Sonny Nagelbush (far right).

The Board of Trustees, Teamsters Local 400, representatives Northern Ohio Food Terminal. Russell Swiler, Manager (far left), Maury (center), next to John Miceli. Don't I look like one of them? Note my slicked black hair and white shirt.

Jim Smith (left), Joe Cavalier Jr., Joe Cavalier Sr., Ron Zdrojewski, Pat Kelly, circa 1980

That is the only way I'll sell them to you."

I was left with no alternative. I had to find someone who would sell them to me at whatever price it would take. I wasn't going to buy 25 or 50 bags of loose beets I didn't need or want. The story does not end there.

Beginning in the late 1940's, bananas were packed in 40 pound wooden boxes with the name of the owner's company stamped on it indelibly. The deposit box was considered the same as cash and you paid a $3.00 deposit on every box of bananas. Since I had made an independent connection for more bananas, I had acquired 33 empty boxes from this particular company. The boxes were not only cumbersome and taking up space, it was foolish not to cash them in. So I asked my houseman to return the boxes for a cash credit to the supplier. They in turn knew that my ration was three boxes of bananas a week.

The supplier was at the end of the dock, at the lower end at street level, so I knew it would take a little more time for him to return. I became a little worried when he did not return and I started to think about what could have gone wrong. When he finally returned, he said, "They insisted that since you don't buy bananas from them, they were keeping the boxes and I could forget about the credit of $99.00."

I have to say I was angry, I should say crazy angry. I was beside myself. How dare they do that to me! The money meant a lot to me at that time because I was just starting my business again after the war. I was not going to just stand by and let that happen. They would have to deal with me. There was no rationality to my thinking! I ran all the way to the supplier's warehouse. When I entered the door, there seemed to be an immediate silence. I shouted out, "Give me $99.00 for my deposit boxes! If you don't, I'll take each one of you one by one." Those owners were not just ordinary looking men. There were five brothers, all of them former athletes, one tougher than the other. Street fighters for sure. If there ever were an occasion to place a bet, you would bet on them. In a couple of cases, two or three of them were bigger than I, tougher, too, I'm sure. But I didn't think about that. I only knew that I had been take advantage of. I shouted out once more, "Where is my credit?" They all remained silent. No one moved. It was like a cloud hanging in mid air.

In the next few moments, I began to think more clearly. I recognized that I was in an impossible position, sure to lose, no matter what I said or did. There was no way I could attack all five brothers. And I could see they had no intention of giving me the credit I was entitled to. Having regained my senses, I made an about face, turned around and said, "We are not through with this yet."

In the space of the few months since I opened my business, my next-door neighbor, who was Italian, had taken me under his wing. He had literally become my Godfather. I can't explain exactly what that means. All I can add is that the Godfather had a certain amount of prestige, respect and power that only he would be entitled to.

I went into his office and told him the whole story. He did not react in any way that showed his disposition. All he did was pick up the phone, mumble some Italian words and phrases, then hang the phone up. Five minutes after his call, one of the supplier's men brought him a check for $99.00. There was a note of apology and they mentioned that I would be receiving special attention to my needs in the future, since I was now a friend of the family!

I look back and remember all of the good things my Godfather did for me. There were many times and places where he helped out, and I am indebted to him forever. It is also worth noting that I joined the Italian-American Club after the banana incident; I attended a luncheon there every week. It was a good time, a place to visit and make friends.

Riding The Highway For Cabbage

If you are a processor of commercial cole slaw, you have to be aware of the seasonal quality of the Danish or Holland cabbage. This variety has great storing ability. Most all of the cole slaw you see in stores and restaurants is prepared commercially by a processor, except for a few supermarkets who process in their main warehouse or at store level.

In fact, long before processing became popular, growers in the Northeastern part of Pennsylvania and New York would store tons of this variety of cabbage in gigantic cold storage houses. It was termed "old cabbage" by the trade because when it was trimmed it would gradually trim to a solid hard white head. It was also highly valued because restaurants preferred this hard variety, which was better suited for cole slaw than the new crop of green cabbage that was softer, leafier and was harvested in the South. The hard head variety can store well for three to six months under proper refrigeration.

Since these storage houses were some distance away, I would often make a trip in my 1950 Chevrolet stake body truck, driving either to Erie, Pennsylvania, or Rockport, New York, for a five-ton load of this hard head cabbage.

I would load 100, 50 pound mesh bags of cabbage, cover the load with canvas and take off. There were no freeways, just straight Route 20 to the storage house. It was a long, lonely drive. I had no radio and the heater worked off and on. The trip took six to eight hours each way. Thankfully, I never got stuck with a blowout or with truck trouble. It was not until later in my business career that I was able to hire a truck delivery person to do this same job.

It is a lot different today because cabbage is more available locally. Processing cole slaw commercially is big business because it is a labor-intensive process that restaurants want to avoid. So the next time you order cole slaw, I want you to think of me driving my red Chevy stake truck with the wind blowing on the canvas top and me saying prayers that I would arrive home safely without breaking down.

As a point of interest in early spring, I would receive loads of the soft green leaf cabbage from Tennessee in cone-like hampers, 50 pounds to a unit. The cabbage, though extremely green, was well accepted by the Southern trade, however, it was not suited to make commercially acceptable cole slaw.

The Carrot Juice Story

Juicing of fruits and vegetables has become an important segment of the marketplace for carrots. However, I don't want you to think that this use for carrots is new. Like most everything it has gone through many periods of change and popularity.

My own history with juicing carrots goes back to the 1950's. I have always been interested in health food benefits, even in my younger years. One of the basic vegetables that I sold regularly to restaurants and institutions when I was in the wholesale produce business was a 50-pound bag of carrots. It was a standard for most places in the 1950's and would cost probably two to three dollars a bag.

Each week, I saw a particular customer come in to buy carrots by the bulk bag. After a number of visits over a long period, I asked him what he used them for. I thought it was odd for a layperson that did not have a business to buy so much product. He explained that he believed in juicing carrots and other vegetables because of their health benefits. Being interested in improving my health and that of my family, I suggested to him that I would trade him a bag of carrots each time he purchased them for a gallon of his carrot juice. He agreed and here is what happened.

The first week I tried to get my children, who were quite young at the time, to drink a glass of juice each day. For those of you who know it, carrot juice by itself is rich and sweet, too sweet by itself for most people. There was a battle going on between my two children and me. They continued to rebel against this healthy product. A number of weeks went by and all of us began to notice that our skin was turning a light orange. This is what occurs when you drink a large amount of carrot juice! When my wife observed this change, both she and the children said, "This is the last straw, Maury. If you come home with another gallon of that vile stuff, you are going to drink it all by yourself." That was the end of my carrot juice experiment, but the story really doesn't end there.

Forty years later on my radio program, I interviewed the Juice man, Jack LaLane, an advocate of juicing all kinds of fruits and vegetables. Over the course of the years I interviewed him three times. He was an excellent representative of his product and he could talk a mile a minute about the benefits of juicing. Soon, the entire country became entranced with juicing. You would see him on TV, hear from him on the radio, see him in person—and he wrote a book as well. National marketing promoted a juice machine he invented. Today, that idea has diminished to some extent, but there are still many adherents.

The unusual aspect of this story is that I always took a negative view when I argued with this author and promoter. The fact remains that juicing fruits and vegetables does not give you all of the essentials you need for good health. The American Cancer Society promotes fiber as a basic protection against cancer. You cannot get fiber from the juices of vegetables and fruits alone: You must combine juice with the roughness and benefits of the natural qualities in the skin and flesh of fruits and vegetables.

Today, you can walk into many health food stores and juice bars selling fresh vegetable juice. They will be hustling vitamin drinks, smoothies and other mixes. So the wheel does not stop, it changes all the time, only the basic idea remains the same.

The Yankel's Pickle Scam

There is no funnier story that I can tell you than my pickle experience, except to relate it just as I remember it. Pickles and cucumbers are two distinct entities. They are members of the same family, but have different properties. Kosher style dill pickles are an ethnic delicacy. Processing them for long keeping is difficult since they do not have any artificial preservatives in their preparation. They are prepared differently than pickles in vinegar, which is a totally different product.

I had some minor success in processing a limited number of kosher style dills under the brand name of Yankel's Pickles. I had figured out how to produce a consistent tasting product and I was making some inroads in that market. After a couple of years in operation, I decided to expand the product sales. It is important to know that in order to maintain good quality, you have to begin with the best product available. I made sure that every shipment I purchased would meet the high standards I set.

When I went for a three-day weekend vacation, my processing manager took it upon himself to buy the next load of pickles that was available. That was an unfortunate move because that entire shipment was poor with many defects. It wasn't long before I discovered what had occurred because we had many returns of poor product that I had to replace.

I approached my manager, trying to find out the details of the purchase. This was two months later and he no longer could identify the lot or the problem. He insisted that the pickles were not at fault, the problem was due to the menstrual cycle of the women who were packing the pickles! There was no way I could get him to change his mind about this, no matter how I argued with him. As you well know, voodoos are a part of the beliefs of many societies—this was one of those situations. What had really occurred was a breakdown in the purchasing of a quality pickle. If they had been good to begin with, they would have processed well. The manager was not willing to accept this concept.

A Gift Basket Business Story

Now we turn to the peak years of my gift basket business. It was called Fruit Baskets by Maury and was located at 3100 Chester Avenue, in Cleveland, Ohio. Starting in November, around Thanksgiving, we would have our most important gift basket season. During the busy season, we would pack and ship 9000 baskets of fruits, boxes of steaks, turkeys and other foods.

We began to hire college men and women beginning at Thanksgiving, peaking in mid-December. We would hire from 50 to 100 young people who worked consistently anywhere from 8 to 12 hours per day during that period. My average work week at Thanksgiving was about 75 hours a week; for the next two weeks I worked 100 hours, then 120 hours. My wife and family members followed that same routine. Let me tell you, it was no easy road, however it was the one I had chosen and I loved the excitement and the drama for 35-40 years, until I retired in 1990.

Cheri Nagelbush creates a basket for shipment, Christmas 1960; Mike Nagelbush (top left). Alan Feren (top right).

There was a policy that I maintained in the workplace: Any employee could eat as much fruit as he or she would like to have. There was no limit. Although there were boxes of cheese, meats, candy and other kinds of foods, they would not be allowed to open any package unless it came in broken or damaged. From time to time, I would open a number of boxes of cookies or candy and pass them out at break time to the employees. The system worked, or at least I thought it did. There may have been exceptions that I didn't know about, but I felt confident I had things under control.

I do remember one year after Christmas, I was walking down the street and a well-dressed woman came over to talk to me. She introduced herself as Mrs. Lieberman. First she said, "Both of my children worked for you this past Christmas and they loved it. You are a wonderful boss. Every night they would bring home cookies, candy and even champagne. In fact, we enjoyed one of your wonderful Polish Hams, which was so good."

I could not believe what I heard, but what was I to say. There was no question that my system had been abused. All I could add was, "I'm so happy your children enjoyed working for me." There was no use in trying to replace what was already gone!

I Attempt To Take My Kids
On An "Intellectual" Vacation

Sometimes your desire to bring intellectuality to your children can backfire: Too little is not enough and too much doesn't always work. Here is how my experience with it goes.

It was my summer vacation time off, about fifty years ago. Since summer was the busiest produce season, each of the brothers only took a three and a half day break in August. I had chosen to take my family to Chautauqua, New York. Why Chautauqua? It was a noted place for learning, good lectures, and a beautiful setting. I was just so sure my children would like it—I didn't say love it—that I decided it was worth a try.

Bess approached me before I made reservations and warned, "Don't you think the children are too young for this kind of an institute?"

I replied with confidence, "Everything I've heard about it makes me believe they will like it. Besides, they have to get some other forms of learning under their belts so that they can learn to be adaptable in this world."

Shelley was fourteen years old and Alan was eleven. Bess continued to advise me that she didn't think my idea would go over well with the kids. She kept asking me, "Don't you want to try something else?" But I was adamant. I thought it was an excellent idea and I was determined to try it. I must give Bess credit; she didn't push too hard for a change, but was resigned to giving it a chance.

We had an uneventful trip driving there. It took five to six hours and was an easy drive. Previously, we had made a trip to Atlantic City and that drive turned out to be real trouble. We had run into bad rainy weather and had to endure Alan crying about going home most of the way. Home was uppermost in his mind. Thankfully the trip to Chautauqua was uneventful.

Upon arrival we had breakfast in the main dining room, but soon there were some problems. Shelley and Alan complained about the sleeping quarters and the fact that the bathrooms were down at the end of hall. The main building was a big sprawling house, with one hundred rooms or more.

"The floors creak," Alan complained. "This place is falling apart."

"I hate the food," Shelley added.

"Me, too!" Alan confirmed.

Now I had a problem. They never stopped moaning about everything.

We attended lectures on Friday and Saturday, and participated in some other activities. There was no playing around; this place was very serious! Everyone we saw was much older than we were; we were the youngest family there. As luck would have it, we saw a movie Saturday night, *Stalag 17*. The kids liked that. I scored some points at last.

Sunday morning we all attended a Unitarian Church service—that clinched it. Even though the service took place in a lovely outdoor setting on a beautiful morning, the family revolted.

Bess, Shelley, and Alan all spoke in unison: "We've had it! It's over! We're leaving!"

Not too far away from Chautauqua, in Pennsylvania, was Conneaut Lake Park. It was not only an amusement park, but also a place where you could water ski. Guess where we wound up. A couple of hours later Alan and Shelley were on water skis, struggling to stand up. I know they don't want me to tell how many times they fell, so I'm going to say they did pretty well. Conneaut Lake Park filled the bill! Bess was right. She was much wiser in choosing activities for the children.

We returned to Conneaut Lake Park several times after that and made some wonderful memories there. I think I was the only one who kept on with the sport of water skiing; the children didn't talk much about it after our first visit to the lake.

The Racquetball Win

Every father wants his son to believe he's the best: It is important in every father/son relationship. In my early years I spent a great deal of time with my son, Alan, as a coach in Little League. Alan had pretty good speed with the softball pitch. He worked diligently on improving his speed and getting the ball over the plate. He concentrated on strikes and I encouraged him. When the action took place, he started out a little nervous and had to settle himself down. Little League was just beginning in those days and as time went on Alan played at higher levels—in a junior league, and then with young adults. I mention all this to emphasize how big a role sports played in our relationship.

Around 1960, Alan's homeroom teacher at Beachwood High School was a superb athlete. You might call him a "jock." He looked the part and played it well. Alan was so infatuated with him that Bess and I invited him for dinner. We discussed sports in general and had a lively discussion!

This episode occurred at the peak of my physical abilities. I was National Physical Education Chair for all of the Jewish Community Centers in the USA. I was known for my racquetball prowess and swimming. Alan thought it would be a great idea to invite his teacher to the J.C.C. for a swimming and racquetball competition. I thought it would be fun, so I extended an invitation.

On the day the teacher came to the Center, my brother-in-law, Sonny, played the first game. It was apparent that the teacher was a terrific racquetball player, and had good general athletic ability. (At that time, racquetball had just come into its own and was known as "paddleball;" the racquet was solid instead of the netting now in use). Sonny tried hard, but the teacher beat him easily. I don't remember the score, but it was an easy win.

Bess Feren, Maury's wife,
painted this picture of her
husband in 1968.

Now it was my turn. I have to say I was a pretty good player—not a champion—but I could play with the best of them. We started the game, each of us feeling out the other. I could see that this was not going to be an easy match. The game was tied at ten points each. We went to fifteen, back and forth, each of us slipping one in from time to time. I was beginning to tire; this guy was making me run! The score went to nineteen all and we battled for the two-point win. Back and forth. I was not going to give up. I said to myself, "You have to win at any cost!" The game went on for two, three more tie points and neither of us would give in. Finally, after a terrific run on my part, I made the final point! The game was over. I had redeemed myself in my son's eyes—at least I thought so.

Next came the swimming competition. There was a ten-year difference in ages, I remember. Anyway, he was no match for me. I won easily.

I turned to my son and said, "Your teacher met his match!"

"You did OK," Alan replied, "but I'm sure he'll take you the next time. He just had a bad day."

How could I win, I ask you?

Hiking and Mountain Climbing

As a young man I was always interested in hiking and climbing, but since my work was so demanding, I never did much about it. I could only dream. One day, when I was forty or forty-five years old, I picked up a National Geographic Magazine and happened to read an article about Justice William O. Douglas hiking the Appalachian Trail in New Hampshire. The story described the joy and excitement he felt during his trip, which included a climb up Mt. Washington. When I examined the photographs, I discerned that Douglas was quite mature in years, so I figured, how hard could it be?

The article stated that there were camps at various levels of Mt. Washington in which you could sleep, but it did not stress the danger of the terribly bad weather that often occurred up there. It also included all kinds of information on how to sign up for a climbing adventure. I became obsessed with the idea of climbing that mountain! More than that, I was excited.

It was 1953 and I was in excellent physical condition: I had been running for a number of years and I believed that climbing Mt. Washington would not be a problem. My next job was to persuade my wife, Bess, that I had to do it. I mean I had to do it! I was determined. It was part of a life-long dream. I had followed climbing stories about Mt. Everest, and I was hooked. I had also read "Annapurna," by Maurice Herzog and was fascinated by the physical toll climbers had to endure. Bess finally gave in and I took off for a three-day hike.

The hike and subsequent climb proved to be all I had hoped for. I had no trouble with my physical stamina, but there were a few small things I should have prepared for. First of all, I did not take mosquito and insect protection. I was bitten up the entire time, and itched all over. Also, I wore long army fatigues instead of shorts. The bottom of my pant legs swept through the wet grass every morning, soaking them and I wound up wearing that wetness for three days. It was not pleasant. I learned that Mt. Washington could be extremely dangerous in a storm, causing climbers to die, but luckily I enjoyed good weather on my trip.

My next trip did not work out as well.

A couple of years later I persuaded Bess that I should take our son, Alan, along on what turned out to be my last trip to Mt. Washington. She agreed to it and the whole family went to New Hampshire together. Unfortunately, my brother, Hal, had recently died unexpectedly and I spent most of our vacation grieving for my brother.

My mountain climbing did not end just yet. Years later, in around 1970, Alan began his surgical internship in Denver, Colorado. Again I informed Bess, "I gotta do this! I just gotta!" and I made plans for a three-day hike at Mt. Harvard, elevation 14,420 feet. I hired a professional guide who furnished the sleeping bag, the food, and all other essentials. He was the epitome of an environmentalist: He did nothing that would harm the earth. The pots and pans were scrubbed with sand, then rinsed in a stream. Our bodily waste was buried and everything we touched was carefully tended. Most of our food was dehydrated, but since I was strictly controlling my diet I carried some additional provisions: a few tins of tuna, some cantaloupe, and other healthy goodies. "You're wasting your energy carrying all that food," the guide advised me. "When you climb to high altitudes your body is not interested in food. You're certain to carry it back down with you." (That is exactly what happened. I left all my uneaten food with the guide).

The climb began at 6000 feet above sea level. "How high do you want to climb today?" the guide inquired.

"Let's see where this will go," I replied. "I'll check with you as we go along." As it turns out, I had no problem and we wound up at 10,000 feet by day's end. I did not feel that I was in any kind of distress. We slept outdoors in our sleeping bags, heads covered up, sleeping well even though we lay on the ground. The guide, a young man who loved the forest and the mountains, was wonderful company.

The next day we had an early breakfast and hiked to within two hundred yards of the peak. I began to feel uncomfortable, so I said to the guide, "This is it for me.

This is my peak." He was just as satisfied as I was, agreeing, "That's it for me, too." We stopped to rest. It was noon and the sun was shining brightly. It felt wonderful! Now I had a different goal in mind: "Get me down the shortest and best way, as fast as possible," I told him. I had attained my goal and had had enough. It was my last climbing adventure. I did go rafting later on, but that's another story.

Suffering At The Shvitz

There are always stories that you remember vividly. This is the kind of story you never forget. The year was 1955. One of our best customers, Dusty Miller, owned a farm stand in Westlake, Ohio. His business was so big that we had to load a full truck of fruits and vegetables every Saturday morning. The produce had to be the best, and it was. We made sure that he received the best of everything.

Here is the rub. I said it was a farm stand. Actually he had no farm! His property was in front of a large farm that sat two hundred yards behind his. That's one part of the story.

How would you entertain a customer who enjoyed his liquor? Sonny and I were not drinkers by any standard, so we decided to invite him for a night out at the *shvitz*, a true Russian-style steam bath located at East 116th and Kinsman. Oh, I could elaborate on the *shvitz* of yesteryear! Once inside the steam room, you would climb three big steps and come face to face with a large Russian man wearing a heavy cloth cap. He was referred to as the *platza man* and would take a shot of whiskey every hour, as he stoked up the steam. The *platza man* soaped and rinsed his customer, then worked him over using a bunch of leafy oak branches. The extreme heat would wear you out, but not the *platza man*: he kept drinking whiskey, pouring water over his head, so that he could keep working.

In those times, the *shvitz* used to accommodate people who wanted to sleep over. It was like a hotel. There were bunks or beds, a hundred or more next to each other, and after the massage and all that heat you would lie down to rest. Oftentimes you would not get up until the next morning! Dusty, the farm stand owner, didn't have that problem. He enjoyed the steam and the glorious rib steak the *shvitz* was famous for. It was his first visit to a *shvitz* and he was in heaven.

I did forget to mention the massages. (I don't know why I call it a "massage," because they were non-professionals who performed the work). The "masseurs" were Russian and their "massage" was carried out with brute strength, no more no less. Sonny was the first victim. He was kneaded with great fervor, back and forth, but never let out a cry of pain. The powerful Russian literally tore Sonny apart, but he never let on. Afterwards, when I asked him how the massage had felt, he said, "Terrific! Really good!"

It was my turn. I got on the table and the Russian started to work me over. I swear he was killing me. He kneaded me back and forth and I thought I would come apart. It was horrible! My body ached all over, but I couldn't let on. When it was over, I crawled off the bed and exclaimed, "What a terrible massage!"

On the way home, I said to Sonny, "How was your massage? You seemed to like it."

"That guy almost killed me," Sonny admitted. "But I wouldn't cry out because you were there. I didn't want you to know how much pain I was in."

"You suffered? I thought I would die on his bed!" I retorted. "Why didn't you say something?"

"What, let you get the best of me?" he answered.

That was the game we played, all through our years together.

Eating Oat Bran For Good Health

Now why would I be writing a story about Oats? Oats are a grain, used mostly as a breakfast cereal. Oats are noted for their health giving qualities: They are recommended for building bones, body building replacing lost Vitamin E.

When I owned the gift basket business, 90% of my orders came over the telephone. Very few clients came to the packing plant and most of my day was spent on the phone. I did have gift packers, so at times I felt a little bored off-season, but not at the holidays.

I had a dear friend, John Smith, who brought in eggs and some farm fresh vegetables from the Amish Country, three days a week, for resale at retail. His stand was behind the wholesale market and you could always find some interesting basic vegetables that were raised under natural conditions. His eggs were exceptional and probably the freshest eggs available at the time, grown in Wayne County, some seventy-five miles away.

You have to take note that the small farmers in Amish Country had no standard packs. There were no paper bags, no cello bags, or any kind of packaging material.

Everything he brought in was in makeshift containers: cardboard boxes, paper containers, newspaper or anything to hold things together—but the quality of everything he brought in was excellent.

Some of you may remember the oat bran craze, sometime in the 1980's or 90's. John Smith had a connection and began to offer twenty-five pound and fifty pound burlap bags of oat bran. I thought it would be fun to repack it and sell it at cost. I advertised it on my radio program, just to see if I could get some interest. The retail price in the health food stores was about seventy-five cents to a dollar per pound. I ordered it at forty cents a pound, repackaging the oat bran in ten-pound bags. I can only tell you the action never stopped! I had regular customers who came to pick up the oat bran. When the price jumped at wholesale to ninety cents a pound, people continued to come. My price was still the most competitive in town and even at the higher price I still beat the market.

I rarely sold anyone of those customers a fruit basket, but people loved to see the packaging plant in action and the beautiful product we put out. When the oat bran craze died off, my oat bran adventure came to an end. But I did have fun and excitement. It was worth it. Where are all those oat bran customers now?

A Mushrooming Market

What a difference the epicurean varieties have made in the mushroom market! I could spend the entire day telling you stories about what has happened to them. The finest chefs have turned to the exotic varieties to prepare innovative recipes that only can be prepared with mushrooms. For years, the mushroom industry was stagnant. Growth was slow and the change was gradual before the consumer began to accept the newer varieties. The Shitake came first, a tender, brown mushroom that was meaty and flavorful; only the finest chefs used them. Next came the Oyster mushroom, the wild Morel, the Porcini and the Enoki, a tender, stem like mushroom that seemed strange to look at but it had great edible qualities. However, when the Portabella mushroom was discovered, a whole new world opened up to everyone who used it. This was a giant brown mushroom with a thick heavy, meaty taste, tender and flavorful, offering numerous opportunities for use in a dozen different ways that had never been attempted before. Its success came overnight and today it remains the star of the mushroom family. It is worth nothing that up until its discovery, no one realized that the Portabella was only an overgrown Crimini, a tender, medium sized brown mushroom. As a matter of fact, the Portabella was discovered by accident when some Criminis were not harvested in time. The Portabella is quite popular throughout the United States, and is still recognized for its versatility.

In the 1980's, during my TV career as an Action Cam Reporter on ABC Channel 5, WEWS in Cleveland, Ohio, I would go out into the field to do any kind of story about food that was current and topical. Anchorwoman Wilma Smith had just become the new co-anchor of the evening news. Wild mushrooms had recently hit the news with reports of a number of deaths that had occurred in Ohio as a result of people picking and eating wild mushrooms. I suggested to the producer that we go to Forest Hills Park in Cleveland Heights to do a story on the dangers of eating wild mushrooms. I found a select area that showed promise: There was a large array of mushrooms popping out all over. The TV piece emphasized the potential hazard of picking wild mushrooms without knowing whether they were safe or not. Indeed, one must take the utmost care to buy wild or exotic mushrooms only from reliable sources.

I also remember how delicate and ladylike Wilma Smith tread through the tall soft grass in her high heels, which were fashionable for a TV anchorwoman at that time. Today she would have no qualms about wearing comfortable shoes. She is a great lady.

SOME CHARACTERS
I KNEW AT THE MARKET

Sporting Men

From the sublime to the ridiculous is the only way I could describe the "Grape Deal" that began in early October. Here it was, a month since there had been any financial activity, or any money coming into the house, and the wine season began. The only way to describe this would be to begin with the characters in this business, if you could call them that.

The men this business attracted were unique. They were interesting, exciting, sporting, and yet they remained plain, simple people. There was Frisco, the curly-headed, lovable guy who had once been to San Francisco. He had many good qualities and a pleasant disposition. Besides that, Frisco was one of the first members of the early Socialist Party and a believer of Marxist principles—until he became an owner of a business, gradually acquiring success, slowly succumbing to the advantages of the capitalist system.

Then there was Meyer-Vy-Sure ("sure" was pronounced "soor"). Meyer was a "money man," a financier, who knew how to handle men, especially his customers. Physically, Meyer was short, with a rotund figure. He always answered any question with an affirmative "vy soor"—hence the name!

Luft was a character who left me with little appreciation for his cultural qualities. He was short, but appeared tall. He dressed flamboyantly, generally in bold bright colors, and always drove a convertible. Women were his greatest weakness, and then came gambling. I guess I never could measure his business ability because whenever I was around him, he made so much noise. Luft was definitely the most exciting figure in the entire group.

Blinky was another personality I got to know. His face was pockmarked and one eye was half-closed. He was the brother of Fat Lou, who was one of the most stabilizing influences in the group. Fat Lou was a warm and friendly person, always with a cigar. He was obviously a wonderful eater; in fact, he looked as if he weighed 280 pounds, carrying most of it in his stomach. Fat Lou was everybody's friend and he had many friends and customers. This was very important financially. Blinky and Lou were as different as they could be. Besides that, they were always on opposite sides and were bitter competitors.

The market can be compared to the jungle, for once you are in it, you must devour your competitor, or he will devour you. This may seem to be a cold, calculating way to analyze it, but it is the only way to emphasize the bitterness of the daily struggle for survival. Life at the market demanded courage and strength.

I must be sure to emphasize that all of these men were bright with high I.Q's. They had adaptability and knew when to use it. Some of them weren't particularly successful out of their daily sphere of activity, but when it came to business, they knew every trick in the book. The odd thing is that each of the market characters hated each other, yet somewhere in their business careers each of them was forced by necessity to become partners. Somewhere along the line they got together, if only for one season!

At the market, interactions between men could be subtle and complex. For example, there was the "walk-space"—an area in which a buyer could walk and check out merchandise that was displayed after it was unloaded from train cars. Signals, such as winking and the use of fingers, were common, and in some cases, when that failed, the "walk space" became dangerous.

It must be said that the produce merchant, especially the seasonal distributor, was considered a sporting man: He always handled a great of money—some of it came easy and some of it came hard—but there was plenty when things were going right. Since there was always money floating around the market, it was only natural that gambling and card playing rooms should flourish. The poolroom was always filled. There was pinochle for the men with time on their hands, craps for the big gambler, and betting on the horses for anyone who was interested. There were fellows who represented the underworld, as well as the little guys who were just passing the time away.

I must note that this was a period when the underworld flourished and the market was a breeding ground for their activities: There were at least a dozen sites—the office of a broker, the claim adjustment office, a room upstairs, or in the restaurant—where a man could place a bet or relax playing his favorite game. The fact that he should have been working that day, or that he was spending money that did not belong to him, was secondary. It never really seemed wrong to any of them, for like all gambler, they thought they would win. The professional gambler made this his habitat, and in many instances, the little guy never had a chance.

There was also another type of personality who was a part of this scene. He was the straight-load huckster, or peddler, who tried each day to pick up a cheap load of some item to sell. It might be strawberries, oranges, potatoes, or what have you. Anything that was a "distress load"—that needed immediate selling—was his forte. The trick was to be able to buy a load every day to work with. This was a possibility, but not a regular occurrence, for most of the hucksters were of the same character as the seasonal produce merchant: If he could buy a very cheap load, he would work; if not, he would spend his day at the card table or in the poolroom, never regretting that he had failed to work that day. In later years, with the demise of the produce huckster, many of these men turned to peddling scrap iron as an alternative.

All these characters made the market way of life the interesting study it was. It did not matter whether the men were Jewish or Italian; they were a part of a way of life that was natural for them. I could not say that had they known better, they would have been different. I don't believe that, for somehow I have the feeling that this is what they wanted out of life. It has been said, with some justification, "Once a market man, always a market man." It is something that gets into your blood, or so it seemed. Even as the years passed, many of them returned to the market, even if just for a visit.

Doing A Favor For Billy K.

It was 1974 and I had just finished my contract with Fisher Fazio. I was taking some time off, trying to decide what I should do next. I happened to meet Billy K., a supermarket owner who used to be one of my customers.

"Hey, Maury!" he exclaimed. "What are you doing these days? I'm going away for a short ten-day vacation and I need a favor. Would you buy my produce for me while I'm away?"

"Sure," I answered. "Are there any particulars that I should know about?"

"Yes, there are. You have to shop only at these three companies for whatever you need," he informed me as he wrote down a list of the three names.

"That's fine with me. These guys are all quality produce merchants," I said as I accepted the list.

Now you must take note of the fact that there are at least forty to fifty merchants who carry the produce that Billy's supermarket would need. I knew why his instructions were so definitive: Billy was indebted to the three merchants, who also happened to be bookies!

I walked into the Jim Jones Market and Jim approached me at once. He was no ordinary looking man, built like a football lineman with muscles protruding from his open shirt. He gave no hello, no greeting, just the question, "How many crates of lettuce do you want, Maury?"

I didn't even have time to answer before Jim walked over and grabbed my arm, squeezing it so hard I thought it would come off. "I'm checking around," I said. "I'll be back after I see what is available."

Jim was not pleased at all. He squeezed my arm even harder and I could barely catch my breath. I was determined not to let him dictate to me. I was angry and upset, but I also had a job with certain restrictions that had to be completed. "Why be a fool?" I said to myself. "I might need this Jim character for something some day." I extricated myself and walked out. After looking around the terminal, I returned to Jim's place and ordered thirteen crates of lettuce—I had ordered the other twelve crates I needed from another merchant. Jim looked puzzled; he seemed to know intuitively that the order should have been for twenty-five crates, but he had no way to determine that for sure. He gave me no thank you, not even a handshake.

A few years later, when I re-established my new fruit basket company, Jim became a regular customer for my prime aged steaks. He and I became very close friends; in fact, I wrote a eulogy for his funeral.

The "Wild Guys"—Truck Drivers Spoiling For A Fight

During July and August, it was not unusual for my company to sell two to three truckloads per day of watermelons to retail markets for resale. It was a labor-intensive process, all of it done by hand: First, unload the watermelons, and then re-load them onto the delivery trucks that take them to stores. There were no tow motors and no shortcuts.

Oftentimes watermelons would be shipped in open trailers with sides that could be pulled off. Those vehicles were driven by men we called the "Wild Guys," or "Jockeys"—They were not particularly dependable and rarely arrived when they were supposed to, but they were hired by the shipper because they charged a lot less than the regular freight haulers. The market opened at four or five in the morning and the truckers were supposed to arrive in time for the opening, but it was difficult to get them to cooperate.

There was always the possibility that the watermelons would arrive with a great deal of bruises and breakage. They also could arrive in an over-ripe condition, due to the open sides of the truck or other factors.

It's 5 AM. There are two trailers of watermelons that did arrive on time, ready to back into the unloading dock. The first driver, who owned his own vehicle, gets off the trailer truck and begins to shout, "I want you to unload me right away! I need to make another pick up and if you don't unload me right now, I'll leave." He doesn't even give me a chance to reply, immediately calling me all kinds of deprecating names. For no reason at all, he's ready to fight.

This is not a new situation for me, so I just stand there and calmly tell him that he will be unloaded in the proper sequence, according to his unloading status. I'm not frightened or upset because I know this is a game for most of the Wild Jockey Truckers. Meanwhile, he is not to be cajoled. He is wild-eyed and begins to scream, "I'm not going to wait! I'm pulling out!" Then he threatens me physically. I wonder if he is on drugs to stay awake.

As the trucker leaves with is load of watermelons, I warn him that USDA regulations demand that he must get a release from the receiver—in this case, me—before he can leave without unloading. I remind him that he can be sued or lose his license, but he does not listen. He is playing a game and he knows he will have to come back to unload, because of the regulations.

Most truck drivers fit into the Wild Guy category. They would always try the same trick. Better yet, they always threatened to fight. This was a way of life they had chosen: being on the road for weeks at a time. Oftentimes they never got home for a month or more, picking up loads in each city that they made a delivery. They always wore a Stetson hat, a checkered shirt, a wide cowboy belt, and Levi's. Yelling and making a lot of noise was standard behavior for them, and I learned that I had to stand up and do some yelling myself, in order to make my point. The thing is, I was always ready to fight if I were forced into it, but I never met a truck driver who would ultimately decide to try me out. It was always the same game of chicken: they hoped they could frighten me into succumbing to their demands.

There were always "pick-up laborers" available, mostly black men who were willing to do the hard work unloading the watermelons. I usually helped with the task. Picture this: Maury the boss, shirt off, covered with the dirt from the truck, and sweat running down my face and body. Do you think I loved the Watermelon Deal? I ask you!

How A Fight Leads To Market Justice

George (Gusty) Damon and his two brothers belonged to the "old school." They were raised in the market, and learned all there was to know about it. Their father was an immigrant and all of the boys worked with him on the truck; it seemed sensible for a man to bring his family into the business, especially when they were young and strong. It was interesting to watch the growth of the trucker who specialized in the delivery of fresh fruits and vegetables to restaurants and hotels; they performed a function that is no longer a part of the world we know.

In the old days, anyone could start a business as a "wagon peddler" simply by buying a truck and stocking it with the basic foods used by most restaurants. They have been replaced by purveyors of complete lines of foods that are delivered only on order. The wagoners were rough, strong men. Their profits were small. The only way they could manage to beat it was to get up early and work late. Competition was intense, but it made this type of business very exciting.

Gusty was just that way. He was a part of the old family group that stuck together regardless of the consequences, whatever they might be. Each one of the brothers drove a truck and managed a separate route. Their father wielded the big stick, for even though his sons were adults, his word was law, and the boys followed obediently.

Physical characteristics of men in the market are meaningless. All of them began to look alike, just blurred images of humanity. They all fit into one category: just busy people, pushing and jostling, struggling to make it. The three Damon brothers were a part of that blur. All I can remember is their size, their dark complexions, and their rough appearance. George was the youngest and of slight build. Jack was somewhat heavier, of medium build, and tough looking. Marty was the biggest, with the kind of look that made you think he might be mean. (Actually, he wasn't as disagreeable as he seemed, but in the feverish hustle and bustle, he acquired an air of roughness that made you hesitate to argue with him).

Parking was always a problem, even in the good old days—and in the market, conditions were as difficult as they could be. My place was a corner unit, with front and side parking that ran parallel to a through street. This created additional problems because of the many people who were in a hurry to load on both sides, as well as those who double-parked for a few moments to load or unload. One truck could block ten people, and in the process jam up traffic for twenty to fifty yards! Even though it caused havoc, people kept parking where they shouldn't. Horns ringing, people shouting and cursing at each other was not uncommon, and no one really took offense at some of the vernacular used.

Those were the days when men tried hard to do all they could to hold onto their customers. George was not one of my customers, neither were his brothers. One day he pulled up with his big, open-sided truck, and I realized that he would be blocking my store for a precious half hour during the busy pre-dawn hours.

"Get out of here, you S.O.B.," I yelled, full of the tension of the morning. "I need that space to load my customers! You're blocking my place with your lousy truck!" Those were harsh works, but a part of the lingo I had come to think of as common usage.

The morning had proven to be a rough one for George, too. He yelled back, "Drop dead! I'm not moving! This market is a public place, and I can park anywhere I like!"

"Like hell!" I screamed. "Move your truck or I'll beat your ass!" I raved, angered to the breaking point, because of his obstinacy.

"Come and get me, M.F.! If you want me out, come and get me!" Solid talk it was, and I was beyond enraged. The blood rushed to my head and I felt no fear, no pain, only the frustration of someone who wanted his own way, no matter what.

The fact that this was a minute incident in a normal business day did not change anything, because I felt that I had lost control of my private territory. I came out swinging, moving recklessly toward George with anger in my eyes and vengeance in my heart. Little did I know what complications that fight was to bring! I swung hard, throwing a right to George's jaw. He wavered for a moment, and then began to fight back, yelling for his brothers. I hit him again, with a left and a right to his chin, to his nose, and then his eye.

By this time, a small crowd had gathered around us. A good fight was always a market stopper, and no one even thought of stopping us. Jack jumped in and went at me flailing both arms like a windmill. Jack and I exchanged hard punches and George added his blows to the onslaught.

"Move the truck you say! We'll move you!" they screamed. "We'll carry you out laid flat in it!"

I danced away from both of them, moving all the time so that I would not be cornered. Out of the corner of my eye I saw another figure, and this was the older brother. I knew I was in for it. Marty was big and strong and I could not see myself fighting all three of them with any success at all.

My anger had subsided a little and I knew I would have to do some fast maneuvering to get out of this mess. That was not going to be easy, for now I was cornered, and fighting three men instead of one. Marty swung at me with all of his strength, and I felt his blow land in my stomach. I moved in closer and swung my arms wildly, but my efforts were futile. I knew I had only one choice and that was to take off from the scene: I had to move fast—speed would be my only salvation. I moved slowly to the right, dancing like a boxer, jabbing with my right and guarding with my left. Jack ducked and I swung hard, making the opening I was looking for. When he moved back from the force of the blow, I dashed forwards, running as fast as I could, away from the crowd, and the market, wondering where I could take refuge.

Refuge was going to be difficult to find, for there was no place in the market area that was not open. All my opponents needed to do was follow me into any one of the stalls, and that would be my finale. As for the freight cars, they were much too far away, and besides, it was unlikely that I could get that far untouched.

I thought of the few choices I had as I ran. I needed a friend, now more than ever, and who could that be? It would have to be someone who knew the brothers well. Many names kept popping into my mind, but only one stuck: my old friend Joe. Joe was the only guy who could help me out of this dilemma—I was sure of that, for he had once mentioned that I could call him if I was ever in trouble.

Joe would be the right choice, I thought, as I circled around the outskirts of the last building in the market terminal.

I headed for Joe's office and, as I opened the door, I screamed out, "Help me Joe! I'm in real bad trouble!" Panting and out of breath, and with sweat pouring off me, I began to tell him my story.

"Don't worry, kid," he assured me. "Those guys will never get you. I'll see to that. All I want you to do is lie down on the floor and take it easy. I'll cover for you. You can bet your life they won't find you here."

"But how an I supposed to get home? And how am I going to come back here to work tomorrow at four in the morning, without any protection?" I asked.

"This will all straighten out, kid," Joe insisted. "You have to trust me."

Joe had befriended me years earlier, giving me business advice and friendly tips that proved to be profitable in many situations. Whenever we appeared some place together, people insisted we were father and son because we had the same features. He was of Italian parentage, living in the US for fifty or more years, but he spoke Italian fluently, knew the lingo, the right people, and was actually more integrated into Italian life than American. (This was an interesting aspect of the immigrants of that era: they would generally retain their European culture for one or two generations). You did not have to be Italian to be his friend for Joe had friends of every race and nationality. He loved people and they loved him. He helped anyone who called on him needing assistance.

Joe understood my problem. He realized the importance of the family clan George and his brothers were a part of. He also knew how much protection he could get for me: Under normal circumstances one would approach the opposing party with a cash settlement, or through a legal intermediary. But here in the market the laws of society were ineffective.

The matter would have to be settled under market law. And in the meantime, I knew the less I talked about my predicament to people, the better.

At about one o'clock, Joe said, "Come on, let's go see Jim." We headed downtown in Joe's car, talking very casually about business, our families, and various other subjects, never mentioning the fight.

Finally my curiosity got the best of me and I had to ask, "Where are we going?"

"To Jim's place," Joe replied. "We are to meet him at lunch time. He's the only man who can settle this situation amicably."

I had complete faith in Joe. If he said it, I believed it.

We stopped at an old fashioned storefront whose sign simply said, "Restaurant." An elderly woman met us as we entered, taking our hats and jackets.

"Jim's expecting us," Joe said. "Have you seen him around?"

"He's right there in the corner, by the window," she answered.

I turned and saw the man they called Jim stand up from his chair. He was a gigantic man, two hundred fifty pounds or more, and at least six foot four in height. He came over to greet us with a warm smile on his face. Greetings were exchanged. Jim sized me up very carefully, following my every move with his eyes casually, as if I was an object he intended to purchase.

Jim looked me straight in the eye. "Like to fight, boy?" he asked me.

"Not really," I replied, "sometimes it just happens. You know how it goes. But I'm not really the fighting kind, especially when the odds are stacked so heavily against me. I'd like to get out of the whole mess."

Jim listened intently as I retold my story. His face was immobile and his eyes showed no reaction to anything I said. "What do you think is going to happen?" Joe asked.

"I don't know, but I'd like to settle the whole thing," I replied. "I'm not one to hold a grudge and I'm not interested in continuing this fight. I want to get it over with."

Jim's face remained immobile. "That won't be easy, son," he stated. "You've spoiled a few faces—left your mark on one of the Damons—and said a few words that weren't too nice. I think I can settle this. Let me see what I can do." As he stood up to leave, he shook my hand, almost crushing it. I left the restaurant with Joe. He dropped me off at my store, waving at me as he shouted, "Don't worry about a thing, kid. Everything is going to be alright!"

The next day things began to happen. Joe called and asked me if I could meet the Damon brothers that night at Jim's place.

"Sure," I replied, "what time?"

"Eight o'clock. I'll pick you up."

I was a nervous wreck the entire day, waiting for my appointment. I wondered if it might have been better to try legal recourse, but it was too late for that. The die was cast.

Joe and I entered Jim's house together. There were many people in the room; George and his brothers stood together, drinks in their hands, and I noticed the tape under George's eye when he looked at me. I was introduced to the other men, though I never found out why they were there. Jim handed me a drink.

"Boys," Jim began, "we've got things to do. We are here to straighten things for both sides. Has anyone got anything to say that I have not heard?"

The room was quiet. Everyone listened without moving a muscle. "I am going to make a decision," Jim continued. "Since both parties are guilty to some degree, I insist that the rights of each individual involved be given equal consideration. I expect no further fighting. Maury Feren is to pay all doctor bills that are the result of the fight. The Damon brothers are to respect Feren's property and privacy, even though there have been differences. Now shake hands and let's all drink together."

I raised my glass, saying, "Salut!" The meeting was over. I felt that great burden had been lifted from my shoulders. I no longer had a dull, sickening feeling in the pit of my stomach. But I was left with a debt to pay to my friends. It did not end that day.

I had experienced market justice—and I don't know what would have happened without it.

Archie, Master Fruit Packer

There is a basic precept in the study of human relations that some people seek out and bring trouble with them. Perhaps Archie McGuire would be considered in that category, but if he brought trouble, it was wonderful trouble while he was around. Trouble was his middle name.

New Yorkers are always easy to pick out in a crowd, but to identify the reasons why they stand out is difficult. Archie, a black man from New York, made his livelihood as a fruit basket packer. He also was an educated black man, which was rare at the time I knew him, in the 1950's.

Archie was knowledgeable about fruit: he knew how to pack it creatively. He also gave each basket a unique look. It would be fair to say that he was an artist because each basket he made was comparable to a work of art. He could contrast colors, mix fruit patterns and wrap them in gold and silver foil. He would polish each piece of fruit on his work apron to give the basket a more glamorous effect. No two baskets ever turned out the same, and if they did, they were not planned that way.

Archie first came our way by wandering in one day off the street. There were no special characteristics that one could single out, but he did have distinctive features. His skin was a medium brown color, with a classic nose, dark brown eyes and curly black hair parted on the side. He had a clean look about him, but this was misleading because his personal grooming habits were not as good as they appeared to be. However, this was not a serious fault, nor did it play any great part in his relationship with me.

To say that Archie was inconsistent, lazy, carefree, self

indulgent, bossy, independent and an enigma to those around him would only be describing a small part of his personality. He was all this and more. He came late almost every day, missing more than his share of planned work. The days he missed would invariably be important ones, yet when he was criticized for his absence, he would strike back viciously, lashing out and demanding justice and equal opportunity.

Archie never regarded himself as an inferior person. He had strong feelings that enabled him to meet most men at their level. When he was sober, and this was a rarity, he could discuss and talk about the current events of the day and do so with great insight. The problem was Archie was hardly ever sober. It was no accident that bottles were discovered all over the nooks and crannies of the store, because Archie made it a point to be obvious about the wine he drank. If asked, when he indulged himself in a bottle that we found, he would reply, "Charge me for it, I am the one who drank it." Perhaps we should have done more to help Archie with his obvious addiction. Maybe part of what drove him to drink was the inability, as a black man in the society we lived in fifty years ago, to excel or come near to fulfilling his potential. He was a talented, intelligent man, and the roadblocks for a black man of talent in those days was formidable. It could drive any man to drink.

I liked Archie, maybe because he added a spark to my day, or because he fought back. I would send him home every other day saying, "You're fired, don't come back, get your pay." The next morning, he would reappear as if nothing had happened. Arguing would be futile, because he would insist that I could not fire him.

"You need me," he would say, "because Archie McGuire is the best fruit packer in the country, and your friend. Besides," he would then add, "I'm Maury Feren in Technicolor!" This was no joke, for in reality, he came very close to the truth.

Archie was a black replica of myself. He loved his work, enjoyed making baskets as much as I did, especially if he could use his creativity. The basic differences were sobriety, flexibility and past environmental influences—and it can't be denied, the limitations society put on people of color in those days made the difference.

I don't know how many times I hired and fired Archie, nor how many times he quit in a huff. The fact remained that he was the most creative packer we had. We needed him for special assignments, spectacular orders and gala events. Archie knew this well, always spelling out his importance to us, usually at our busiest periods, threatening to destroy his work if we failed to recognize his talents. But, I just couldn't accept doing without him: I would fight, beg, cajole and ask him to stay sober for at least the two important Christmas weeks. He would promise and swear his allegiance to me, yet it wouldn't take much to get him back to his old ways.

Archie was trouble. Not a day went by that was not beset by personal arguments between the two of us. However, I loved him too much to give him up. One day, he became so drunk, vulgar and violent that I was forced to call the police to have him taken away. I was astonished when I found him back in just a matter of a few short hours. He had persuaded the police that he was accused unjustly and they let him go.

It is also important to recognize that Archie was a pre-revolutionary black man and that civil rights and liberal thinking were the furthest thoughts from his mind. Equality and justice, as it was meted out to the white man, was what he sought—but not in terms of militancy.

He believed he had talent and knew his job; therefore, he was entitled to every right anyone in that position should obtain. The funny thing was, he got it by continually laughing about it. He really believed he was Maury Feren. If you questioned that, he would reply, "Who makes the most artistic baskets? Who does the creative work and who makes the place go?" Archie insisted that he did. The fact that he was only sober about half the time, missing at least one day out of every three and that on most days he would be sent home early because of some problem, would not be included in any of his thinking.

Archie believed he was indispensable to the company, the whole earth and possibly me. Positive thinking is what I would call it, and he made that reality come to life.

When I think back, I recognize that Archie was a weakness of mine. I didn't want to lose him because he brought drama, pathos, fight and challenge to my everyday humdrum activities. He was lazy and never fulfilled his responsibilities, such as hiding when it came time to unload trucks. He arbitrarily refused to do dreary work. Obviously, the other employees resented him because of his indifference and the special consideration he was given by me. However, Archie was admittedly the best of the basket makers, "The New York Champion," which was another name he tagged on for himself. The name was significant, because New York meant the best. That was Archie, the best and the worst simultaneously.

Archie did finally leave my employ. He had to. We both knew it was inevitable. He left and I did not hear from him for a couple of years. But one day, early in November, I got a telephone call. "Hi, Maury, this is Archie. I'm in Washington, but I'm ready to come back to work. I know you will need me for Christmas. Send $100 dollars. I'm broke, but I'll pay you back as soon as I start working." Do you know that my head began to whirl with new ideas of basket making, now that Archie would be back? I could see him working once again, with that silly grin that was so representative of his mannerisms. And I almost sent him the money! If not for my wife stopping me, Archie would have been back, and my life would not have been the same—again.

Curly

A market is a world of its own. The people who live in it are set apart, living in a closed sphere of existence, never truly aware of the world beyond their own. Like many people in various professions, those that work in the food terminal concentrate on the things that affect them—and they shut out the rest. There are a hundred characters in any marketplace, and the Northern Ohio Food Terminal was no exception. Many of those characters had nicknames, falling readily into a Damon Runyon category: "Louie the Pimp," Hymie Short-Hand," "Meyer Vy Sure," "Blinkie," and "Fat

Louie," were just a few of the characters that were part of the picture there. Each of those characters has a story to tell, and this is the story of one of them, "Curly."

In any situation, one or two personalities stand out in the mind and in memory. Curly was one of those individuals. He didn't have a stand in the market, nor did he own a business. He just covered the territory and that meant that he sold his own goods in the Northern Ohio Food Terminal, which is still located off Woodland Avenue between 37th and 40th Street on Cleveland's near east side. This was the boundary he set for himself and rarely would he change his pattern.

When I first met him he was a young, handsome black man with real style. This was back in the 1940's. It was easy to recognize that there was something special about him. He was as slick as they come, yet you wanted to believe him! He had hidden charm that surfaced when you came in contact with him, and even if you were not completely aware, you immediately became receptive and ready to accept his message.

Curly was a dandy. (Perhaps a better word, though less used in this sense today, is "dude"). His clothes were cut in the latest fashion, perfectly pressed and tailored impeccably. His pointed shoes were always polished to a mirror shine. His hair was cropped short, and slicked down with his own special brand of sweet smelling pomade. When I first met him, he would wear a light colored felt hat, large brimmed and cocked slightly to the side. His topcoat would generally be form fitting and slim looking, lending a racketeer effect, especially when he wore the collar up. Although the styling was very pronounced, the colors were solid, usually black or dark brown.

Curly never made the acquaintance of the merchants in the area—not that he wasn't interested in them, but they did not play any part in his plans. His targets were the many truck drivers who came from every part of the country to bring produce to the market. In the late 1940's, trucks were replacing freight cars in the transportation of perishable goods. A truckload of produce could arrive in Cleveland quicker and in better condition than a similar trainload, with enough other advantages to give the truck a preferred position in the perishable goods industry.

Truck drivers were, and remain, a strange lot; they don't fit into any specific category, but they are "different"—they have to be, for who would want to travel thousands of miles by himself in a trailer cab, living on coffee, cigarettes and amphetamines to keep awake. It is a life of travel, little excitement, loneliness and yet it has a fascination all its own. Once a truck driver, always a truck driver. It gets in the blood.

Many drivers wear Texas hats, colorful kerchiefs, cowboy boots, and tight fitting jeans that sport wide belts with huge buckles. Even on the coldest days of winter, they will walk around without coats because they live in heated cabs and they leave only for comfort stops. The cab area and sleeping section is their home. From time to time, you will see a truck driver with his woman traveling with him. In most case, she is young and has a particular style that makes you think of Appalachia. In summertime, there might even be a baby or a child along with the couple. This is not to say that all truck drivers are like this, but it is not an uncommon sight, even today. In some respects, little has changed. It is still a gypsy life that does not allow for the ordinary amenities of living.

Curly found that truck drivers suited his style, were easy to work with and to talk with on an equal level. As to how Curly made his living, he went to work every morning on schedule at eight o'clock. He would go to the wholesale jewelry house and purchase his supplies for the day's business; this would consist of "ersatz" earrings, necklaces, men's watches, women's jewelry and an assortment of bright looking pieces.

Packed in an attractive box, with a gold embossed triple price tag inside, the jewelry would sparkle and glitter as the box was opened. This is where Curly's style served him best. It was Curly's way to walk over to a truck driver, casually. "Hello," he would say, "do you want to buy a hot watch for your gal for less than half price?" The truck driver would turn, shake his head, and not even bother to carry on a conversation. However, Curly was not stymied so easily. "Don't you want this beautiful necklace and earrings set for only twenty-five dollars? It's worth at least seventy-five. Look at it and see if it isn't the best looking jewelry you have ever seen." By this time, the driver's curiosity was aroused and he began to think to whom he might give the jewelry — Edna, his wife? Jerri, his girl?

For that price, who knows how valuable the gift might turn out to be? The jewelry glitters in the sun, the gold-embossed price tag stares at him boldly, almost shouting "Seventy-five dollars!" and he continues to think. After a moment of pleasure, the box is closed. Curly, with an instinctive sense of timing, puts it back in his pocket, looking around carefully, protectively, as if to be sure he is not being watched. If you didn't know Curly, you'd swear that this was not an act, and that his jewelry was indeed hot, and if he weren't careful, he would be caught red-handed.

By now the truck driver's curiosity is stimulated and he asks to see it again. Curly draws the box out of his pocket slowly, carefully, turning his head in both directions, as if looking for a strange face. Opening it slowly, he studies the truck driver's expression in order to determine his next step. "Twenty-five dollars," he says. "Better take it, because you'll never get jewelry like this anywhere for double the price. Look at the label! *Guci*, the biggest name in jewelry on 5th Avenue in New York." The driver thinks he recognizes the name, not realizing that *Gucci* and *Guci* are two very different companies.

From that point the truck driver will make his own move and the deal will be consummated at some point between fifteen and twenty-five dollars. Curly has had enough experience to know how hard a bargain he can drive. Rarely will he push to a point where he will lose the sale. This is how he earns his living, and you can see him walking towards his prospective truck customers every morning from eight in the morning until early afternoon. New trucks arrive daily, with new prospects. From time to time he will hustle the same prospects, possibly in the same season or perhaps the following year, but the pitch is always the same, and the act goes on, almost like a play. The audience is different daily, but the stage is the same.

Curly went home to his wife and family every day. He had good and bad days and the going got rough certain times of the year, however, as Barnum once said, "There is a sucker born every minute," and Curly was determined to find them!

Curtis

I first saw him standing in the cold morning air, a tiny waif of a boy, dressed shabbily and without regard for the weather. He seemed to be a boy of about twelve or thirteen years old. He had clean, classic features and a light black skin. His hair was curly and tight, but delicate in texture.

A food marketplace is the same anywhere in the world. The same kinds of people gather in it and live from it. All one needs to do is transplant the language and customs and the market will seem to fit together just as if it were a piece of the same jigsaw puzzle. Curtis was a product of such an environment, and as such was living the part when I first met him. I didn't consider it strange to see one so young "hanging around," and that is the term literally, for it was not an uncommon sight then, or now. People, who need somewhere to go or some temporary way to try to get out of their rut, turn to the market for companionship and sustenance. Age is unimportant, and in some ways, neither is time or place. There were hundreds just like him.

So that is how Curtis came to be there. After I first saw him, something within me attracted me to him. Perhaps I felt that I could help him get the start he needed and maybe this is why I called him over to me and began to talk to him.

"What's your name?" I asked. "Where do you live?"

"Down the way," he said, pointing to a distant string of apartments.

"Why aren't you in school at this time of day?" I queried.

"Well, today is a holiday for our teachers and we are off too, so I thought I might make some money working somewhere in the market. Do you have any work for me?" he replied. "I can do anything you need, such as sweeping, cleaning, running errands or just fill in where you need me."

He looked quite intently at me and it seemed as if he awaited my answer with the fate of the world in his eyes. His youthful seriousness reached out to me. Even though I knew that there wasn't much he could do around the market, I could not say no to such a request so earnestly delivered.

Actually, meeting a boy like Curtis was not a new experience for me, as there had been many more before him, looking for work. They too had seemed to have this freshness and youthful charm when they first started, but before long they became just another story. I have always believed that it is possible to change the direction of some young boys if they are given some proper help and guidance. I guess in reality it just doesn't work that way too often when you have so much working against you: a broken home, lack of love and attention, racial discrimination, very little good food and perhaps just missing many of the essentials of a good upbringing. Many came from the ghetto where hundreds just like him strive to just break out of this type of life.

Curtis worked that day, and many Saturdays after that. He learned to do the things he needed to do, well and without complaint. Perhaps he had already acquired the wisdom that man's lot is a hard one. While others spoke about baseball, boxing and football, Curtis never let himself go that route. Now that I think about it, there was very little he would talk about. While he worked, he seemed to be a part of the total machine, helping to create the things that make sales, whatever that might be. There was nothing that was too difficult for him if I asked it, even if it meant lifting up the heaviest boxes. There was also an inner gratitude that seemed to appear in his face whenever he looked at me, and the confidence he inspired in me made me proud and happy to be of help to him. Sometimes it takes a small boy's trust to make an adult mature and strong. Perhaps this is why I was constantly searching for someone to protect, guide and lead, especially after my own children had grown into adulthood.

Weeks went by, and then came summer. Curtis became a part of the regular crew and took his place, arriving in the early morning. Oftentimes, his face would have an unwashed look and I would ask him to perform his morning ablutions before I allowed him to begin work. I doubt if he had many breakfasts at home, and if he did, they couldn't have been of much consequence. Sending him out for coffee gave me a chance to give him some extra change for breakfast. Of course, when he returned, there was a smile of affection on his face.

The weeks turned into months, the months into a year and before I realized it, Curtis had begun to look like a young man. He had become a regular feature in the store, and we counted on him to bring coffee for the fifteen-minute break as well as a dozen other jobs he learned to do without being asked; rarely did a day go by that Curtis did not go home with a sizable pocketful of tips.

Fourteen is not old by our standards, but in Curtis' world I'm sure it was an adult age for him and many of his friends. It is true that many people including myself grew up in rough environments, but when you make a factual comparison, it certainly would not be comparable to his background. This doesn't change the situation as I have always heard that you can become a better person because of life's hard knocks. I am sure that most of us refer to people who have come up the hard way and succeeded as a "Horatio Alger" story; I hoped that it would work out that way for Curtis.

Curtis had won the affection of all whom he worked with and I doubt if anyone felt any different than I did in our admiration for him. We believed Curtis was on his way to becoming a good, hardworking adult.

The warm weather always seems to bring out the best in our cleanliness habits, and with summer almost on our doorstep, it happened to me, too. The dirt and grime of winter was still upon us when I decided to have the store painted. If you have ever had a store painted during working hours, you know how irritating it can become. The constant moving of materials and fixtures made every day more difficult, for something was always in the way or out of place. It also meant staying later until the painters completed their work, which made my day even longer. I decided the weekend was the best time to finish the painting job. Even though we were less busy on the weekend, the job was not finished on the day as I planned it and they had to return on Sunday to finish the job.

Suddenly, I knew I had the answer to my problem: Why not let Curtis watch the painters after I opened the store, then there would be little chance of anything happening? I suppose it wasn't fair not to trust the painters, but with so many good things surrounding them, the temptation might be too much. Besides, Curtis could be counted on to keep them honest in any event. So I made the arrangements, a perfect set up. I could have Sunday off and that is what I wanted most of all. My thought was that six hard days of work was more than enough for anyone.

Finally the painters did finish, and the store looked bright and shiny. It was really worth all the trouble, now that it was all over. The biggest surprise, however, was yet to come. Upon my general inspection on Monday morning, I discovered a case of beer with some of the contents missing and the box in an unusual position. "Strange," I thought to myself, "how did this get here?" I asked my men if they knew who had placed it there or who had opened it, but no one seemed to know. I dismissed my feelings with some misgivings until later when I met with the policeman who patrolled the market.

"Say, Mr. Feren," he said, "did you give your boy, Curtis, permission to take beer from your store on Sunday?"

Beer? Curtis? It all came back to me in a flash. "I'd have to be foolish to do something like that," I replied.

"Well, that may be so," the officer continued, "but I saw him walking down Woodland Avenue carrying a case of beer and a bag in his other hand. I stopped and questioned him. All his answers sounded plausible, but I took the beer away from him because it still seemed strange."

I thanked the officer and told him his suspicions were

correct. In those few short minutes, everything I had dreamt about for Curtis disintegrated in thin air. All of my hopes had vanished and it was a great disappointment to me.

It was hard to believe what happened, but the evidence was there. I never saw Curtis again, or at least he never returned to my store. The reason why Curtis would do this is what bothers me most, for I felt that we both were on the right track. Maybe we were, but I was off of it from that moment on—until the next boy that reminded me of Curtis came along! Hope springs eternal.

FRUITS AND VEGETABLES
A TO Z

At 94 years old I find myself reflecting back on times and people of the past. Living as long as I have—and staying as active as someone at my age can be—I begin to see patterns in people and produce, and I realize that they are both inexorably intertwined. After all there is nothing closer to a man's body, that has more to do with his well being, than what he chooses to eat. And from the market comes those choices! So this is a story about the people that have made my professional life interesting, and the wonderful fruits and vegetables that drew us together.

Nowadays people eat a wide variety of fresh produce, but this was not always the case. I firmly believe that fresh air, good regular exercise, keeping the mind busy and eating lots of produce has been the key to my vitality for nearly a century.

In this book you will find not only wonderful stories, but also valuable information about buying, preparing and eating the bounties of the earth. As a dealer and as an "expert" in the field, it is now my pleasure to share what I have learned with you. If your century has as much great change, wonder and happiness as I have experienced in my century, you will be lucky indeed.

Enjoy my story and good eating!

Maury

Maury at produce exhibition, Public Hall, 1950

Looking back only a few years, you might remember when vegetables were considered to be foods that you were supposed to eat because they were good for you. This idea prevailed as a permanent part of the vegetable's status until relatively recently. In fact, up until 1970, only a few nutritionists and food "mavens" believed that the doors would open so wide for this market.

The frozen food boom in the 1960s, '70s and '80s expanded the use of the basic vegetables. The Bird's Eye brand, which first emerged during the 1930's, was a leader in this regard, first with its staple vegetables and later with innovations in variety. During this period, few of us recognized that using vegetables for their freshness and good taste would add so much to their usage. Besides this, there was a decided boom in the resulting nutritional information that was being discovered.

While all this was occurring, a number of creative chefs and cookbook authors, as well as food afficionados, began to recognize that the addition of fresh fruits and vegetables into the diet would change the entire landscape of food. Salads and fresh herbs began to find their way into the national food scene. Soft lettuces, greens, sprouts and other fresh ingredients began to find their place as regulars on menus all over the country.

There was also a boom in the use of many forgotten vegetables of the past, as well as some newer ones. Broccoli, for example, came out of the blue in 1936, zooming almost to the number one position on the vegetable chart. Vegetables such as cabbage, Brussels sprouts, spinach and cauliflower returned to their once popular status. However, this also was due in part to the amount of research that was done on antioxidants and their effectiveness against cancer.

I wouldn't have dreamt then that after years of eating meat and potatoes, you would find salads of every description as regular offerings on everyday menus. This dramatic change was slow in coming, but each year there was a steady increase in this category.

Phytochemicals, antioxidants and folic acid studies

flooded the medical journals as well as the news media in the 1950's and 1960's. Vegetables found their place on top of the USDA Food Pyramid in the last twenty years. The Mediterranean Diet placed vegetables on top of its list; this is still recognized as one of the most healthful diets in today's world.

Most vegetables are cholesterol free, low in sodium, low in calories, mostly fat free and a good source of fiber. There are exceptions to this rule, but only in limited situations. Of course how they are served is the determining factor in most cases.

When purchasing greens such as lettuce and other vegetables, look for crispness, bright color on the butt or leaves and lack of bruises. Freshness in tomatoes is delivered by a bright, uniform color, firm flesh with no cracks and a shiny skin. Pinkness and changing red color are important to indicate ripeness.

The five-a-day program established in 1988 through the National Cancer Institute Grant was developed to educate consumers about a more healthful diet. Today, this program is handled through the Produce for Better Health Foundation. Interestingly, this has aroused so much interest that there has been a positive increase in vegetable consumption in the last twenty years.

The advent of the exotic red and yellow pepper and other colored varieties grown hydroponically has stirred interest not only in peppers but also in every phase of vegetable consumption. Although most common varieties of bell peppers will turn from green to red as they mature, the hybrid successors grow yellow, orange, purple, black and brown, creating new markets and uses for these delicacies.

The cluster tomato has also brought about changes. There also are many new varieties of tomatoes of this type moving into prominence throughout the United States. The Cherry 100 and the cherry grape are two new varieties in the miniature group that have made their mark; others will surely follow.

As you can readily see, the world of vegetables has

changed and is constantly in flux. Yesterday's standard of head lettuce, cooked carrots and over-cooked cabbage has given way to a potpourri of new choices. Packaged fresh salads, herbs of every description, prepared foods that include fresh vegetables and imported foods from every part of the world have changed the landscape. The introduction of the Mesclun lettuces and exotic greens has also created an even more dramatic environment. However, this is only a beginning. Today's newest entrants will be the standards of tomorrow. I hope that this book will be a guideline for you for today and the future.

My experiences in sixty years of buying, selling and storing produce led me to believe that I have had a unique relationship with many of the fruits and vegetables which I write about in this book. It is not only the produce that attracts me, but also how these foods relate to me personally. Certain fruits and vegetables bring stories to mind that relate to my own life, as well as to certain ethnic communities.

For example, in writing about black radishes, it is essential to mention their history and uses. They are a vegetable of Eastern European origin with the same biting taste as the long or round white radish. It is also worth noting that in the Depression years, it was a basic food served in many European Jewish homes as an appetizer. It was served with sliced onion and covered lightly with chicken fat (schmaltz). It was not the healthiest dish, but a good filler when you were hungry and didn't have a lot of money to spend.

By the 1960's, there were only a few farmers who would grow black radishes, so it became more of a specialty vegetable and thus, gradually diminished in popularity. I learned from experience that I had to be able to store them under refrigeration in order to have supplies in January. In the 1950's and '60's, refrigeration was a limited possibility because of costs. As a substitute, I used blocks of wet ice to protect all of the perishable produce items. Wet ice, in turn, would discolor the black skin, which destroyed their appearance and color. To protect them from the damage of the melting ice, I would cover each layer of peck baskets with a burlap sack, then place wet ice on each layer. Since all of the local produce was packed in uncovered baskets, this was the most practical method to protect the outer skin.

I became the king of the black radish dealers, but my crown disappeared in the next generation of offspring. Strawberries, too, were a part of my life. I remember carrying a case of twenty-four quarts of strawberries, thirty pounds or more, on my shoulders in the hot sun, offering them for sale at twenty-five cents a quart in the poorest neighborhoods, in 1932-1934.

Later on, when I owned my own wholesale produce business, my specialty was locally grown berries in season. I was well known in the industry for the broad selection that I offered and the top quality berries that you could find almost every day. Since strawberries were not processed at that time to any great degree, there were times that I was unable to sell all of my purchases successfully that day.

Gradually, as my wholesale customers began to fail me, I decided to try the retail market by advertising in the local newspapers. *The Plain Dealer* and *The Cleveland Press*, addressed customers who were interested in processing their fruit—canning or freezing it. My ads in the local newspapers met with some success, but the location of my business between East 37th and 40th Street at Orange Avenue in Cleveland was not considered desirable, limiting my business. A twenty-four quart crate of berries sold for $10 to $15 at that time. Oftentimes, it would devaluate to $5 or $7 at the end of the day because of their perishability.

There was a great variable in quality and appearance by many of the local growers who specialized in strawberries. An interesting evaluation of the growers could be found in the way they dressed. Even in overalls, a clean, neat appearance would enable the purchaser to know what the packaging and quality would be. Casual or sloppy clothes would tell you that the produce would look the same way.

A family farm would generally consist of a husband and wife farming five to ten acres of land or more, and a slew of children ranging in age from five to eight years old or older. Once children were strong enough to do the chores on the farm, they were put to work, either before or after school hours.

Market days were Tuesday, Thursday and Saturday. That is when the produce was brought to market. No matter the weather, the farmer would arrive at the farmers' market at 1 or 2 a.m., his children half-asleep on the back of the truck. When the selling began, each child, boy or girl, was an important part of the operation, unloading boxes or baskets, whatever the need. It was not a question of what was good for the child; the child was raised primarily for the help he or she could bring to sustain the farm. In contrast, today we try to protect our children. In those days, the strawberry patch was generally the obligation of the older children to tend and care for. It is labor-intensive work. With the advent of McDonald's and other fast-food franchises, the children gradually came to the realization that they could make more money working in one of those businesses rather than picking berries.

In time, the local berry farm lost its base; its glamour and the family enterprise began the road to extinction. The price of land in the outer farm areas skyrocketed, which helped to make most of these family farms available to local housing or industrial developers. It was more profitable to sell the farm than farm it.

These are just a few examples of what you will find in the book. There is a great deal of basic information, but there is also a story of a life—my life—that goes with it.

ANISE

Fresh anise, Italian style. It used to be great fun to refer to anise whenever I dealt with an Italian who spoke the language of his forebears. "Fenocchio nevoie," I would cry out, meaning that the anise was fresh. Speaking their language gave me a more personal relationship with customers. Remember, this was a time when there were many immigrants who had been in this country for just a few years.

Today, many cooks use anise because it offers many opportunities for innovation; gourmet cooks have turned to it for some most unusual recipes. Using anise in a stuffing with meat or an equivalent substitute is one of the more exciting ways to use it. When you cook anise in a covered pot with butter and water, the anise will turn soft, leaving behind a flavorful glaze. It has a taste similar to licorice, but it is not as strong.

The green stalks of the anise should be bright green and the base should be a bright white. It is essential that this vegetable be kept at temperatures of 35° to 42° for best results. Wilting leaves detract from its essential good taste. You can cook anise in a variety of ways. The feathery stalks are used for soup seasoning. Cut the bulb raw, using it for salads, boil it for use in a casserole or serve it as part of an omelet for a specialty dish. It is available from local farms in Ohio and in ethnic markets. California and Texas are the major national suppliers. It also has a large amount of vitamin A and vitamin C, plus potassium.

APPLES

Apples are known to have grown wild in the regions from the Caspian Sea to the Atlantic Ocean. There are records of them from the Stone Age period of Europe. Even wealthy Romans enjoyed apples. In America, Robert Prince in Flushing, Long Island first produced apples commercially about 1730. The famous Delicious variety was found in Peru, Iowa, about 1881.

There are many apple-producing states. Washington is the leader, followed closely by New York, Michigan, Virginia,

California and Pennsylvania. Apples are available almost every month of the year, with peak periods from September to March. With the innovation of the atmosphere-controlled processes to ripen apples, crisp flavorful apples are available throughout the late spring and often in late summer.

Although there are more than 7,000 known varieties, a few select types have become universally accepted. The Red Delicious, a medium to large red-striped apple with five points at the calyx end, is used mostly for eating and salads. It's sweet, crisp and juicy.

The Golden Delicious is similar in size, shape and appearance to the Red Delicious, but not quite as distinctive in its calyx indentations. A sweet, yellow apple that is good for eating out of hand and for salads. It is also used for cooking.

The McIntosh is, a reddish, green-tinged apple that ripens early and easily. Crisp, juicy and mildly tart, it's a good pie or all-purpose apple, and it is excellent for eating.

The Rome Beauty is a highly colored, generally large red apple. It is a dry type that is excellent for its baking properties. It's also a late keeper that is sometimes preferred for eating, if you enjoy a full, dry taste.

The Stayman, a striped apple noted for its wine like taste, is colored red to mixed red and is juicy, aromatic and an excellent all-purpose apple. I think it is one of the best of the present-day varieties.

The Winesap is a very late apple harvested typically in October. It has a crisp taste that is juicy, not too sour or sweet, and is generally mild in favor. This is a good, all-purpose apple that has great long-keeping qualities.

The Cortland is a softer approach to the McIntosh and is noted for its snow-white flesh. It is an excellent apple for salads and is a good all-purpose apple.

The Newton, an apple that California prides itself on creating and growing, is a yellow apple tinged with russet dots. A juicy, firm crisp apple that is good for cooking and eating out of hand, it is also one of the best keepers.

The Pink Lady is shipped from Washington State from

December to May. It is both decorative and distinct in flavor. It is also grown in California.

Some other varieties that once were popular are The Northern Spy, the Rhode Island Greening, the Ben Davis, the York Imperial and the Jonathan, which are the best of the old-time varieties. They are more difficult to find today.

Other summer varieties of apples that have gained acceptance are:

- Summer Rambo - one of the best early green apples

- Williams Red – a very light-dry apple that becomes overripe almost overnight

- Transparent – a soft, tart, cooking apple that was once the most popular on the scene

- Fenton and Miller Red – harvested in August and accepted primarily for their red color, but not too flavorful

- Gravenstein – a striped, red and green apple noted for its flavor and is very popular in the West. This is an excellent dessert apple and good for salads.

- The Fuji, the Honeycrisp, and the Matsu have become standard varieties with exceptional flavor and taste.

There are many other varieties, too numerous to mention, but these have established themselves as the best in their field.

To identify good fruit, shop for clean, bright, attractive apples. They should be firm, free of soft spots and bruises. Good color indicates maturity. A dull look, scalding or browning should be avoided, as well as soft, mealy fruit. Apples should be kept under refrigeration and served when cold and juicy. It is a mistake to allow apples to lose their crispness out of a refrigerator.

Summer fruit is very perishable and should be used at once. Any bruising will affect the apples internally. Late apples often blacken inside during the latter part of their storage period. This occurs especially with the Delicious variety, beginning in March. Your best protection is solidity and a healthy appearance.

Apples are noted for their nutritive values. They are good as a mouthwash to clean the palate and prevent tooth decay. They furnish bulk for good digestion. They are also low in calories, very filling and have a fair number of vitamins. Apples supply some Vitamin A and appreciable amounts of Vitamin C. They are unequaled in the variety of their uses: They can be used raw, cooked in numerous ways, candied, canned, preserved or dried.

RELATED FRUITS:

Crabapples are a small fruit averaging from one to two inches in diameter. They are almost identical in shape and form to the common apple, except for size. They cannot be eaten raw, but they are a wonderful processing fruit. The fresh market is almost extinct for crabapples, with most supplies going to processors. They can be used to make delicious preserves, jellies and marmalades. Crabapples have a very distinct, sharp taste, even when processed.

Sapote is known as the Mexican custard apple. It is shaped like the Pippin apple, but ripens like a pear, with a smooth green texture. Grown in California, it's available July through May.

See also: Cider

Maury, the Farmer

Marketing apple varieties has changed considerably, particularly in the past few years. We are seeing the advent of many more apple varieties than we had been accustomed to in the past. Fuji, Matsu, Braeburn, Empire, Gala, Pink Lady and others have moved into the forefront. There are many doomsayers who believe the Red Delicious will become a minor variety; its future does not look that promising.

One of my first jobs of importance was working for the second largest commission merchant in the Northern Ohio Ford Terminal, the Thomas M. Rini Company. They represented the best produce in the marketplace and you could always count on them to feature the finest produce. They were the purveyors of the top fruit and vegetable lines available in the years before World War Two, until the 1970's.

I started working for them before the advent of atmosphere-controlled apples, which enables apples that are harvested in the fall to be stored effectively for six to nine months without losing flavor or appearance. In the 1930's and 1940's, it was a rarity to find good hard apples in the early spring months. Even under the best conditions, there was little apple stock available. There were some dry, hard varieties available that had good color and looked good such as the Ben Davis, the Gano, and the Winesap, but they did not have good flavor and you could taste the dryness.

In 1936, there was a well-known apple orchard for sale in Amherst, Ohio, called the Darby Orchards. You may have heard me mention that certain genetic qualities of both fruit and vegetables give them special characteristics. The Darby Orchards were renowned for the late-keeping qualities of their fruit. They specialized in two varieties: the Baldwin, a hard apple, and the Jonathan, a tart, juicy apple that was prized by both the Jewish and Italian trade in the 1930s and 1940s.

After they had purchased the orchard, the Rini Company wanted to make sure that the crop would be harvested properly and put into storage without any delay. This would help maintain the crop so it would store well and come out of storage in early spring looking and tasting its best.

Since there was no manager on the farm who understood commercial packaging requirements, I was sent to the orchard to take charge of the harvesting and packing in mid-September. I can laugh about that experience now, because I certainly was no farmer. However, I did know what was required as a packing expert and I learned to use that knowledge effectively.

The standard package in the 1940s was the bushel basket with a ring-faced top. You would have to place each apple in the inner circle of five separate circles of two inches or less on a metal ring facer. Then you would place this ring face on top of the bushel basket which weighed forty pounds or more, turn it over - bottom up, bringing the ring face to the top. A laborious process, but it would bring a perfect ring faced top that lined up the apples exactly in the circle. It would also show off the best looking fruit. Today, the fruit is poured into loose apple boxes with no "face" whatsoever.

I had five farm girls working for me at the Darby Orchards and I was in my early twenties. They were about the same age as I was, so there as some interplay verbally, but not much of anything else. This was hard work. Turning 40-pound bushels over required strength, but they were strong and didn't complain at all. I don't remember much about their feminine attributes, but I'm sure I must have taken notice of them. I was invited to dinner at one of their homes and the food was well prepared and there was lots of it. I had no trouble enjoying their good cooking and the bountiful harvest. The work was hard and the air was cold, with the wind blowing into the packinghouse, so I wasn't choosy about the food. I ate whatever they served.

I spent all of September and early October during the harvest period on the farm. I wore overalls and tried to act like a farmer, but I'm sure I never fooled anyone. The apples came out of storage in April looking great, so my work was a success. I always look back on that experience as a survivor: I wasn't born to be a farmer, but I learned fast. It was a time I will always remember.

See also: Cider

APRICOT

The apricot has become one of our fading famous fresh fruits. Each year it seems to get more difficult to obtain fruit that is satisfactory, yet more and more apricots are being sold to the processing industry. The apricot is mentioned in many early histories, with its origin dating to China as far back as 2000 BC. It is part of the plum family. It has great medicinal properties.

ARROWROOT (GOO, ARROWHEAD)

This is often referred to as the Chinese potato. It is a ground root vegetable rich in iron and vitamins, and is shipped from Japan.

ARTICHOKE

The artichoke is an ethnic vegetable that has found its way to the American scene, enjoying great popularity. It is a native of the Mediterranean areas and is a prized delicacy of the French, Greeks, Italians and Spaniards. Its history and origin appear to date back some 3,000 to 5,000 years. Although it is noted for its nutty flavor in its fresh form, it seems to have become more popular in its processed form – as an appetizer or hors d'oeuvre.

The artichoke is a semitropical vegetable with the cactus-like appearance of a pinecone. Its tender buds are flowerlike and it is regarded as one of the most unusual vegetables grown in this country. Since artichokes require the most ideal growing conditions, production is limited primarily to the mid-coastal area of California.

To select good artichokes, shop for fresh green leaves, with no wilting, black spotting or blemishes, and a tight, compact head that is fleshy and globular. Artichokes must be fresh and crisp to be good and should be refrigerated when storing. An attractive looking appearance can help you determine the condition of the vegetable. The artichoke is available most months of the year, with peak periods in March and April as well as in both late fall and winter.

Since its introduction as an entrée, it has begun to take on more importance as a gourmet food. The larger the artichoke, the higher the price. The ideal size is from three to four inches in diameter. This vegetable is highly perishable and should be used as soon as possible after its purchase. Artichokes can be used as an entree, an hors d'oeuvre and as a fully cooked vegetable.

Artichoke Memories

I can remember when the famous Italian store in my neighborhood, Alesci's, in South Euclid, Ohio, would feature prepared stuffed artichokes in season. However, the demand was so great, they were forced to freeze the artichokes ahead. It was not too long before they realized the labor involved was too costly, so they had to discontinue selling this delicacy. Only a few restaurants feature them today; one of my favorites is "Tuscany" in Beachwood, Ohio, who makes them available in season, stuffed with cheese. I have also found that marinated artichokes with hot pepper, parsley and olive oil have become quite popular. Giovanni's Restaurant on Richmond Road and Chagrin Boulevard, is noted for its great artichoke recipes, as well as other Italian delicacies. A five star restaurant.

One of the most outstanding experiences of my produce career was to visit the artichoke farms in Castroville, California, in season. I have never seen a prettier picture than a field of artichokes in full harvest bloom, ready to be picked. It is a sight to behold! Unfortunately, I was unable to visit the artichoke fair that same week, when numerous vendors prepare and sell artichokes many different ways: Fried; marinated; steamed; as an appetizer; or as artichoke hearts, stuffed with cheese. Delicious!

If you talk to any Italian chef about artichokes, his face will light up. Every one of them will have a recipe that will use a cheese or meat stuffing, baking it in the oven allowing the cheese or meat to penetrate the entire inside. Processed artichoke hearts in olive oil have become a popular appetizer and are often times used in salads. Braising can turn even the toughest artichokes tender. You can microwave artichokes for six to eight minutes until a petal near the center pulls out. To serve, pull off the lower petals and cut the stems to one inch or less. Cut the top quarter of each artichoke and then wash under cold water.

Look for green, plump artichokes with tight leaves. Oftentimes you will see blight, which are little black spots which is caused by early frost. It will, however, not affect the taste.

ARUGULA (ROGUETTE, ROCKET)

This highly perishable green-to-reddish herb has a peppery, watercress taste. Used in salads with goat cheese and to add individuality to any fresh dish, it has become a byword for the true epicurean. It is available year-round in Mexico and the United States. It has become very popular in salads.

ASPARAGUS

Asparagus is one of the most highly regarded vegetables produced in this country. Although its origin has never been determined because it grows wild, there are records of its cultivation in the Mediterranean area some 2,000 years ago. For many years it was regarded as a medicinal cure-all because of its unusual qualities; boiling the juice of asparagus to cleanse the kidneys was a common practice.

Today it is prized as a gourmet delicacy. Modern agricultural technology and air transportation have created a highly publicized crop, developing a demand for this product that puts it on top of the list of the most desirable foods. Although only thirty percent of the crop is sold in its fresh form, it manages to hold its fresh customers because of its exceptional, distinctive flavor. Frozen and canned asparagus are important markets, but asparagus tastes best when it is served fresh.

It is essential that we distinguish between the dark green variety and the all-white type. There are only a few varieties of asparagus and there is a continuous effort to graft the stronger varieties with the weaker types. The Martha Washington and the Reading Giant are the most important in this group.

Asparagus is highly perishable and must be watched carefully at all stages of distribution. It is in season from March to June, with the major shipping areas consisting of California, Washington and New Jersey. Today it is flown in from Chile and Peru out of season. To select asparagus, look for bright, clean, green stalks. The tips should be firm and compact with no signs of deterioration. Any wilting or general breakdown in the appearance of the stalks will determine whether the eating quality will be satisfactory.

Asparagus is graded to size, with premium prices paid for the thick, colossal stalks. There are many people who prefer the thin or medium-size stalks which taste equally good. This is only a matter of personal preference, depending on how you intend to prepare it.

If it is purchased fresh and cooked properly, this vegetable will prove to be one of the most enjoyable dishes that you can serve. It is also a highly recommended vegetable for good health, containing large amounts of Vitamin C, Vitamin A and some iron.

I don't think my mother ever analyzed the nutrients of the foods she prepared, but I know she wanted to give us healthy food based on whatever she knew about it from her own experience. She knew about steaming vegetables. She served us steamed asparagus in season, which she prepared in an elongated coffeepot. It would come out just as tender and flavorful as it could be. This was truly a great treat because we would top it with wonderful melted butter. Today the butter is a definite no-no for me!

Back in the 1920's and 1930's, the asparagus season lasted a couple of months. When California and Washington finished shipping, we were able to buy locally grown asparagus packed in 6 lb. peck baskets. The season finished off in Michigan, with excellent tasting quality. I don't want to forget New Jersey, the Garden State. Their asparagus crop followed Washington and it matches the best of them. They also produce a myriad of other truck garden vegetables.

In Europe, white asparagus dominates the scene, however, in the USA, it has never received any degree of success. White asparagus is achieved by covering the green headed spear once it just pops out of the earth. It is then covered with straw and even animal manure (on occasion) to heat-up the earth, which bleaches it to its fine white color. Both varieties of asparagus, all white and green, receive high marks for their distinctive taste and delicate spears.

The Greeks and Romans held asparagus in high esteem. It appears to have been cultivated in the time of Cato the Elder in 200 BC. If you really want to taste asparagus at its best, try warmed or steamed asparagus topped with your favorite Hollandaise sauce.

AVOCADO

A product of South America, Mexico, and the warm areas

of North America, the avocado is as ancient as some of these countries' ancient civilizations. Avocados are known as "alligator pears" because of their pear like shape. They grow on trees that are cultivated for the purpose of supplying avocados. Many years ago the name "Calavo", which was a brand, was the only name used by the avocado trade because they were distributors nationally. Today, we recognize the name "avocados. "

There are some varieties that have an alligator like rough skin, which also accounts for their name. Avocados are grown in the US primarily in California and Florida. They are available every month of the year, with their peak periods in March, April and May. The California Fuerte variety is popular because of its rich nutlike flavor. The Lula, the Florida type of avocado, grows much larger and has a smoother skin, although it does seem to be more watery, with less flavor. Also, the Haas variety (dark blackish green) is the most popular variety. With the advent of pre-ripened avocados, more people have come to recognize how good they can be. There are many offshoots of these varieties, but these are the most highly developed commercially.

To select good fruit, shop for bright, clean avocados with a heavy feel to the body. The fruit should show some signs of softening before you use it. Any black marks, bruising or dark sunken spots will penetrate the skin, damaging the flesh. Size is unimportant; the best buys generally are in the medium sizes.

The avocado is recognized as a high-energy food with many minerals of importance. There is a high proportion of iron and potassium, and it is a good source of Vitamin B1. Avocados have a high-calorie content, with about 245 calories a serving (half an avocado), yet low in cholesterol, enabling an avocado to be served almost as a meal in itself. Avocados are easily digestible and can be used in salads, as a spread or a garnish. Once they are fully ripe, they should be cut open and served. Storing the cut halves in a refrigerator and sprinkling them with lemon juice will retard the darkening of the flesh. Covering the halves with foil or a polyethylene bag will also be of great help in storing. The avocado is an excellent salad fruit that blends well with grapefruit or any variety of vegetables.

With the advent of Hispanic culture in the US, avocados have achieved a success that has surpassed the wildest hopes of the avocado growers. Demand has become so great, we are receiving year-round shipments from Mexico (a new law permitting this) as well as seasonal shipments from Latin America.

Guacamole has become a favorite recipe for this wonderful tasting fruit. In a veggie sandwich, it adds its unforgettable, rich flavor. The avocado grapefruit salad was once an old time favorite that still has good acceptance. Avocados have so many wonderful qualities; there are even a number of cosmetic products that are made from it commercially.

Avocados are available year around. Chile and Peru have become major suppliers during our winter months (which is their summer).

BANANAS

Bananas are one of the world's most precious fruits. Known since prehistoric times, they probably originated in Southern Asia more than 4,000 years ago. Since bananas grow so profusely in the tropics, they are considered to be one of the most important foods in their tropical settings.

A great many changes have taken place in the banana industry since they made their debut from Cuba in the early 1800's. Bananas are grown in every part of the tropical world, but only a few varieties have the capability of traveling long distances. Today, Central America is the most important supplier. Ecuador, Honduras and Guatemala lead this group, with Costa Rica, Panama and Colombia next in line. Bananas are also grown for local consumption in Israel and some other countries.

Bananas do not ripen well on the plant and, contrary to the normal ripening processes of other fruits, they ripen best once they are picked. Today the fruit is shipped in 40-pound cartons, cut from the stalk. Each "hand" (stalk of bananas) is carefully laid on a nest of paper to protect the bananas from bruising. The amazing factor is that this process has enabled the shippers to select bananas that are mature enough to ripen. The fruit is picked green, packed in refrigerated cars and checked from the railway car to the ship. The bananas are then sent to the final truck that carries them to their destination. If they are too green upon arrival, they are then ripened in carefully controlled "banana rooms," oftentimes with gas.

Bananas are available every month of the year, with spring and early summer the peak months. The most popular variety that is shipped commercially is called Gros Michel. The Valery also is well accepted. The plantain, or cooking banana, is a favorite of Puerto Ricans and other people of the Caribbean area. Plantains are generally sold green and must be cooked to obtain its best flavor. The Red Banana is available only from Guatemala. It is much drier and used primarily for cooking, however, it also can be eaten fresh. The Manzana, also called baby or apple banana, is shipped from Mexico year-round.

Hanging stalks of banannas displayed at
M. B. Feren Produce Company, 1950's.

Select plump, well-filled fruit that is turning a yellow color, with no bruising or soft spots. Color is important, for discoloration indicates immaturity or the inability to ripen well. Bananas that are allowed to speckle attain the full color that gives them their superb flavor. Most people prefer solid-yellow fruit. Bananas can be kept in the refrigerator, but it is preferable to let them ripen at room temperature. Overexposure to heat or cold will be damaging, so it is best to protect them from either extreme.

Bananas are used in many kinds of diets for good health, for babies and heart patients and for those on soft diets. They are an excellent source of vitamins, calcium, potassium, phosphorous and carbohydrates. They are well received everywhere because of their flavor and universal appeal. Bananas are generally served fresh, but they can be used for baking and cooking.

Bananas by the Hand

When I think of bananas, I always remember the days of long ago when they arrived piled on top of each other in big stalks weighing 40 to 100 pounds. They were hung on hooks, individually handed down through an opening to a gas-heated room where they were ripened for three to six days, according to their maturity. I want you just to think about this process for a moment, and the labor involved: There was the individual who had to lift the stalk; another person to hand it down, holding its weight in his arms; and finally the person who would hang it on a hook from the ceiling. It is much different today, because they arrive pre-cut in hands (a hand of bananas is trade lingo), packed 40 pounds to a container.

BASIL

Available year-round in the United States and Mexico, basil has a distinct taste of licorice or anise. There are at least twenty-five different fresh basil herb varieties, but the two most important are sweet and bush basil. It is used as a standard in soups, stews, pastas, and salads, and is great combined with tomatoes, dried or fresh. Many people prefer the deep purple basil varieties, such as opal basil for its distinctive taste.

You will see rack displays of fresh basil plants in many varieties in some stores. Years ago, dried herbs in packages would be the only way you could purchase basil. The essential difference in taste that basil offers has created a strong following for the enterprising home cook, as well as the commercial chef. You will find variations in flavor, including cinnamon, lemon and the beautiful deep purple opal basil. Some interesting recipes for pasta marinara include basil in the sauce.

Basil is available all year long, grown locally in the USA, as well as in Mexico. It may be one of the most popular herbs grown.

BEAN SPROUTS: The Rise of Bean Sprouts

It is only recently that people know about or use fresh bean sprouts. California restaurateurs discovered its fresh attributes and bean sprouts became commonplace in most salad bars, in sandwiches and definitely in Asian food. Marie Callenders' restaurants in California were one of the first to use them on most of their sandwiches, and then their popularity zoomed.

During my produce career, I was one of the first merchants to recognize their potential, at least one of the first in the Midwest. I began to purchase fresh bean sprouts from two Chinese restauranteurs who grew them in a special area in the back of their store. At that time, few people knew about them or accepted bean sprouts as part of the mainstream, so sales were limited. Bean sprouts are also highly perishable, needing instant attention for good marketing.

I furnished them for a major supplier. He in turn would supply them to a supermarket once a week. Since there were two profits taken in this commodity, I lost my competitive edge. As bean sprouts became more popular, I lost the account because the supplier found his own supplier. It was just about that time that they became a regular produce commodity that you could find in most markets.

Purchase firm, bright attractive sprouts. Keep them dry. Bean sprouts can remain fresh under refrigeration two to three days. You will find the California bean sprout grows much longer and seems to be a stronger variety. I am unable to explain this, except to refer to their soil and genetic background. Bean sprouts are available year round, mostly from local suppliers. In Cleveland, the Shuhei Restaurant, on Chagrin Boulevard, features bean sprouts as part of every fish dish. They add freshness and flavor, contrasting well with the colors of the fish and orange color of the carrots that complete the total picture.

BEANS: Limas, Pole Beans, Black Valentine and the Kentucky Wonder

Lima Beans - When people think of lima beans today, most of them visualize lima beans in cans, frozen food packages or in dry form. At one time, lima beans were a popular fresh vegetable. They have lost their appeal as a fresh product because of the time that is expended in their preparation. People in the South also call lima beans "butter beans" or "fordhooks". This is a truck garden crop in most parts of the East and Midwest. The major producing states for commercial processing are California, North Carolina and Maryland. Since most of the crop is sold processed, there are only a few months—August, September and October—when this vegetable makes any great impact in the fresh market.

Select well-filled, clean, bright fresh pods that show little signs of shrinking or aging. The shelled Lima should be of a bright light-green color and should appear tender. Lima beans are sold shelled in some specialty markets, but since they deteriorate rapidly, it is preferable to shell them yourself when you are ready to use them. It is best to store them in their shells in the refrigerator to keep them fresh until time for preparation. I predict that this market will continue to diminish in its fresh form because of the versatility of the processed lima beans that are sold as a pre-prepared food product.

I always think of the days when fresh lima beans were a

standard vegetable. Fresh lima beans had to be shelled by hand at that time, but it seemed to make no difference, as people were willing to expend the energy. If you received a good heavy lima bean shipment, it would bring a premium price. I would pay special help to shell the beans and pack them in pints and quart boxes. This was labor intensive, but that made the beans a more valuable asset. Even though there were canned lima beans, frozen lima beans had not yet come on the scene.

Green, Wax Beans or Pole Beans – there are many varieties of beans and history indicates that the snap bean (which is another name for the fresh product) originated in Central America. Fresh beans are a highly regarded vegetable with a great deal of universal appeal. The vegetable is available almost every month of the year, with a peak period in June and July. With modern pre-cooking methods and excellent transportation, we have become accustomed to fresh beans of excellent quality throughout the winter months.

Green beans must be young, tender and free of stringy qualities to be good. The Contender, a long, slender, thick green pod with tiny seeds, has gradually replaced the Black Valentine, an old favorite. When shopping for beans, snap them to hear them crack. This will determine their freshness. Always look for bright, clean-looking beans that have a fresh appearance. Black spots, withering and dull coloring will detract from their flavor. When selecting wax beans, use the same guidelines except for color. Shop for a bright, yellow-colored bean that is free of spots, and look for freshness.

The Kentucky Wonder or Pole Bean is another green bean that is gradually taking on more importance. It is long and wide, with an outwardly tough appearance. This is an excellent meaty bean that has a delicious flavor. Avoid curling or misshapen beans in this variety. A bright green appearance that is fairly smooth looking will help determine freshness.

Fresh beans deteriorate rapidly and should be used at once. They can be stored for short periods in your refrigerator. Green beans are a good source of ascorbic acid and make other important contributions to the diet. They are at their best when served fresh. Fresh beans are noted for their cooking attributes, but they can taste good raw or marinated.

The French Bean (Haricot Vert) has become a specialty food for the epicurean. It is deep green in color, very slender with a delicious tender taste that singles it out. Prepare steamed or in a microwave. High in potassium and Vitamin A, it is available year-round.

The Chinese Long Bean is also known as Dow Gawk, Dow Gong and Dow Kok. It is available all year round from Mexico and California.

The Fava Bean is an Italian member of the bean family, shipped from Mexico and California in the spring.

Mr. Herrick's Excellent Beans

During my wholesale produce years, the most important part of our operation was being able to obtain the best quality produce. Interestingly, there were only a few farmers that raised green beans that were young, tender and tasty. Green beans are a difficult product to raise: An extra day in the field could make the difference between tender, tasty and attractive green beans and overgrown beans. As a result, I valued my relationship with every one of the growers; they were the key to my success. At the peak of the green bean harvest, the pickings would be so large that it was not possible for any one merchant to handle all of the sales. Therefore, the farmers would ration out smaller parts of the crop. One particular farmer by the name of Herrick, who had a farm in Vermillion, Ohio, always had the best quality beans. They would be perfectly shaped, beautifully green and they would be so fresh they would literally break in your hands.

It was Herrick's custom to split his load and distribute equal amounts to a half dozen merchants whom he favored. He also preferred to consign the beans instead of selling them outright. This meant that the seller would try to get the best price for them and then deduct 10% for his commission. Actually, this made for competition between the six merchants to see who could get the best price.

During this particular week of the harvest, the market

was loaded. There were all kinds of beans available at any price you wanted to pay. However, Herrick's beans were exceptional. Even in an overloaded market, they would still bring a premium price. Oddly, my carriage trade buyers were reluctant to pay a high price for Herrick's beans that day.

Unfortunately, I was the lowest producer in price that day. There was so much difference between my returns compared to the highest price that Mr. Herrick received from his other favored sellers that he became very upset. He insisted that he was being cheated and that I was not giving him an honest return for his green beans. There was no way to discuss this matter with him or get him to change his mind. He left with a sense of bitterness. Since his belief in honesty was so powerful a force, he never sold me any of his produce for the rest of my days at the market. I was never able to change his mind about my returns for the beans he consigned to me that day.

There were many times I saw Mr. Herrick at his stand in the market when he was stuck with his produce. That made no difference to him. He was firm in his beliefs. He would rather dump the produce than to sell them to me.

It is worth noting that the farmer-buyer relationship was always built on trust. I was always proud that I had maintained such good relationships with growers and with family farmers who were all so important to my success. This was my only failure. It still remains a thorn in my side more than fifty years later.

BEETS: Borscht and all that

Although fresh beets have lost some of their impact as a truck garden crop, they still manage to retain some interest during their productive periods, which is the late spring and summer. Bunched beets with tops were once considered a delicacy, and many people used the beet tops as well as the beets in preparing special dishes.

The table beet is more contemporary than most vegetables; its first usage seems to have been recorded in Germany about 1550. From there it moved on to England and then to

Italy where more cultivation was introduced. Since most of the recipes for this vegetable come from Eastern Europe, its most successful inroads were made in that part of the world. Borscht, the famous beet juice prized by the Russians and Slavs, is the most important entry in this field.

Supplies are available practically every month of the year, with the heaviest shipments during June, July and August. Local garden crops create the most interest in this vegetable. There is a question in the minds of some people whether to buy beets with or without tops. This is only a matter of preference, however, any fresh bunched vegetable will retain its nutrients better with the foliage remaining.

Shop for young looking beets of medium size that are clean and bright appearing. Avoid a rough, tough appearance for these beets will have a woody taste.

Beet tops should be fresh and green if you are going to cook them. On the other hand, the tops do not affect the flavor of the beet, even if they should decay. Refrigeration is essential for this vegetable and it can stay fresh for long periods at the proper temperature. Beets are low in calories and have many minerals and vitamins. The tops also have considerable amounts of Vitamin A and iron. Serve beets cooked, pickled or use for decoration. Today beet salads are an epicurean delight, found in the best restaurants.

If you are an orthodox Jew, you might prepare your own borscht (beet soup at Passover). These beets have to be unwashed, with the dirt of the earth still remaining on them. This is the law of that tradition. It may sound odd, but in my wholesale produce days in the 1940's, I was one of the few merchants who sold unwashed beets. The growers loved me because it saved them so much work. I would purchase 100 half-bushel baskets of beets, unwashed. They would bring a premium price because they were a specialty item.

I had no refrigeration in my warehouse in those days because I had just opened my business. Each night, I would cover all of my perishable produce with fresh ice over burlap sacks to keep the produce fresh. It did the job, but think of all the hand labor that was involved! I had to go to the ice warehouse each night and purchase 50-pound blocks of ice to protect the produce. Then there was the labor involved to cover it. It was not until many years later that I was successful enough to purchase a large refrigerator for my warehouse that would take care of my refrigeration needs. Today, it is essential that the entire warehouse from one end to another be refrigerated. You cannot operate a produce business without it.

Specialty beets such as white, striped and off-colored baby beets have become treasured by the famous chefs who use them. Tiny beet greens have also become part of the epicurean scene. Swiss Chard is closely related to the beet green family. You can find some similarity in the taste of beet and chard leaves. Beet greens have found their niche, but they should be classified as one of our most healthful vegetables. Beets are available year around, grown locally in most states and sold with the beet greens attached in most areas. Texas and California ship fresh beet greens all over the country.

See also: Swiss Chard

BERRIES: The Berry Story

Blackberries - The blackberry has gradually declined in popularity and is now seen in only a few specialty stores. This has occurred because of the change in food tastes and a change in family demographics.Cultivating blackberries and picking them was always a family project. As the labor market shifted to the city, farmers could no longer afford the cost of picking and the blackberry patch began to disappear.

Wild blackberries are recorded in North America from its earliest history. From these berries, cross breeding helped produce some of the best varieties of blackberries we know today. They are also called "Dew Berries."

Black Raspberries - Those of you who have experienced the joys of eating black raspberries from Ohio, New York and Michigan, can appreciate their wondrous taste. Small drupelets with tiny seeds distinguish the black raspberry from the blackberry. A good blackberry is larger and the druplets (the attached berries) have a sharper, bitterer taste. Each of these berries can be eaten whole, but the black raspberry is smaller and more closely related to the Red Raspberry.

Loganberries are dark red and of good size. They are similar to the blackberry and also have a slightly bitter taste.

The Boysenberry is a hybrid, seeming to have both the qualities of the blackberry and the loganberry. Made famous by the Knotts Farm in California, it is well known for making exceptional tasting preserves. The fruit is a deep red, of good size and has a sweet taste. It is difficult to obtain, except in season in epicurean markets.

Blueberries have made tremendous inroads on the American scene since World War II; before then only a few people who knew of their fine qualities used them. Consumers have now discovered the many uses of this berry and its widely used and enjoyed by consumers throughout the country.

The blueberry's origin appears to have been in the Northern Hemisphere with some records indicating a European background in the 1600's. Blueberries were called Huckleberries at first, a name that has remained with them in some parts of the country. They were also called turtle berries in England and blackberries in Scotland. Native Americans found many uses for the blueberry, passing on this information to the early colonists. Blueberries grew wild and little was done until the early 1900's to develop cultivated varieties. Today, this industry is based on the cultivation of more than 100,000 seedlings.

New Jersey, Michigan and North Carolina are the major producing areas, with smaller areas in New England, New York and Indiana. May, June and July are the peak months for Carolina and New Jersey; August and September are the high production months for Michigan. Limited supplies come from Ohio. The season is quite a long one, giving the consumer an opportunity to enjoy this fine-tasting fruit throughout the entire summer. Blueberries are noted for being high in anti-oxidants. They are recognized as one of our most healthful fruits.

Blueberries should appear bright, clean and dry and free of leaves or stems. The color should be a shiny blue-black, indicating maturity and freshness. Avoid off-color or green fruit, overripe berries that are weak and dull-looking and seem moldy, which indicates decay. Blueberries must be refrigerated at once and should be used as soon as possible after purchase. They taste best when served cold and can be used in the same ways as other berries, serving them with cream or milk.

As with other berries, blueberries can be frozen for later use by simply washing the berries well and storing them in a plastic container. They are easy to process and thaw out in a very solid form, which enables the consumer to use them throughout the year. The blueberry muffin has helped make this berry famous. These berries continue to gain in popularity as more people learn of their sweetness, flavor and versatility. Chile has become a major supplier in our off-season periods. They rank high in healthful nutrients, and have received high marks for their benefits.

Gooseberries - When we think of gooseberries, we refer to "Merry Old England," where the first gooseberries originated. England is still a popular home for this fruit, while here in America it is hardly recognizable as a factor in the fresh fruit industry.

The gooseberry was never used in this country as a fresh fruit. It is served in England as a ripened fresh berry; in American it is used only as a processing product. Early homemakers would pride themselves on the combinations they made of currants and gooseberries. Jams and preserves were another important use. Only a small part of this tradition remains with us, and the gooseberry is well on its way to extinction as a fruit in the United States.

There are two types of these berries, the reddish gooseberry which is made into jam, and the New Zealand Cape Gooseberry, which can be eaten raw, cooked or dried as well as made into preserves. The fruit of the Cape Gooseberry is quite small, a tiny yellow orange fruit to which the calyx is attached to surrounding dried flower cups.

Look for fresh looking, plump, firm berries. The skin should be unmarked and free of spots or blemishes. They are available from February to August in very limited quantities except for Oregon, which is the major producing state. The only other supplies are grown for local markets.

Raspberries - Cultivated raspberries are not quite as old as most of the other fruits we know, since they were introduced in England about four hundred years ago. Yet wild raspberries are a fruit that has been with us for thousands of years, with no positive record of their origin. Today, wild raspberries can be found in the hills and mountains in many parts of the country.

First, we must distinguish between the Black Raspberry and the Red Raspberry. The major difference is not only in color but also in the solidity of the berry. Black raspberries are rougher tasting, more tart, with hard seeds. The red raspberries are shaped the same but are softer in taste, with a mild tartness. Red raspberries have become a popular dessert fruit noted for their flavor. Winter supplies have been shipped successfully from Chile.

Currants - These are small berries of deep red color that once grew wild on the shores of the Mediterranean many years ago. They are primarily grown in temperate climates. Today, most of the currants grown are used commercially for preserves, jellies and some light wines. There are also some varieties that can be dried. They are available in the late summer.

All berries decay quickly so they should be used as soon as possible after purchasing. Shop for fruit that is plump and fresh appearing; greening in spots will detract from their sweetness. Overripe berries will appear to be dull and soft looking; you can oftentimes discover this by the stains on the container in which they are packed.

Berries From Across The World

Thirty years ago, no one ever expected the development of the berry industry that has taken place today. Genetic engineering has made these developments possible. Oregon, Washington and California ship beautiful red raspberries almost every month of the year. They are shipped by air and arrive in perfect condition. The varieties are big, fully colored red raspberries that have a firm body and a sweetness all their own. They are not as tart as the original berry you have known in the past, but they command respect and recognition for their own rich taste. Chile has also become a major factor in this global world. Who would have believed that we would be enjoying red raspberries from a country 9,000 miles away in midwinter? That has happened and you'll find them in your supermarkets and finer restaurants during the cold winter months. What a treat that is!

In July, the first red raspberries would come to the market, followed by black raspberries. What a treat they were. Packed in 24-quart containers, they were the premium fruit in the 1950's and 60's.There was only a few good growers and because of their high perishability, it was a struggle just to get enough good quality berries to supply my best trade. My customers literally had to stand in line for the product. Of course, that didn't go on for too many years.

See also Strawberries

BOK CHOY

This vegetable is also known as "white cabbage." A Chinese chard, it has had a favorable reception by American cooks. It's sometimes called Boy Toy or Pak Choi. Today it is in great demand by American chefs who have discovered its versatility. Choy Sum is a variation of Bok Choy, with only the heart. It is a very tender eating vegetable.

BREADFRUIT

Breadfruit is a round, thick-skinned fruit that is grown in the tropics. It is never good until it dries out completely and it is generally processed by being ground into flour. It is also known as PoiPoi in the tropics and noted for its long storage qualities. This fruit is rarely seen in American markets. It also can be prepared by boiling, then peeling the entire fruit and serving it with a butter sauce.

BROCCOLI

The broccoli family is closely related to the cauliflower as well as to some varieties of cabbage and fresh kale. The history of this vegetable is vague, with some material indicating that its origin took place 2,000 years ago somewhere in the Mediterranean area. Although there were many varieties of broccoli, or the sprouting plant as it was called originally, what we see today and accept in America is an adaptation called the Calabrese variety.

Broccoli has an interesting background, perhaps more so than many other vegetables, because it is a contemporary American form that has made its mark only in the last forty years. In the early 1920's, the D'Arrigo family in Boston decided to market broccoli on a national scale to people of Italian descent. It took years of hard work and education before the vegetable caught on. As the American consumer showed more interest, broccoli became a regular featured vegetable on most counters. Today, fresh broccoli is accepted at an even higher level, with supplies available almost year-round.

Peak periods are in the fall from October to December and in early spring from February to April. California is the major shipping area with some assistance from New York, Oregon, Pennsylvania, South Carolina, Virginia and Arizona. Although some of these vegetables are sold prepackaged, they do not hold up well this way. It is best to buy them in a loose pack so that you can see all of the head and leaves.

To select broccoli, look for a bright, clean appearance with a dark or purplish-green color. The head should be compact with small, tight flowers and solidity indicating freshness. The stalk should be tender, from one to two inches in diameter. A thick stalk may oftentimes denote a woody taste. Any sight of flowering, wilting or damaged leaves will detract from the flavor. Broccoli should be refrigerated at all times and used as quickly as possible for best flavor. Since it freezes well, it has become an important frozen vegetable, with a large percentage of the crop sold this way. It is one of the few vegetables that retains its fresh taste enough to maintain its popularity as a processed product.

Broccoli is also noted for its vitamin and mineral content. It is an excellent source of ascorbic acid and has high food energy content.

An offshoot of fresh broccoli is a similar vegetable called rab, rape or rapine. It's actually the forerunner to broccoli. Mediterranean in origin, it is prized by people of that region. This vegetable has the outward characteristics of broccoli, but it has a bitter taste. A product of the turnip family, it is tender, with broad green leaves and a thin stalk that is quite flavorful. Rapini can be steamed, boiled, sautéed or braised, and has a dandelion, spinachy taste. It's highly perishable and must be used at once for best taste.

Chinese Broccoli is a green vegetable with a long shank and a large flowered leaf. It is also known as Gui Lou and Guy Lou. It should be cooked like chard. It makes me feel good to know that I've been around long enough to remember receiving the earliest shipments of broccoli marked Andy Boy when I was working at my first job in the wholesale produce industry.

I've often wondered, "What would the Chinese restaurants use if they didn't use broccoli in their stir fry dishes?" It is the most popular vegetable found in their cooking, even though it is not an original Chinese vegetable; it seems to fit well with all of the vegetables they use.

It is available year around, with California, Arizona, Maine, Texas and Colorado, along with some local producers in some other states filling the gaps. Mexico also ships broccoli during short seasonal periods.

What's your choice: Broccoli au gratin, broccoli rabe with Parmesan cheese, broccoli stem slaw or cold broccoli soup? Packaged broccoli florets has made terrific inroads as a primary vegetable and many people like to use it instead of the whole unit, including the stem. Oftentimes, the young thin stem is the tenderest part of the broccoli. It is excellent in salads, or served as a side dish.

BRUSSELS SPROUTS

Brussels sprouts never have achieved their goal of universality.

If they are prepared properly, they have wonderful eating properties. They also have lots of Vitamin A, potassium and phosphorus. Brussels sprouts are also known as one of the primary nutriceuticals that have protective anti-cancer properties. They can be braised, broiled, steamed and sautéed and they also do well in soups.

Brussels sprouts moved into the market place slowly. When they were first introduced, they were packed in twenty-five pound drums, filled with ice for protection. There were processors who could then repack them in quart boxes for institutional use and for retail markets. They seemed to be most marketable at holiday time in the 1950's and 1960's. Gradually, people began to learn more about them and the packaging became smaller, in pint boxes and also in bulk.

If you really want to see a beautiful sight, you must visit Castalia, California. When you go here, you will see Brussels sprouts that grow as a bush, tightly winding around a long stem, sort of like cherries on a vine, but with no space in between. They grow so closely together they present a most interesting contrast. You will stop and hold your breath as they present such a gorgeous picture. It is a sight you will never forget as you look out at rows and rows of these beautiful green bushes of Brussels sprouts. California is the major producer, with Long Island, New York filling in from time to time; Brussels sprouts are available all year, with the peak period between November and December.

CACTUS LEAVES:
Don't Forget To Dethorn Them

I can remember when I first saw a display of cactus leaves in a Hispanic market in California. I wondered what it tasted like and how it was served. It did seem strange to me, quite strange. In speaking to a local woman, I asked her that same question. She said, "It is a tasty delicacy once it is dethorned, however, it must be fresh to be good and it is used primarily as a stir-fry vegetable. When cooked, it is tender, but crunchy and slippery."

You will find that there are six to ten cactus leaves per pound and they do shrink to some degree. They are available in California and Mexico year round.

Cantaloupes: see Melons

CARAMBOLA (STAR FRUIT)

There are two varieties of Carambola, one is sweet and the other is tart. It is grown primarily in Florida, with some occasional shipments from Mexico. It is also known as Star Fruit because when it is sliced, each slice will be star shaped. Its decorative potential does make it more interesting, but to date, it has not achieved great success for its taste.

Many years ago, I did taste a processed star fruit jam, but it was so costly, I never found it anywhere again. Brooks Brothers in Florida is staking its hopes on achieving a more universal appeal. The skin of the fruit is tender and has a glossy golden yellow color when ripe. The flesh is translucent and exudes a juicy fragrant taste. It is available from September through March from Florida and Mexico.

CAROB BEAN:
The Carob Bean and Johnny Bread

I don't think that many people know that Carob and Johnny Bread are one and the same. For the traditional Jew, Johnny Bread is served on Lag B'Omer, a festive holiday of thanks during January and February. (This is a holiday based on the Jewish calendar, which follows the lunar cycle). Johnny Bread is offered along with dried dates, figs and raisins as part of the holiday tradition. In mystical terms, there are some Biblical interpretations that seem to indicate that the carob bean was the sustenance "manna" for the Jewish people after their liberation from Egypt, while they traveled for forty years in the desert—however, no one to date has been able to substantiate that theory.

For the health food aficionado, carob flour is the fruit of the carob tree that has been finely ground. It is used as replacement for cocoa, chocolate and in some cases, sugar. It is high in calcium, phosphorous and has lots of iron, copper and magnesium. Each pod can contain up to fifteen seeds.

CARROTS

The carrot has a long history of development and change. Botanical records indicate its origin in Middle Asia, and there is some research validating its use more as a medicinal herb than as a food crop. Carrot seeds were found dating back as far as 2000 BC in the ancient lake area near Zug, Switzerland.

The fresh carrot is available year-round. California is the most important producer; Texas, Michigan, Arizona and Canada are also good producing areas.

With the advent of the packaged baby carrot, machine tooled in some cases, carrot consumption has zoomed. However, once the consumer began to recognize its beta-carotene qualities, the carrot became a household standard for its nutritional benefits.

Many varieties of carrots are sold mostly in a pre-pack form, covered with a polyethylene bag with the tops removed. Some consumers still prefer the bunched carrots with the tops because they believe that this practice retains flavor and freshness. There is evidence to prove this, but the fact remains that the prepackaged carrot has improved the general eating qualities almost one hundred percent because freshness is maintained.

Shop for fresh looking, clean, bright carrots that are free of blemishes and black spots. The carrot should be firm and solid, with no indication of softness. A clean, smooth carrot will be easier to prepare and will not be wasted. Avoid shrinking, rubbery or discolored carrots.

The carrot is one of the most highly rated sources of Vitamin A that we know. It is a low calorie vegetable, loaded with healthful vitamins and iron. The medicinal properties of this vegetable are often overemphasized, but nonetheless carrots are recognized by food experts for their nutritional qualities. It is one of our most versatile vegetables, offering many opportunities to help make meals more interesting. They can be served raw in a salad, cooked in soup or stew or served as a buttered vegetable. Carrot sticks are an excellent lunchbox item. However, be aware that these are not baby carrots, but are machine tooled from a giant carrot variety.

The French Carrot is a tiny carrot, generally from one to two inches long and is very sweet. It is ideal for roasts and stews. Oregon is the major American producer of this variety of carrot.

The Red Carrot has been genetically produced to double the beta-carotene phytochemical it produces. It has a beet red color and the red shows up in its outward coloring. It has received some minor acceptance because of this. However, carrots by themselves have had a wide acceptance over the years. Their nutritional qualities are well known. With the advent of the impact of the (punched out) baby carrots, sales have doubled over the last decade.

CAULIFLOWER

Cauliflower never has attained the popularity it is entitled to because of its counterpart broccoli, another member of the cruciferous family. Many years ago, someone recognized that a smaller package of just the florets would work out well for the individual consumer; it is recognized as one of the more popular prepared packages.

There are also new varieties that have made some impact such as purple cauliflower, also a baby green variety, which is quite tender and more colorful, and a combination cauliflower and broccoli variety, as well as baby cauliflower.

Steamed baby cauliflower served when it is completely tender is an excellent side dish, served with a favorite dressing. Fried cauliflower has always been a standby treat in our home, as well as cauliflower soup. You will find cauliflower florets on many vegetable trays, but I've never seen a lot of takers, even if they have an excellent tasting dressing, or Hollandaise sauce. Cauliflower is available all year around; California is the biggest shipper, followed by Long Island, New York. You will also find some local areas that grow cauliflower seasonally.

CELERY:

Remembering The Real Pascal Celery Hearts

I can't tell you how disappointed I was in the holidays when I expected one of my premium Pascal celery heart growers to fill my holiday order, only to find out my ration had been cut. Often, the celery hearts would not meet the high standards I set. In order to obtain the premium growers' product, I had to be in the market at 1 AM. on market day.

In order to bleach celery hearts, they are stored underground, covered with straw and manure; the heat this generates bleaches the celery. In the bleaching process, black spots can appear which are caused by overheating. When everything went well, I was the proudest produce man in town. Those celery hearts were the talk of the town, bleached to a sunny white perfection, crunchy, crisp and flavorful. It is an art that no longer exists in our farming society. The labor involved is so intensive, that it is no longer practical. Today you rarely see the bleached celery heart. We have become accustomed to the large green California Pascal.

Celery stalks with a flavorful dip make a great appetizer. Celery is great in soups, salads and in stir-fry. Celery stalks must be covered to stay in good condition; a good way to keep them crisp is to place them in an ice water container under refrigeration.

Selling to Restaurants

It may come as a surprise to many people that the quality of food that the restaurants used in the 40's and 50's was quite different than it is today. Most restaurants concentrated on a meat and potato menu, which limited the amount of fresh vegetables they would consume. There were always the basics: lettuce, potatoes, onions, celery, tomatoes, cabbage, peppers, carrots, etc. The Forum and the Colonial Restaurant in the Leader Building on Superior Avenue were two of the few restaurants that served a variety of vegetables, mostly fresh, with some canned and frozen. Higbee's Silver Grille Room also prided themselves on their variety and quality of food. Even there, however, there was nothing like the proliferation of salads that there are today.

Let me tell you a little about the Chinese restaurants that I served from the depression years up until recent times. Every restaurant I served fifty years ago would use "basic" quality vegetables; they had to pass first grade inspections. Few restaurants went for US #1 Fancy Grade or any of the higher-grade produce we had.

I recall the story about Pascal celery hearts. The Pascal term in those years meant a highly bleached, crisp celery heart, almost totally creamy white.The discarded outer celery leaves would be packed loosely, washed individually and then packed in a wooden crate. Most of this celery was still fresh and good and I would sell it as a box of celery leaves; it would wholesale for 75¢ to $1.00 a crate in the 1950's.

When I would deliver an order to a Chinese restaurant, most of the shipment would consist of only the following items: a box of celery leaves, a crate of celery cabbage (Napa cabbage), a bag of large Spanish onions and maybe some lemons.   Although communication was difficult because these restaurant owners had just arrived in the USA, they knew about numbers. Somehow, we managed to consummate a deal.

Chinese food at that time was very limited. The major restaurants were located off St. Clair Avenue and there were probably a half dozen that were popular.

Only a few restaurants attained great popularity because Chinese food was just coming into its own in the 1950's and 1960's. It was not until the 1970's that Chinese food took its place among the recognized, widely popular restaurants of that period. Today there are more than two hundred and fifty Chinese restaurants in the Greater Cleveland area.

CELERIAC (CELERY ROOT)
Trying To Find The Root

I was so entranced with the taste of celery root that I made up my mind that I would make it available to all of my customers when it was in season. Since it is harvested in the fall, the old time farmers stored it in the ground all winter. The so-called under ground storage unit would not be uncovered until spring, so there were no supplies most of the winter.

It was my custom to attend every International Fancy Food Show in New York once a year, to purchase epicurean delicacies for my gift basket business. I came upon a line of processed glass jars of Celeriac from Germany, which I purchased and offered for sale as a replacement for the fresh product. There was a great deal of interest, but the pricing limited sales.

Celeriac, (Celery Root) has Eastern European origins. The root is excellent for salads, and adds great flavor to soup, including Cream of Celery soup. The stalks are seldom used and many chefs peel the skin, while others use them as they are. It is considered a delicacy today.

CHAYOTE SQUASH
The Earliest Squash We Know

Today we have come to accept and utilize all of the exotic fruits and out of season vegetables that we see in our markets. In the days when I first became involved with the produce industry, the only exotic fruits that were available were avocados, cranberries, chayote squash, seeded grapes through November (with an occasional shipment in December out of storage), Spanish honeydews from Spain in December, pineapples from Cuba and peppers, cucumbers and tomatoes from Mexico. It doesn't seem like a great variety, compared to the 39% of imported fruits and vegetables today.

The Chayote is actually a member of the squash family. Why it was named originally as the Chayote pear is a mystery that I have not been able to solve. Prepare any way you like— baked, steamed and seasoned to taste. Look for solid green, fresh appearing chayote squash when you purchase it. It seems to have a Hispanic appeal, and is used basically by this segment of the population. It is available from California, Mexico and local growers, who serve Hispanic populations.

Also: see SQUASH and GOURDS

CHERRIES

No Sweeter Time of Year Than Cherry Time

There was a time when the best cherries were "ring-faced", every big cherry in place. ("Ring-face" means a neat presentation of the most beautiful fruit in the container, presented right up front). That was when the cherry growers packed the premium large sizes as a specialty package.

It was also a time when cherries were a luxury. When the cherry season rolled around, we knew it was a short season and everyone who could afford it would make sure to get at least a taste of them, regardless of price.

I would love to pick out the largest and best red cherries, nine or ten-row size, packed in eighteen pound refrigerated boxes, ice cold. I would open the box with the cold sweetness just pouring out, and I would eat as many cherries as I could. I probably ate three to five pounds of cherries myself at one sitting and divided the rest with my two brothers, who participated in this big feast as well. It has never been the same since then. The cherries are no longer ring-faced. They even taste different. I think so, even though we get those same big Bing varieties in season.

Now, cherries are available through the entire month of July and part of August, with shipments from Washington, Oregon, Colorado and Utah finishing off the season. They are also atmosphere controlled for late keeping. Once we get our fill of them and the newness wears off, there is less interest. It isn't until winter, in December and January, when we taste the cherries from Chile, that we remember what we've missed!

Sour cherries have a life of there own, great for pies and used as a filler for an old Jewish recipe called "Varnishkes". Sour cherries are grown in Michigan with a short season during July. Most of the sour cherry crop is used commercially.

Then there is the Royal Ann, a light, creamy white and red cherry that has a delicious taste, and is also premium priced.

CHESTNUTS

Roasting Chestnuts By The Fire

Many chestnut trees once proliferated in Ohio. However, they were obliterated by disease and today there are only a few remnants. Ohio chestnuts never attained great size, but they were tasty and had good flavor.

Today, Italy is our main supplier, with shipments beginning in early December through January. Look for shiny, solid chestnuts with a full brown color, no softness, and a bright appearance. Size is unimportant; most people purchase the medium sizes. During one holiday season many years ago, I rented a chestnut roaster. For fun I set it up one day in a busy spot and stood there personally roasting chestnuts, selling them for cost just to do something different. I wanted it to be like New York!

The easiest way to prepare chestnuts is to cut their outer shell just deep enough to avoid the flesh. A cross is effective. Put them in your oven at 350° for five minutes for best roasting. If they are handled properly, they can become a great "nosh." New Yorkers love to buy them on the run from the roasters who hustle them on the busy corners of the business areas. This is still considered a major treat. Another popular way is to use them in stuffing. Both the French and Italian people use them extensively in their cooking. You may see them processed in liquor, or just the shelled meat itself. However, once these processed jars are opened, they must be used at once or their quality disintegrates. Chestnuts are never refrigerated.

CHILI PEPPERS

Hot peppers have become the most popular pungent flavoring for the truly innovative chef. There are a dozen different characteristics of each variety of hot peppers and each chef has his own favorite. I have particularly enjoyed the Anaheim hot pepper, which is a medium size green hot pepper, but more on the milder side. The Vietnamese cut them into small ringlets to use in their soup with rice noodles, meat, chicken or vegetables. Hunan Chinese cooks make good use of the tiny red chili hot pepper in their spicy dishes.

I enjoy spicy food, but I've been fooled many times when biting into a chili hot pepper; sometimes they are so hot that I've jumped almost to the ceiling! I also have bitten into a pepper that was so hot I could not catch my breath. I have to rank the chili hot pepper as one of the hottest. The long yellow hot peppers are considered to be of Italian origin and have their own sense of hotness. I've tried to use small pieces in a salad, but they just are a bit too hot to enjoy. Cutting small slices into pickled dills will give them that extra pungency that makes the pickles taste better. Many years ago, I purchased jars of long yellow Hungarian hot peppers for personal use. They were produced by a homemaker who was looking to make a little extra money. They were terrific, with just the right taste, medium hot and not too much vinegar.

Look for a fresh appearance, no softness, and good color. Red generally signifies a hot quality, but the dark green can be just as hot. Hothouse growers have developed sweet varieties that have similar shapes to the hot peppers. They have to be marked to identify them, and are a specialty item. Dried hot peppers offer another kind of pungency and are used extensively in the Hispanic community. Habanero is the world's hottest chili, however, the orange Scotch Bonnet pepper will give you a good run for the money. The green Jalapeno is the unripe version of the red hot peppers. Both the red and green Serranos have a very powerful heat; they look like a tiny chili, but more expanded. The Poblano is the very best for roasting and stuffing. It is available all year and is grown in Mexico, the Caribbean area and in the USA.

CHIVES

I don't know how many people remember when green onions were considered a delicacy in mid-winter because they were only shipped from one source. Periodically, I would receive six to eight barrels of green onions packed solidly in ice, twenty-five dozen to a barrel, shipped by Railway Express from Louisiana. At holiday time they were so scarce, I would ration them so that each one of my customers would receive their fair share. But I did have a chive pot plant in my home all winter. I never ran out of chives because I would cut off just enough for a meal.

Chives are a member of the green onion family and have a mild onion flavor. When cut, they grow back rapidly. Chives have been cultivated for thousands of years, originally being grown in ancient China. Chives were considered a luxury in the 1940's. They were grown in hothouses, packed in eight, four-inch pots to a basket. They were a specialty item that received little attention, but also played an important role as a flavorful seasoning.

Today, chives are available year round. They are a mild form of the green onion family. They also make a good substitute, if you enjoy green onions, but prefer a lighter version.

Also: See Leeks, Onions

CIDER

Oh, For A Glass of Old Fashioned Apple Cider!

I know that many people would be surprised to know that before there were protective regulations ordered by the FDA (Food and Drug Administration), there were no quality restrictions on the apples that were pressed for cider. Until these regulations were policed, some farmers would press apples that dropped off the trees (originally referred to as "drops"). They may have even lain on the ground for a few days as well. Other apples had black spots or pockmarks, but there was no one to inspect them, so apples were pressed if they looked fairly good. There were exceptions. Many farmers only used their good standard fruit pickings, singling out particular varieties that gave the cider good flavor.

However, with the advent of the e-coli bacteria, the restrictions became more severe. E-coli problems played a major role in the change of pressing practices. In the new rulings, all cider must be treated, or it cannot be sold. Actually, it becomes apple juice in this process, but it is not refined to that extent. It still is perishable within seventy-two hours; otherwise it will sour almost immediately, even under refrigeration. Cider vinegar was used extensively in the past, but it has lost some of its popularity—except among old-timers.

See also: APPLES

CLEMENTINES
Oh My Darling Clementine

Clementines first made their debut in the United States in the 1980's. Many people were totally surprised how good Clementines taste, and how easy they are to peel. The first shipments made a tremendous impact on the citrus market, arousing a great deal of interest. Spain and Morocco are the original producers and have established themselves as the top Clementine growers in the world.

The Sanson Company of Cleveland sent my brother-in-law, Sonny Nagelbush, to Spain, to contact some new growers. When he returned, he could not stop raving about the beautiful orchards and the magnificent growing areas. He said, "This is Clementine heaven, there is no other way to describe it."

Today, there are other growers who produce Clementines in California, Chile and Israel, as well as other countries. They grow similar varieties to the Spanish variety, but they don't compare in taste. The fact remains that the genetic qualities that appear in Spain and Morocco cannot be duplicated; they dominate the citrus market in December through March. Clementines also have proven to be powerful competitors to the California Navel Oranges that are marketed at the same time.

Look for firm, well-colored fruit that show no signs of softness or decay. Under refrigeration, they maintain freshness for two weeks or more. Eat them out of your hand like candy.

See also: Temple Oranges

COCONUTS

The newest innovation in fresh coconuts may change the whole dynamics of their use: They are split open at point of origin, closed and sealed in a vacuum pack ethylene cover. They can stay fresh under these conditions, allowing the customer easy access to the sweet luscious flesh within.

Fresh coconuts have a wonderful taste. They can be used in fruit salads and baked desserts. Freshly grated coconut can keep well for three days under refrigeration. Drained coconut milk can be frozen. The Caribbean countries are the major suppliers, with Puerto Rico following closely behind. Processed coconut products dominate this market.

COLLARDS

Would you believe that fresh collard greens in their heyday were a mainstay for most Southerners, particularly the African-American community? In my produce career, we would sell two carloads of fresh greens each week, possibly1000 bushels, which would include at least 400 bushels of collards of 25 pounds each. Today fresh collards still have a smattering of followers, but they have lost their importance because fast food and frozen packs of collards have replaced them. They are high in Vitamin A, Vitamin C and calcium. Cooked young collard greens can be added to a mixed green salad.

Collards are available from early spring to mid October. Local suppliers dominate in the Midwest, Florida and Texas. California fills in during the winter months.

CORN

King of Corn, But Does That Matter?

During my wholesale produce years, I was known as the "Corn King" by the many retail outlets that depended on me for supplies. I had to be in the market at midnight or 1:00 am if I wanted to be able to purchase the best quality product. Bi-colored corn in the early 1950's had not made an appearance. However, there were a number of varieties that had good taste and appearance such as the Golden Bantam, the Iowa Sweet, the Blue Farmer and many others. People would look with astonishment when I would bite into a raw ear of fresh corn, picked at random. That was my personal test of sweetness and flavor. In those days, there was no genetically engineered corn; they were all heirloom varieties, grafted and mutated over time. Today, there are a dozen new varieties appearing every year, including the Super Sweet variety, which has moved to the top of the favorites list. It dominates because it has wonderful flavor and good keeping qualities. Under refrigeration, it can retain its best properties for at least a week.

My best story relates to a major purchase I had made from a reliable farmer who was known for his excellent quality corn. The purchase I had made was for 500 baskets (three dozen to a basket) of Golden Bantam corn. The entire load was to be delivered to a supermarket the next day. However, even under refrigeration, when I opened the door to the truck, I found that the entire load had dried out. It seemed as if something had struck the corn because every ear had signs of deterioration. I never found out why this happened and I was unable to salvage my loss. The farmer insisted that the corn was absolutely fresh when I received it. He said, "You probably did not handle it properly." It was a lost cause. However, that is one of the risks in a perishable industry. Produce lives and breathes like human beings. It needs water, avoidance of extra heat or cold and proper care, be it refrigeration or heat.

Fresh corn in today's market is one of the great eating pleasures ten months of the year. Local supplies go from early July through October. Florida and California fill in during the fall and winter months.

CRANBERRIES
The Health Drink of the Future

In the late 1940's, a scientific study was made on cranberries. There were some indications that cranberries were carcinogenic. You can imagine the impact of that announcement! Sales of cranberries came to a halt. One half of the crop was dumped. No one wanted to buy or use them. In fact, it took two to three years before the study was renounced and people recognized that it had been a fluke—Cranberries are not carcinogenic—and marketing returned to normalcy.

Today, cranberries are regarded as a health food. Cranberry

juice is recommended for bladder and kidney problems. It improves blood pressure and oftentimes is served as a cocktail drink, substituting for alcohol. Cranberry-apple juice is quite popular as well as cran-apple relish. No Thanksgiving dinner would be complete without a cranberry relish dish. Dried cranberries have become a standby and you will find them in supermarkets as well as in health food stores. You can freeze fresh cranberries in their original bags for as long as six months. Maine, Massachusetts and Wisconsin are the biggest suppliers, available in late September through January in their fresh form. Processed cranberries have become more acceptable as part of regular menus, particularly when turkey is served. Cranberries cannot be eaten in their fresh form. They must be processed in some manner to be consumed.

CUCUMBERS

To purchase fresh pickles, look for a clean solid appearance, no soft spots, good color that varies from light green to a whitish tinge. Size is unimportant, except for specific uses. The most valued sizes are medium for barrel processing and the smaller sizes to place in jars. Avoid misshapen pickles or any with defects.

Pickles are excellent in salads because of their sharper taste. They also do not create digestive problems because they have much smaller seeds, so they are less gaseous. They are available in late August to October in the Midwest, with Florida and Texas the main suppliers the rest of the year. Mexico fills in the gaps. Stored under proper refrigeration, kosher style pickles will stay well for months. The garlic, spices and fresh dill singles them out from all other pickling processes and gives them their singular flavor.

English cucumbers, also known as the Western Reserve Cucumber are grown in hothouses and are available year round. They are noted for their crispiness, small seeds and good digestive qualities. They are an important part of this market.

Yankel's Pickle Recipe

Makes Six Mason Jars of Pickles.

Yankel's is a traditional Jewish pickle recipe that has served me well for many years. I hope you enjoy it!

1   Peck basket of pickles, about eight to nine pounds. They should be fresh, green, firm, and 4" or less in size

20 Cloves of fresh Garlic

6   Teaspoons pickling spices

1   Small branch of dill. Wash carefully and cut it up. Use it all: tips, seeds and stems

3 1/2 Quarts of cold water

1/2 Cup pickling salts

Hungarian hot pepper optional

Wash pickles in cold running water. Scrub them, using no soap. The pickles should be fresh, handled carefully and prepared at once. If this is not possible, keep soaking overnight in a sink or a pail of cold water.

Pack pickles into sterilized jars. Also put in three cloves of garlic and the tips of dill into each jar, maybe 1/2 ounce, along with one teaspoon of spices. Also add one teaspoon of salt. If you want a sharper flavor, add one Hungarian pepper, medium hot. Then fill these sterilized jars with boiling water, within one inch of the top.

Screw on zinc lids, but not too tightly. Keep at room temperature for six to nine days (for half sour pickles, four days). Brine will begin to ooze out in two or three days. If necessary, keep filling with liquid to keep out air.

Fill again with water. Then, tighten jars very tight and keep cool or refrigerate for longer keeping. You can use a cool cellar area, however it is not as effective as a refrigerator and will not keep for more than a month. Under refrigeration, the pickles will stay good for three to six months.

DANDELIONS

If you talk to any old time Italian cook, he will tell you, "There is no healthier vegetable than dandelions eaten in the spring." In those so-called olden days, he would go out into the fields and pick the greens of the dandelion before they flowered.

New Jersey is the first state to ship them in the Midwest and they hit the markets in late March and early April. The season is a short one and the dandelion lovers can't wait to try them out. The Texas Dandelion has longer leaves and tastes different because it is a cultivated variety. It is available in January through early spring. It has its aficionados as well. Look for fresh appearing greens, no wilt, with little sign of yellow or flowering. Some Midwestern local areas also ship dandelions in season. A good way to serve them is as a stir-fry vegetable in olive oil, seasoned to taste with pepper, garlic, oregano or basil.

DAIKON

Daikon is a strange looking vegetable. Totally white in color, it has the appearance of an overgrown elongated white radish. Daikon looks exceptionally large, but it can be cut into small pieces. It does store well under refrigeration. Daikon makes a great cocktail appetizer along with a dip; cut it into small squares or long strips, whatever your preference, and serve with Hollandaise sauce—its sharp pungency will give it the right edge as an opener. Look for an attractive white color, no softness, and a bright fresh appearance. Refrigerate at once. It is available locally and from California year round.

DATES
A Date You Won't Forget

You owe it to yourself to visit a date farm in California. It is a special treat, one you will never forget. On a recent visit, I was astonished to learn how little I knew about dates. Would you believe that even dates need male fertilization contact? One male tree, using pollination by human hands, can fertilize one hundred female trees! It is enough to drive anyone mad when you hear this. These date farms, which are limited to only a few farms because of declining interest are deserving of their own story. I left the gift shop, having purchased date candy, date cake and a beautiful package of Deglet Noor dates. Dates store well for six months under proper refrigeration.

At one time, dates were a delicacy appreciated by most everyone, especially at the Christmas holidays, but now people avoid dates because they're considered to be fattening and high in carbs. At the height of my gift basket business, I always made sure to offer a special gift package of the best dates available, usually the Medjool dates.

The principal variety is the Deglet Noor, a large date with good flavor. California grows the Halawi and Khadrawi, both considered to be of the semi-dry variety. Dates store well under refrigeration for as long as six months to a year. Pitted dates are used mostly for baking. They do make a great "nosh" stuffed with cream cheese or nuts.

Pre-World War II, most of our dates came from Iraq. Today, California is the leading supplier, offering from September to June every variety known to man. Dates may have the highest potassium rating of any fruit or vegetable. A serving of dates has only twenty-three calories, which includes thirty-one grams of carbohydrates plus loads of fiber. This makes it one of our most healthful fruits.

DECORATIVE KALE

Whoever dreamed that decorative kale would take on the importance that it has today? With the advent of the colorful light green, bleached yellow and light red hearts of this decorative vegetable, you are likely to find pieces of it contrasting with the food on every plate in some of the finest restaurants you visit. Oddly, in spite of its beautiful color, it is not as tasty as its green cousin, but it adds a dramatic and colorful touch to any dish.

DILL

Anyone who has ever prepared kosher dill pickles knows that fresh dill brings out the real pickle flavor. You may note that the commercial processors of pickles do not use fresh dill, but substitute dill seed, which is a fair substitute. (The reason for this is that fresh dill clouds up appearance, looking more like black spots through the glass jar). However, if you plan to make your own dill pickles at home, be sure you use fresh dill for that true dill flavor.

Look for fresh appearing green dill. It can be used dried, as well as in its fresh form. Dill, however, will have a stronger taste in its fresh form. All parts of the dill plant are aromatic, with both the leaves and the seeds being used. The name dill comes from the Saxon word "dilla" and it means "to lull," which is appropriate as dill has a mild, calming effect when used as a herb in cooking. It is also taken to help aid digestion. Seeds can be chewed to sweeten the breath and dill infused tea can help promote sleep. You only need a small amount in each jar for good results.

Dill as an herb will add taste to boiled new potatoes, as a seasoning on fish, poultry or wherever you would like to add its distinctive taste.

EGGPLANT

The Eggplant That Almost Cost
Me My Future Wife

Whenever I think of eggplant, I always remember the first time I introduced my wife to my family. Every ethnicity has its favorite recipe for particular foods. Eggplant was a family favorite of ours and we served it Romanian style. In this recipe, the eggplant is baked, chopped finely, with a base of olive oil or canola oil and chopped onions. It is served as an appetizer known as "Forshpize". At its best, it is not an attractive dish. My future wife was introduced all around the table and was invited to share the appetizer with the family. Being a lady, she graciously accepted her serving of the eggplant concoction. After the first taste, I could see she was very uncomfortable. She finished the entire serving and then excused herself to go the bathroom.

When we were returning to her home, she did not make any fuss about it. She did say this, "Don't ever ask me to eat Romanian eggplant again!" It may come as a surprise that she learned to make and enjoy this same eggplant recipe because she knew I enjoyed it. In fact, it became one of her star recipes.

There are dozens of variations of eggplant: Sicilian Purple, baby eggplant, Japanese eggplant and many others native to the Mediterranean area. They are served in as many variations as you can think of: stuffed, fried and as an appetizer. In Israel, they have become a popular specialty entrée.

ROMANIAN EGGPLANT

1 medium eggplant

1 small onion

1 clove garlic or 1 tsp garlic powder

2 tablespoons oil (olive or canola)

1 tablespoon pickle relish

Select a firm eggplant, medium size. Cut off the stem, puncture in several places in the flesh. Place the eggplant in a meatloaf size casserole. Put in a microwave on high for 5 minutes, maybe a little more if larger in size.

When soft, to the touch, scoop out of the shell the flesh. Dispose of the skin. In a bowl, add to the flesh garlic or garlic powder plus the minced, raw onion. Use any oil, preferably olive oil or canola (you can also use vinegar dressing if you prefer). Add a tablespoon of pickle relish and mix all these ingredients well. Add additional garlic or onion to taste and add additional oil for consistency as desired. Put in refrigerator and serve cold.

Can be used as an appetizer or hor d'ovures, served in a small dish with crackers. Will serve 6-10 people as an appetizer.

FIGS

Don't Miss Out On This Delicacy

If you never have enjoyed the sweetness and flavor of a fresh fig, you must be sure to try one the next time you see them in the market. Since I was a wholesale produce merchant, I had access to all kinds of produce. Fresh figs were always one of my favorites. It was not a specialty item for me, so I always purchased them in season from a neighboring merchant. I would wait until mid-season when they achieved full natural ripeness. This was when I would purchase an entire box for personal use.

They are packed in an egg carton type box to prevent bruising. For starters, I would gobble down eight to ten fresh ripe figs at one time. A dangerous thing to do. Fresh figs are a natural laxative that works every time. You'll find that it works better than Metamucil.

My personal favorite is the Black Mission variety, although the green Kadota Fig when fully ripe oozes out a delicious sweet taste. Fresh figs are native to the Mediterranean Basin. California is the largest American producer.

Select plump, fragrant figs that have a little give when touched. Avoid hard   or mushy figs that show mold. Figs do ripen well at room temperature. The best way to serve them is to eat them out of hand. They can be used in salads and also as part of a dessert. Today, many chefs combine figs in many different ways. I've seen them featured as an entré, fried with chicken breasts in a combination with prosciutto. Fresh figs and goat cheese are a great combination. When ripe, figs have a shelf life of three days.

GARLIC

Can You Hold Your Breath?

Garlic is indigenous to many ethnicities, particularly from the Mediterranean area. My family was not an exception. From the first day of our marriage, I suggested to my wife, Bess, to season most of my poultry and meat dishes with fresh garlic. Garlic has always been a staple in our home, even though it did create a problem. I learned early in my community volunteer career, that garlic was offensive on my breath. I then made sure that when I attended evening meetings where I met other people, I avoided the use of garlic in my food.

Since my business had become more of a gift packing

business, I would often work along side one of my assistants. I learned that eating garlic the night before such work was not a good idea! The problem is one that few people understand: the odor of garlic may be eliminated from your breath, but it will be exuded from your pores, even the next day. I was left with a choice, do I use garlic or not?

I have not had the opportunity to attend, but I have heard that the Garlic Festival in Gilroy, California is one of the outstanding events on the Coast. This takes place the last weekend of July. Gilroy is known as the garlic capital of the world.

Look for fresh garlic heads that are plump and firm. Store in a cool, dry, dark place. You can also store garlic in your refrigerator (in the hydrator). To peel a garlic clove, place the clove on a work surface and cover it with the side of a large chef's knife. Press down firmly on the side of the knife to crush the clove slightly and the dry skin will slip off easily. Elephant garlic has made new friends because it is milder in flavor. It also is a hard compact variety. Garlic powder and garlic salt have made positive inroads as a substitute for the fresh.

In the past, we received shipments from Chile, Italy, Spain and China. With the advent of the imports from China, the California market is threatened by pricing which makes it almost impossible to compete. At this time, California is our major supplier, but it is besieged by the Chinese imports. Their quality is equal to ours.

At the garlic packaging rack, circa 1960.
Frank Cavalier (left), Joe Cavalier Sr. (right).

GOURDS

I don't know of a more beautiful form of any kind of produce that can compete with gourds—there are so many magnificent colors and shapes. In autumn, gourds seem to thrive and you will see them displayed wherever you go. During the Jewish holiday of Succoth, Jewish traditionalists will decorate their outdoor huts called "Sukkots" with hanging gourds and other fruits and vegetables symbolic of the harvest season.

Every geographical area grows different varieties of gourds. The shapes and colors differ from state to state or country of origin. While visiting my children who lived in Decatur, Illinois, I discovered a giant gourd that resembled an alligator; it had a long extended knob hook and it was much larger than any of the gourds I have seen in Ohio. I still use gourds as an item of interest in my lectures on food.

Also: See SQUASH

GRAPEFRUIT

Do You Like 'em Red, Pink or White?

It should be noted that scientific studies indicate that the pink and red varieties have more vitamins and nutrients. Scientists are unable to explain this.

In the 1930's, before the Cuban boycott, grapefruit was not as well known as it is today. We would receive the first white Duncan Grapefruit (with seeds) from the Isle of Pines, off the island of Cuba; this was a highly regarded import that received high marks for its luscious juice and flavor. It was not until years later that the pink and red varieties appeared on the scene. Texas was the original discoverer of these grafted hybrid varieties. Today, the Ruby Red and the Star Ruby Red, its advanced counterpart, dominate the grapefruit world not only in Texas but also everywhere they are grown. Indian River, Florida is also famous for this fruit.

Do you remember when every fine restaurant would serve a half of a large grapefruit with a red maraschino cherry on top as a breakfast starter? There were also special grapefruit spoons! A salad consisting of grapefruits segments along side half an avocado attained great popularity during that bygone period.

The Pummelo, the original grapefruit before it mutated and was grafted into the varieties we know today, has also found its own niche. It is grown extensively in Israel and is a well-accepted specialty fruit grown in California, however, it is not a popular citrus fruit in the USA.

GRAPES

In the early stages of my produce career, I sold wine grapes as a part-time job. At the time, in the 1920's, the1930's and early 1940's, there were many European people who had recently come to America. They brought with them many of the customs of the countries they came from. Making wine was as traditional to them as preparing a meal. No one of that generation would consider buying a bottle of wine to serve in his or her home. My own father, who was of Russian Jewish extraction, made one hundred fifty gallons of wine every year—three barrels of it! It was as basic as food. We drank wine with every dinner until we drank it all.

Wine grapes are harvested in October. They are different from table grapes in terms of variety and are used differently. The most popular grape in Ohio is the Concord. This is a deep purple grape with a soft skin and a wine-like taste. It is grown in New York, Ohio, Michigan and Pennsylvania. It is used not only in the making of wines for everyday use, but for sacramental wines that are recognized as "kosher" or kosher style wines.

Another variety of grape popular with home wine makers is the Carignane. This is one of the most popular grapes for making wine and is blood red in color. This often is used as a substitute for the Zinfandel grape. Both varieties have black skins, but the Zinfandel is the ideal mixing grape. The Muscat, the large amber colored grape has a wonderful raisin-like quality when it is harvested. This gives it a rich, mellow and strong wine flavor. It is one of the most flavorful varieties for richness of taste. Other popular kinds of wine grapes are the golden Malaga and the Grenache, as well as the Mission variety. This rounds out the list of the most important varieties of grapes used traditionally in home winemaking in this area.

Also: see Raisins

GREENBEANS: see Beans

HONEYDEWS: see Melons

HORSERADISH

Do You Like It Hot or Maybe Sweet?

For years, you could buy a piece of fresh horseradish and have it grated by a professional at the West Side Market in Cleveland for a nominal fee. This was a common practice because few people wanted to grate it as it made your eyes tear and your nostrils flare. Both the root and the leaves of horseradish were used as far back as the Middle Ages for seasoning. Japanese horseradish, known as Wasabi, is undistinguishable from its cousin in taste, but its bite is much stronger. If you use too much of it, you'll jump as high as a kite, it is so hot!

Horseradish is traditional for both Jews and Christians at Passover and Easter. In Jewish ethnic circles, adding beet juice would soften the blow by modifying horseradish's strength. Processed horseradish is used for shrimp sauce, cocktail sauce and mustard. Horseradish can be stored in its natural root form for a year under proper refrigeration. St.Louis, Missouri is famous for its productive horseradish root crop.

JICAMA

Today, Jicama is much better known in this area than it has been in the recent past. I first discovered how versatile Jicama is when I attended a cocktail party where it was served cut up in little squares with different dips to accompany it; it is a very versatile cocktail vegetable. Since I was not familiar with it, I asked my host what it was. Actually, it tastes better in its natural form, without sauces because it has a nice refreshing bite to it this way.

Jicama generally grows to a large size. This makes it difficult to use unless you have a large family or are planning a party. It must have a fresh attractive look, free of softness, black spots or wrinkling. It stores well under refrigeration, but it must be covered with an ethylene bag once it is opened. It is available year round, grown in California and Mexico

KALE

The Toughest Green of Them All

A member of the cabbage family, kale is a native of the Mediterranean and Asia Minor. It is a form of headless cabbage whose history goes back about 2,000 years. It made its entrance in our own country about 1700, in Virginia, where it is still one of the important vegetables grown in the South.

Virginia, New Jersey and local areas supply most of the kale produced in the US. It is a winter vegetable that is popular in late fall through early spring and available most months of the year. Since it is hardy, it can withstand cold temperatures better than any other vegetable in the field, even as low as 30º Fahrenheit.

When selecting kale, look for young and tender greens. They should be dark green in color. The kale should be crisp and free of dry or yellow leaves. Many people have learned to buy this vegetable when it is clipped (with the greens cut off), but you will find the stem to be tender eating if it is not coarse and aged. Kale is more popular in the South, but it is still used to some degree in other parts of the country. Kale is losing some of its impact in its fresh form, but is making gains in the frozen product field. It may be that clipped kale will help to maintain sales and production. Kale requires refrigeration and immediate use for best results.

Kale is a recognized source of Vitamin A. Each serving also contains 100 percent of the daily Vitamin C requirements for most people. This vegetable is one of our most useful suppliers of iron and minerals and contains many other valuable nutrients. Its outstanding nutritive qualities make this vegetable an excellent component of a healthy, balanced diet.

See also: Cabbage

KIWI

From Obscure To Most Popular Exotic Fruit

I was always interested in locating new fruits that would be marketable and fall into the exotic group. Some forty years ago, I heard about a new fruit called the Kiwi that was shipped from New Zealand. Expressing a great interest in this fruit, I learned that the importer who was the sole receiver was located in Brooklyn, New York. I was determined to contact him and to see and taste this fruit personally.

The reports were so good on its sweetness and general qualities; I believed it would be worth a visit to New York to check it out. I took a cab from the airport to be sure I would not get lost. I don't remember the cab fare, but I do remember how long the trip took and how difficult it was to find this distributor. After finding him, I discussed the possibility of obtaining a preliminary shipment of one hundred cases when the next arrival by ship would take place. I was so enamored with my discovery that I carried two boxes as a small suitcase, bound together on the plane. They were flat boxes made of solid wood, containing forty to fifty kiwis; they were not heavy, but cumbersome. Clearly, it was the most expensive fruit I ever bought, having gone to all that expense to simply find the distributor!

Upon my arrival home, I contracted three or four of my most interested supermarkets that would be likely to purchase exotic fruits. My first customers ordered an initial shipment of ten cases. One client ordered twenty-five cases. My first sale went well, but then interest diminished because of the high price. I ordered three more shipments in the next few months, but there was little response because of the lack of consumer education and no demonstrations.

 I was disappointed then, but think of how bad I feel now

knowing that kiwi fruit is grown all over the world—in the United States, Chile, Israel, and the Caribbean countries—and it is now recognized as one of the premier exotic fruits grown. Sales of this wonderful tasting fruit go into the millions. And to think that I let this opportunity go by when I had the first chance to become an importer! It is worth recognizing that of all the fruit grown, kiwis from New Zealand still have the most interesting taste of any growing area in the world.

The origin of the Kiwi fruit is unknown, but it is thought that it was first discovered growing wild in New Zealand. It's also sometimes known as the Chinese gooseberry, a name that indicates some relationship to Asia, although this has not been verified.

 The fruit is generally the size of a small egg, with a brown, fuzzy surface that could be considered hairy and similar to coconut. The inner flesh is lime-colored with a symmetrical pattern of striping that gives it a beautiful color. The flavor is tropical; combining the blandness of papaya with the tangy taste of the mango, but its flavor is unique and cannot be identified in any other way except as kiwi fruit.

 The fruit is named after the Kiwi bird of New Zealand. To identify good kiwi fruit, look for firmness and fresh appearance. Avoid bruised fruit because it will be damaged internally. It is ripe when soft to the touch and can ripen well at room temperature. Kiwis have excellent keeping qualities, but it is preferable to begin ripening them at once for best results. The fruit is rich in Vitamin C. Kiwis are used in a variety of dessert dishes and taste best when mixed with other fruits. They can be eaten raw, scooping the flesh out, or better yet, by blending with ice cream.

 Golden kiwi fruit has become a minor addition to the market. It is identified mostly by its outer skin, which has a golden-like color. California is a major producer.

KOHLRABI
You Don't Have To Be Hungarian To Enjoy This

Originating as a native of Northern Europe, this vegetable

does not have a long history. It was first discovered in the early 1500's, having been used in Germany, Spain and Italy quite extensively. In the United States, it probably made its most significant contribution during the heavy Eastern European immigration in the late 1800's and early 1900's.

Kohlrabi has not enjoyed the popularity of one of its cousins, the turnip, but is still deserving of your interest. This vegetable looks a great deal like a small head of cabbage that is tightly closed, growing on a light green bunch of leaves. It generally attains a diameter of three to four inches, tasting almost like a turnip with some cabbage-like effect; this is one of the reasons it is referred to as a "cabbage turnip".

Kohlrabi is available about nine months of the year, with Texas, California and New Jersey the leading suppliers. Local growers furnish the necessary supplements during the heavy summer and fall growing periods.

When selecting kohlrabi, look for fresh, tender, young leaves with a bright colored globe. Kohlrabi should be firm and free of any discoloration.

Although Kohlrabi is gradually disappearing from the scene because of its limited ethnic appeal, it may remain popular for a few more years because it is tasty, tender and good eating, offering a contrast to the heavier tasting turnip.

Kohlrabi is an excellent all around nutrient, adding many vitamins and minerals, such as calcium and ascorbic acid to your diet. It is generally prepared as a cooked vegetable and in soups or stews, but also does well sliced in a salad, adding a water chestnut type taste.

LEEKS

I Never Knew How Good Leeks Tasted

Many years ago, I did a TV series on public television on twenty-six ethnic communities. The theme was the cooking style of each group. I was surprised to find out that leek was the recognized symbol of the region of Wales in the United Kingdom. It is also used extensively by the French in a great many of their dishes. The leek is also famous with Hungarian cooks. It is a member of the onion family and can be baked, broiled, braised, pureed or stewed.

In America, it is just beginning to become well known. Potato leek soup is far and away one of our most popular ethnic soups, although leeks have innumerable uses. They can be served as a green replacement for chives, scallions, onions and garlic tops. The tender green leaves can be eaten as is. Leeks have a pungent odor and an acrid taste. Clean thoroughly before serving because the compact leaves tend to retain mud or grit. Leeks are available year round from California, Michigan and Virginia.

Also: See Chives, Onions

LEMON GRASS

Available year round in Asia, South America and the United States, lemon grass is a thin, lemony flavored stalk. You can use it to flavor soups, stews or even add to tea. Lemon Grass will stay fresh for long periods of time, even at room temperature.

LEMONS

If Lemons Are So Good For You, Why Are Bad Products Referred To As Lemons?

Lemons are an ancient fruit said to have a history dating back to 900 AD. All the information pertaining to its history indicates that China or Upper Burma is where it originated. The importance of the lemon in world history will never really be known, but this much is certain: Lemons have played an important role in the history of the early travelers and explorers who brought lemon seeds back with them to plant in their own countries. Columbus planted citrus seeds in Haiti when he wanted to establish a new colony for Spain. The Portuguese brought them to Brazil, and Ponce de Leon introduced them to Florida.

California and Arizona are the major producing states that supply the entire country year round with this excellent citrus product. Florida is also producing some commercial crops for processing on a smaller scale.

The lemon has many uses, some of which are unknown to the consumer. The lemon is important for its citric acid, which is used in dyes and extracts. It has medicinal properties, such as pectin, a soluble dietary fiber that is found in the membranes between segments and helps to control blood cholesterol levels. The lemon is easily one of our better foods, containing many nutrients and vitamins, especially vitamin C. It is also a low carbohydrate fruit.

In my market days, if I cut myself, I would apply the juice of a fresh lemon to the cut before bandaging it. The older Italian men I knew would cut a lemon in half and use it as a mouthwash anytime of day. I found that it worked well and would use it the same way if my mouth were dry or parched. The Italian men claimed that it whitened their teeth, especially tobacco stains, but I was never able to prove that. Another old time remedy for coughs, used long before the advent of cough drops consisted of equal parts of lemon juice with honey, taken every two hours, a tablespoon at a time.

If you go to any good restaurant, you'll find lemon slices in your water and often times a slice of lemon along side the fish serving; in the more formal settings, they will wrap it in cheesecloth. The oil is used as a pharmaceutical ingredient and in certain cosmetics. The colorful skin, also known as zest, is an important ingredient in many products. Lemons' best usage stems from its excellent blending quality in flavoring foods. It is probably one of the most highly regarded food flavorings in the field of cookery.

The fresh lemon continues to maintain its position as a leader in the citrus section because it meets all of the requirements of the consumer in its fresh form. A fine quality lemon should be thin-skinned and heavy to the touch. It should be firm and of good color, emphasizing its yellow appearance. A bright shiny look is important; a shriveled appearance will indicate diminished juice content. Storage is best at refrigerated temperatures although lemons can be kept at room temperatures for a short while.

Meyer lemons are an epicurean delight. Thin skinned, loaded

with juice- a premium lemon that every worthwhile chef or cook treasures. Only a limited amount is available, mostly through specialty stores.

Also see LIMES

Sweet Success With Lemons

Few people remember lemons the way I do. For those people who were a part of the Depression, this story is an easy one to understand. Fresh lemons were a basic fruit that people used every day. If you are cognizant of those years in the 1930's and 1940's, you know that there were no frozen lemon juices, no concentrates and no substitutes for a fresh lemon of any kind. Summertime lemon prices would always skyrocket since the fresh product was the only one available. Speculators made sure that they would store the best of the late spring crop to take advantage of the higher prices. However, there were situations when supplies were exceptionally low because the storage lemons decayed too rapidly. This was also a time when we would receive lemons from Italy, individually wrapped in artistically designed paper wrapping. The Italian lemons would produce a wonderful lemon scent because of their mature ripeness, but these shipments would also exhibit a great deal of decay, a situation that made the useable crop very expensive.

When I was a young man, I wanted to make some money in any way I could. An uncle suggested that I buy a box of lemons, put it on my shoulders and sell the lemons to anyone who would buy them. Think of me carrying a forty-pound box of lemons on my shoulders and walking down the street selling them. "Three lemons for a dime!" I shouted. "Three lemons for a dime!" Don't you think I had takers? By the time the day was done I had sold the entire box, one hundred sixty to a case, and probably made $3.00 to $5.00. That was a good day's pay in those days.

Also see LIMES

LETTUCE
Wouldn't You Like To Be a Head?

Lettuce is known to have grown wild, long before its acceptance as a salad vegetable some two thousand years ago. The Romans, Greeks and Chinese mention it in many of their early writings. The early types of lettuce had little shape and were formed more like loose-leafed leafed lettuce than the solid heads we know today.

Lettuce is available every month of the year and could be considered our most popular salad vegetable. California and Arizona are the largest producers with Michigan, Wisconsin, Texas and New York augmenting the western states. May, June and July are the peak months, when east and west combine their energies to bring you the best in lettuce.

Iceberg lettuce, or head lettuce as it is called, was once the most important type grown, with the Great Lakes and Imperial varieties the two most highly developed varieties. Head lettuce of good quality should be fresh and green looking. Tip burn or discolored outer leaves, seeded lettuce and swelling at the top in a knoblike head should be avoided. Over-trimmed lettuce is not a good buy because it has been trimmed too closely. There are many periods when lettuce has inner damage or burnt tips that are only visible after you have shopped. This occurs generally in extremely hot harvesting periods, and there is no protection for the consumer for this defect. These deficiencies are even harder to find when the lettuce is packaged in polyethylene bags.

For best results, lettuce should be stored in a refrigerator and used as quickly as possible. Many people prefer the loose heads to the tight, firm compact head, but this is only a matter of preference. Lettuce is a good food for balance in the diet. It has a high Vitamin A content and is considered low in calories.

Romaine is a dark green, leafy type of lettuce noted for its tender stiff leaves that are coarse and yet sweet; it's a good blending salad vegetable. Romaine is enjoying tremendous success as a salad vegetable since consumers have discovered its versatility. Romaine lettuce is used as the Caesar salad base and has proven to be one of the best vegetables for this specialty dish.

Leaf Lettuce is a loose, non-head of leaves that are long and tender. It is grown especially for its use as a contrast in decoration when serving meats, fish and fancy trays. It is grown extensively in hothouses. Hothouse or greenhouse leaf lettuce is of a milder taste and is generally of a much more desirable shape than field grown lettuce.

Bibb, Boston and Limestone are known as the Butterhead Lettuce group. They have a delicate texture and sweet taste. Dandelion greens when young fall into this group. There are many new varieties of lettuce we now classify as Mesclun types, which have a distinct bitterness. They also are available year round.

Mache (Lamb's Lettuce) is used in most Mesclun mixtures because of its mild, succulent taste. It has tiny, green pear-like leaves and mixes well with most salad greens.

Lollo Rosso is a fan-shaped, red leaf lettuce that is greenish farther down the leaf. It is one of the most flavorful of all the leaf lettuce family. Used fresh, it adds color and taste to any fresh salad.

Mizuna is another green-leaf vegetable, with jagged edges and a lighter color. It is tender and mild when it is absolutely fresh.

Oak Leaf Lettuce (both green and red) looks like small oak leaves and adds crispness to any mix of Mesclun. It is used as a basic lettuce for most mixtures.

Red Mustard leaves are both spicy and peppery in taste and make an excellent addition to any Mesclun mix. These dark purplish-red leaves have a greenish tinge as well. Hothouse varieties are quite common.

The Return of Head Lettuce

Processed lettuce may have that fresh look, but once it is cut open, it may lose forty percent of its nutrients in terms of nutrition. There are strong arguments about this from the processed lettuce producers, but the science can go either way. The fresh crispness of a head lettuce just cut cannot be reproduced.

Head lettuce has probably suffered the most as a solid head product because of the advent of the packaged salads. However, for those consumers who demand freshness, it is gradually making a comeback. Packaged salads have a place in the market, but they do not offer the consumer the freshness and flavor of the solid head product. Once a packaged salad is opened, then stored, a great deal of freshness and some nutrients are lost. Many restaurants have returned to head lettuce as a featured appetizer, offering it quartered, garnished with bits of eggs, caviar, sprinkles of parsley and other enticements. Combined with tasty French dressings, this newer innovation has made a significant impact in the marketplace.

I Never Thought I Would See The Day When Lettuce Would Be Shipped Without Ice

Years ago it was known as Iceberg Lettuce, because it was packed in a 40 pound case, covered with wax paper and totally surrounded by a solid chunk of ice. I just want you to imagine backing a truck into a freight car and getting ready to unload 25 to 50 cases of lettuce to bring back to my warehouse. If the weather was hot, the ice would melt rapidly and the water from the crate would be all over the rubber apron and boots I wore for protection. If the weather was cold, my hands would become numb, even though I wore gloves. But that wasn't all of it! At the warehouse, if the lettuce wasn't sold that same day, it had to be re-iced: 50 cases with 48 to 60 heads to a case.

Think of today's packaging: The lettuce is picked and packed right in the field, washed and cleaned at point of origin, immersed in ice cold water long enough for pre-cooling, then cello wrapped in a dry paper box container with no ice and the ability to stay fresh for a week without refrigeration.

Head lettuce in its original form still has its popular adherents. However, processed head lettuce and other mixed salads have made tremendous inroads in this market. Available all year, California and Arizona are the main suppliers. Some local areas produce small quantities. Colorado is a strong local supplier.

Look for a firm, fresh appearing green head, free of blemishes, dry rot, yellowing or withered leaves. Oftentimes, the lettuce may be softer, but the rules remain the same. You many note that at certain times of the year, particularly with lettuce from Salinas, California, that the lettuce is firmer and has a crispier taste with just a touch more sweetness. Lettuce is loaded with Vitamin A and Vitamin E.

LILY ROOT

Shipped from California, this vegetable is also known as Lotus Root, Lin Ngow, Lily Flower and Gun Furn. It is dried, generally two to three inches long, and has a golden brown color. It is noted for its garnish flavoring effect.

LIMES

Can I Use Limes Instead of Lemons?

The lime is a tropical fruit that was first introduced to Asia around 570 AD by Arab traders; Ponce de Leon is considered to be the person responsible for its introduction to Florida, in the early 1500's. Missionaries brought limes to California.

Fresh limes are available year round. Peak supplies are available in summer and midwinter, with Florida a major contributor for all of our supplies. Mexico augments our domestic supplies with light shipments during the sparse periods.

Although limes can be used in the same ways as lemons, they have not attained the universality of the lemon because of the lack of education in their usage. Yet in countries like Mexico and similar tropical areas, they have achieved the same kind of success as the lemon. Limes are high in Vitamin C but otherwise do not have the same nutritive qualities as the lemon.

They are excellent for seasoning, for juice and for flavoring drinks. You will find fresh limes more flavorful and potent than their imitation substitutes.

To select good fruit, look for a deep green lime that is bright and shiny. The fruit should be firm and heavy with a smooth skin. Off coloring, brown spots and a hard appearance affect the flavor of the lime and are signs to avoid. Limes are long keeping and can stay well under refrigeration, although it is not required. Because of their unusual flavorful qualities, Persian limes are one of the most important commercial varieties used in the United States.

Many people believe that the small limes from Key Lime, Florida, have a superior flavor. There are limited supplies of this product, so in most situations the limes that are used in Key Lime pies are from many different areas during the seasonal patterns. However, the name remains as a branded product that has made a definite impact on this market.

Also see LEMONS

LOQUATS

Grown in the United States and Israel, this pear-shaped fruit is about three inches long and it tastes like a sour cherry. It is used mostly for jams, jellies or baked in desserts. It is highly perishable but delicious when ripe.

Loquats are best when they are eaten very ripe, uncooked. They can be added to fruit salads or blended with other fruits to make a delicious fruit drink. They have a strong component of Vitamin A.

LYCHEES
You Don't Have To Be Chinese To Enjoy It

The lychee, an ancient fruit of the Chinese, has been cultivated since 1059 AD in that country. In the United States, the lychee fruit is grown in Florida and Hawaii, with Florida the major producer. Lychees have attained their most significant success as a processed fruit that is sold in cans. In its fresh form, this fruit is available from mid June to July. There is some indication that frozen lychees may improve the popularity of this tasty fruit by extending the marketing period.

The fruit is a bright red oval shape, measuring about 1 to 1.5 inches in diameter. Lychees are harvested in small clusters of medium size, numbering from three to twenty in a bunch resembling grapes. The flesh is a white, pale color, with a dark brown seed, which is characteristic of this fruit. It is held in high esteem because of its delicate taste. It can be compared to a grape, but is it different enough to achieve the individuality it is noted for. It is best when fully ripe.

Since Chinese cuisine has become so influential in the culinary world, lychees have become better known. They are served canned and fresh as a dessert. The white flesh has a delicate, sweet taste and a rich flavor. When served cold, they add a finishing touch that is delightful and refreshing. They are grown only in California and are available in the months of May and June. They are very delicate and should be handled with great care.

MALANGA

Available year round in the United States, the Caribbean and Central America, this tough looking root vegetable resembles a yam or potato. It has a woody taste with a touch of black walnut. It should be peeled and served boiled or fried. It can also be deep-fried. It is used mostly in Puerto Rican and Cuban cuisine.

MANGO

The English Brought The Mango Back To Life

This tropical fruit, once known only to people in the temperate climates, is ancient. Its history goes back to India and Malaysia almost 4,000 years ago. Most of the Mangoes we receive are imported, with Mexico and some of the outer islands supplying us with our needs during the off seasons. Florida is the largest domestic producer, with heavy shipments in June to September.

There are many varieties of mangoes. The most popular one in the United States is the Mulgoba. It is of medium size, oblong shaped, weighing about three-fourths of a pound. It has a soft bright color, with some scarlet or light red coloring as a contrast. Other varieties you will note are a dark green with some shades of lighter coloring. The softer colored varieties that change as they ripen seem to be the best tasting.

When selecting mangoes, look for fruit that gives to the gentle pressure of your hand. Shop for clean fruit that is free of black spots and blemishes. The fruit should appear bright and have a look of freshness that would indicate it will ripen.

Although many people eat this fruit out of the hand, it is best known for its uses in a fresh fruit salad. Its rich, tangy taste gives a special flavor to the other fruits as it blends with them. It is also excellent for pickling preserves and chutney.

The Magnificent Mango

What a difference a few years has made in this product. More and more consumers have become acquainted with its remarkable qualities. When perfectly ripe, the flesh and juices have a rich, magnificent flavor. Since the global marketplace has made mangoes more reasonable in price, they have gradually become a mainstream fruit that is available almost every day of the year. The Tommy Atkins variety has attained the most popularity because it seems to ripen so well. Mangoes are used as a basic food in almost every part of the world. You will find them grown in every subtropical area in different shapes and varieties.

The versatility of mangoes as food offers unlimited possibilities. Major Grey Chutney originated in India, first concocted by a noted British officer of the same name. Today, there are hundreds of chutney compounds that are used every day by people who know them as a native ethnic food.

MELONS
Will My Melon Be Sweet?

The Casaba Melon, a large Honeydew type of melon with a taste of squash and cucumber combined, is one of the popular late harvest varieties. It is a deep yellow, with a thick skin and creamy yellow flesh. It has limited acceptance because of its unusual flavor. This melon is grown primarily in California and is harvested in September and October. It is gradually losing its popularity to the Crenshaw and the fall crop of Honeydews, which have been scientifically developed for more sweetness.

The Casaba can be juicy and sweet if it is at full ripeness, emphasizing the flavor of honeydew when it is fully ripe. Persian Melons are a member of the muskmelon family, with a history that takes us back to ancient Iran. The oldest records of these melons are found in Egyptian writings about 2400 BC, though it is not certain whether it is a Persian melon they referred to or a Netted Melon that was quite similar.

Persian melons are available from June through late fall. Most of the fruit is grown in California, especially the central and northern areas. Although the Persian melon was once one of the most highly regarded melons in the muskmelon family, it has begun to decrease in popularity because of changes in the taste of the consumer. It is gradually being replaced by other varieties of melons.

The Persian grows quite large; most are two to three times larger than cantaloupes. The flesh is a deep orange. If the Persian melon is fully ripe, it is one of the finest tasting melons you can eat. The difficulty lies in the fact that it is generally picked green and ripens very slowly. This does not satisfy the consumer who does not understand why the melon has no flavor. The Persian melon should be allowed to ripen to an orange color at room temperature for best flavor, and this may take as long as a week

To select a Persian melon, look for a fully covered, thick netted melon. The fruit should be firm, free of soft spots and blemishes and give to the slight pressure of your hand. A light green melon that has a change of color that seems to look orange is a good sign of ripeness. Persian melons can be kept for short periods under refrigeration. They eat best when fully ripe and should be used as soon as possible.

The Crenshaw, the most popular offshoot of the Persian melon, is the grafted result of many experiments with both the Persian and the cantaloupe. This melon is the finest tasting in its field. It grows to a large size with a solid skin that turns from a soft green to a medium yellow color, indicating ripeness. The flesh is orange with a small center and a rich meaty taste. It is available from June through October.The late varieties in August and September are the most flavorful. California is the major producer with light supplies shipped from some other parts of the United States.

This melon is difficult to obtain at its full ripeness so it is essential to select it carefully. Look for a solid melon that is highly colored and free of spots or blemishes. Bruising will affect the inner flesh. Allow the Cranshaw to take on more ripeness at room temperature for best results. A green melon seldom attains the full flavor this fruit is noted for. It is always luxury priced, but if it is a good melon the price will be secondary. The Turlock area in California is famous for its outstanding tasting melons, cantaloupes in particular.

For best results, pick a cantaloupe with rough netting, free of black spots, blemishes and softness. It should show a tendency to orange color. Cantaloupes ripen after harvesting, at room temperature. Honeydews do not.

 Bitter Melon, also known as Foo Gwa, Fooh Quar and Balsam Apple is the size of a cucumber. Primarily, it is served cooked or steamed. It is shipped from California and Mexico.

Kiwano Melon, or Horned Melon, is grown in New Zealand and the United States; it is a cucumber-like melon in taste, with an added touch of lime. Since it is difficult to obtain ripe, its light green meat must be served with other fruits. This is a prickly fruit best served baked or boiled.

Pepino Melon, also grown in New Zealand and the United States, is a small, pear shaped melon with a soft, edible skin. It is generally striped with shades of green, some red and purple. The flavor reminds you of cantaloupe, honeydew and cucumber. It is not very sweet and is difficult to ripen once picked.

Winter Melon is a squash-like melon weighing about twelve pounds; it is watermelon shaped. Also known as Tung Qua, Dong Qua and Dong Gwa, it is a product grown in California.

MUSHROOMS

Do You Eat 'em Wild or Not?

It is important that we distinguish the wild mushroom from the cultivated. This listing will encompass only the cultivated mushroom that is grown in mushroom mines and mushroom fields.

Mushrooms have increased in popularity over the years with an early history that is interesting as any food we can talk about. The history of mushrooms dates back to ancient Egypt in the first century BC; Horace wrote of mushroom's epicurean qualities in Rome. The true gourmets of the world have always emphasized mushrooms' rare qualities, however most of the mushrooms used in the early days were wild. Although wild mushrooms were prized as a delicacy, they caused many fatalities.

Mushrooms are available every day of the year, with supplies reaching us by truck and plane from the cultivated mine beds in Pennsylvania, Ohio, New York, Illinois, California, Delaware and Maryland. These are the largest producing states.

The most common variety of mushroom is known as the Snow-White or White King Mushroom, which has all the perquisites for good eating. Look for a white or nearly white cap that is not misshapen, but if the mushroom is darker in color, the flavor will not be affected. The stems should be of medium size and the entire mushroom should be clean and free of dirt. A mushroom should be firm and fresh looking. The cap should be tightly attached to the stem with no open spots. When a mushroom opens and expands, it loses some of its flavor. Size is not an important factor in determining taste, even though there are marked preferences for the smaller button mushrooms, which are considered tenderer.

Large mushrooms are preferred for commercial uses, and there is some question as to which tastes better. It appears to be a matter of preference. Since mushroom growing is so highly developed, the entire crop is used for processed soups and for canning. There also is a big market for dried mushrooms, but most of these are imported from Poland, Japan, and China.

Many mushroom recipes have become standbys in the cooking world, and their popularity seems to grow by leaps and bounds each year. Mushrooms are highly perishable, but stay well under refrigeration for a short period. It is best to use them when they are fresh since they retain most of their good qualities in this form.

There is growing evidence to substantiate mushrooms' health-giving value: They are a good source of iron and copper, nicotinic acid and riboflavin; they are also a fair source of Vitamins B, C and K.

MUSTARD GREENS

Who Is The Greatest of Them All?

Mustard Greens are not to be confused with the mustard seed that is used for condiments and medicinal preparations. The large leafy green, which originated somewhere in the middle of Asia, is only one of many varieties that were grown there. Mustard greens have had an important influence in the Southern part of the Untied States, but have not as yet met with much success outside of that area. They are available year round, with Georgia, the Carolinas, Texas and California supplying us during the winter months.

Mustard greens are used primarily in cooking, although they make an excellent addition to a salad. They have a pungent, strong taste that mixes well with salt pork and ham. Since they are so green and leafy, they seem to absorb the fats of these meats when they are cooked simultaneously.

Mustard greens are low in calories and are an excellent source of vitamins and minerals. They are noted for their high Vitamin C content and for the good supply of calcium (6000 I.U. per 100 grams), loads of phosphorus and iron, and just about anything needed for good health. No other vegetable can compare to mustard greens' excellent health giving qualities.

When selecting mustard greens, look for fresh, bright green

leaves. The leaves should be firm with no signs of wilting or yellowing. Clean mustard greens are easier to handle; if they are dirty, you will find them difficult to wash. Since they are highly perishable, they must be used as soon as possible after purchasing.

Alas, many fresh mustard green-eaters have disappeared from the scene because of the advent of low-fat and low cholesterol diets—mustard greens don't taste the same without a bit of fat meat, ham or hock! Unfortunately, people are missing the health benefits.

You will find small amounts of mustard greens used as part of a Mesclun salad mix, but a few old timers still use them as a cooked vegetable. Take note that the strong odor of cooking mustard leaves will dominate the room! Many people purchase the frozen packages of mustard greens since they are already cleaned and ready to use. As a member of the soul food family, mustard greens still take their place as one of our most important vegetables. At the peak of my wholesale produce business, we would sell 1500 bushels of fresh "southern" greens every week: one third of those sales were mustard greens, the remainder were collards and turnip greens.

NECTARINES

Who Is The Sweetest of Them All?

The nectarine, one of our important modern day fruits, aroused a great deal of controversy in its genetic pattern because of its similarity to the peach. Contrary to most opinions, the nectarine is not a grafted fruit, but a smooth skinned peach variety. The nectarine has had a long history dating back to the early Christian era. Early writings by the Greeks and Romans refer to it as "nectar," or the drink of the gods. This may not have been true in its early form, but with the advent of new agricultural technology, the nectarine has become one of our most highly regarded fruits.

There are many varieties of nectarines, with supplies available from June through September. The early nectarines are a different species than those we receive during the peak of the season; they do not have the flavor and sweetness this fruit is noted for. The Quetta, a popular yellowish red variety, the Sun Grand and Le Grand are the best representatives of fine eating in this industry. California and Pennsylvania are the biggest producers, with 90 percent of the crop coming from the West. Imports from South America during January through March play a small part in this economy.

One of the major difficulties when purchasing nectarines is how to determine ripeness. Nectarines can ripen at room temperature off of the tree and should be served only at full, ripe maturity for best results.

"Freestone" is a term used to describe certain fruits—such as nectarines and peaches, that have a center seed—in which the seed separates easily from its inner flesh. This contrasts with "cling fruit", in which the seed clings to its inner flesh, making it difficult to separate.

Nectarines must have a fresh appearance, clean and free of bruises, if you wish to select good fruit. They should be firm, of good color and free of damage or brown spots. A yellowing red or an orange color is desirable, while those with a greenish tinge will not ripen well.

Refrigeration is good for nectarines after they have full ripeness, but it is best to ripen them at room temperature before serving; this will give them the full, robust flavor you are seeking. Nectarines are recognized for their high food energy value since they are very caloric, with 303 calories per pound when eaten raw.

Nectarines Over Peaches

Nectarines have become so popular that it seems as if they have replaced peaches as a mainstay. This has occurred primarily because most of the stone fruits are picked mature green and expected to ripen at room temperature. The failure has been that peaches do not ripen as well as nectarines. The consumer has come to recognize this fact and has turned to nectarines for more flavor.

Initially, the yellow-reddish varieties of nectarines were more acceptable. Today, the red varieties seem to dominate the industry. However, in the last few years, growers have discovered that the white nectarine has special characteristics that single it out. There is a big demand for this variety because they seem to be sweeter and juicer.

People are arguing constantly whether the nectarine is a separate fruit or a grafted variety. Most of the scientific studies indicate that they are the result of a strange mutation that has produced the smooth skinned peach they are so closely related to.

In the days when local growers in the various states dominated the markets, there were a few specialty farms that grew nectarines in Northeast Ohio and Pennsylvania. In Ohio, there were some outstanding producers in Perry, Painesville, and Geneva. The "Lake Erie Effect" seemed to give them added flavor and sweetness of taste. The "Lake Erie Effect" comes as a result of the warm water from the lake making temperatures near the lake more temperate at the end of the growing season. The Ohio-grown nectarines never attained large size, but their color was exceptional and they possessed great flavor. Because of their sweetness these nectarines were in such demand that I had to ration them to my customers! Everyone wanted them.

However those few Ohio fruit growers disappeared from the scene by the 1970's. The land for development in Lake County increased in value to such a degree that it overpowered the economies of farming. Family farms that had been owned and operated by the same family for generations became housing projects. The great farm as we once knew it disappeared from the scene. Even the apple growers sold their land for the same reason.

Also: see Peaches

OLIVES

Did You Know That Olives Must Be Pickled?

The most interesting story I know about fresh olives has to do with the way the first Italian immigrants I knew made such a fuss over them. Green olives would be shipped in early fall from California in their natural state in 20 pound wood boxes. They would be a solid green color, hard as a rock and washed clean. I did not know that they had to be pickled to be eaten. I tried one, bit into it and spit it out at once, because it was bitter as gall.

That did not stop me from having a little fun with some of my women acquaintances. I was young then and fun was the name of the game. I would offer an olive to anyone I knew well. Their reaction was no better than mine. They spit it out, made a sour grimace and told me off. They did not think it was funny at all. I guess I was a little off on that one.

My Italian friends could not wait for the olives to be pickled, a process that took a number of weeks. This was a treat for them, reminding them of home. That generation is gone. Today, you will rarely see any shipments of raw green olives. Variety olive bars have replaced them in the gourmet specialty section of the best supermarkets. Canned and pickled olives of all kinds can be found there as well.

Olive oil has moved to the forefront as the number one healthy oil. It is also used as a base for many salad dressings. You may discover that chopped olives have become a standard in most fresh salad bars. Martini olives have become the rage, while black Greek olives have taken on new dimensions. There are as many varieties of olives as there are shades of color. There is also a big market for stuffed olives. These small to large size olives are usually stuffed with almonds or pimentos.

The olive tree is a symbol of peace and purity. The victor of the Greek Olympic Games was crowned with a wreath of leaves from the olive tree. Spain is a major producer and accounts for twenty percent of the world's production. You will also find olives from California, Israel, Greece, Italy, and Turkey; they will all differ in taste as well as genetic variations that define their flavor.

ONIONS
Am I Hot Or Not?
How can you identify whether an onion will be hot or mild?

When the skin is tight, the onion is more likely to be hot. A loose outer skin that shows the leaves ready to fall off and displaying the inner skin will always be much milder.

In today's marketplace, even a three-pound bag of onions may be too much for some families or a single person. There are all kinds or processed substitutes: onion salt, onion flakes, battered onion rings, etc. Onions can be stored in season with proper dry conditions for as long as three to six months.

Onions can be braised, boiled, steamed, baked, fried, grilled, stuffed, roasted, used in stir-fry, as a part of a hamburger sandwich raw, or deep fried. They come in red, white, or yellow brown. Some restauranteurs prefer the red onions for added color in a salad. Sweet onions have made their mark and the Georgia Vidalia onion has made history as the sweetest onion of them all! In fact, Georgia is known as the Sweet Onion State. We also grow sweet onions in Colorado, Hawaii, Washington, California, and Texas. Onions are imported from Chile, Peru and Uruguay out of season. Medium size onions are available year around from almost every state of the union. New York, Michigan, Minnesota, Indiana, Iowa and Ohio are major producers of regular onion crops.

Onions have a history, going back five thousand years. They are mentioned in Numbers 11:5 in the Bible: "We remember the fish, the cucumbers, melons, leeks, onion and garlic, which we did eat freely in Egypt." The Romans ate them regularly, while the Greeks used onions to fortify athletes for the Olympic Games.

I can remember when onions were considered a basic staple in most European ethnic families; it was not uncommon to find a twenty-five-pound bag of onions in any of these homes. We had them in our own home when we were growing up. In the 1940's and 1950's, the standard retail pack was a ten-pound mesh bag. Later, it decreased to five pounds, while today, three pounds is the standard package. However, most people use onions sparingly, except for knowledgeable cooks. A number of processed onion products have appeared which are easier to use, but not necessarily as good. Onion powder, onion salt, dehydrated onions and prepared fried onions.

Immediately after World War II, onions were so highly regarded they were put on the OPA (Office of Price Administration) list at a regulated price, which created a temporary shortage. There were no extra supplies and people had to limit their purchases because of the shortage. There were pricing abuses because of this, making it almost impossible to purchase any quantity at the regulated price.

Also: See Leeks, Chives

Oranges: See Clementines and Temple Oranges

PAPAYA

The Hawaiian Papaya Is A Hermaphrodite

I never realized how wonderful papayas could taste until I ate them on my first visit to Hawaii 30 years ago. They tasted so good, I ate them for breakfast, lunch and dinner and I never tired of them. I would awake each morning and they would be on the hotel table along with a slice of lemon. Talk about good!

Obviously, eating any ripe fruit just picked off the tree is going to make a difference. I have discovered in my work that shipments by air from Hawaii are affected by cold weather and the papayas lose some of their taste. They also don't seem to ripen well at that time so you will find a variation in the degree of ripeness. Warmer weather is helpful and you can enjoy the flavor much more if they have a full yellow color. The volcanic ash the Hawaiian papaya grows in gives them their special taste. These are known as the Hawaiian Solo. The female strain of the hermaphrodite papayas is preferred by nature, while growers thin the male out.

About ten years ago, the Caribbean pink flesh papaya made its debut. It has made a tremendous impact and more people are enjoying its flavor. The pink flesh variety has a distinctive taste and is more consistent in flavor because of its location just off the coast of Florida; proximity to market makes a big difference. There are many variations of this wonderful fruit and you may see larger versions, almost the size of a football, from the Caribbean Islands. Papayas have wonderful digestive properties and are known for their pepsin qualities that aid digestion.

PARSNIPS

The Army Made Me Wary of Parsnips

Parsnips were a huge part of my diet in basic training in Spartanburg, South Carolina during World War II. They were served so frequently, I dreaded even hearing the word. I never thought they would turn out to become one of the vegetables that the famous chefs chose for their unique taste. Since that time, I have developed a higher regard for them, having discovered how good they taste as a flavor enhancer in many dishes beside soup.

Historically, parsnips were cultivated as far back as Roman times, noted for their long white flesh and edible root. Look for firm, fresh-appearing parsnips with no sighs of wilt, soft spots or decay. Store in the refrigerator in a cello poly bag and they can stay for at least two weeks. You will appreciate using them in many recipes; their adaptability makes them valued.

I have to call attention to the fact that people used to grow parsnips, turnips and carrots in their gardens. Since there was no refrigeration, they would be trenched in the earth and covered so that they would not freeze. The temperatures below the ground kept them firm and fresh throughout the winter. Oftentimes, the earth would be covered with hard, dried manure, which produces heat.

PARSLEY

When I was probably seven or eight years old, my mother would send me to the fruit and vegetable store for five cents worth of soup vegetables and greens. I would get a piece of celery, one carrot and one parsley root with greens. In contrast to today's marketplace, parsley root falls into the exotic class because it is used so infrequently. However, any European cook who is proud of his or her recipes will always include parsley root and greens in the soup they prepare. Since it is so limited in its use, it is a high priced vegetable today.

The early spring parsley root greens that arrive in April or May have a special flavor. The late crop in September is also one with great taste. These are generally local crops. Texas parsley root has a wonderful green appearance and good taste; it is shipped from January through April and I've seen no other parsley root shipments that can compare to them. Regular users of these greens will freeze them and package them in small units using them as needed throughout the year. Fresh curly parsley is used more as a garnish than the cut Italian or French flat parsley; it is also much sweeter in taste. Curly parsley can also enhance your breath, with its chlorophyll effect. Parsley is rich in Vitamin C and is believed to help with rheumatism.

PEACHES

I Am Peachy

There was a time that Georgia was called the Peach State, but that is no longer true because Vidalia onions have become the insignia of the state. There are more shipments out of Georgia than there were in the past, but they have been overshadowed by California and South Carolina shipments.

I can remember the first peaches that were shipped from Georgia back in the 1930's, packed in one-half bushel containers, ring-faced, graded 1.75", 2", 2.25" in diameter and up. They were full colored, hard, juicy and mostly the free stone, Elberta variety. It wasn't until many years later that we began to receive layer-pack boxes, packed like eggs, and loose thirty-two pound packs.

Both California and South Carolina vie for top honors as the biggest peach producer in the US, and there are times when one outshines the other. However, the varieties are much different, modified and grafted to attain their full color and taste. Oddly, peaches have suffered most, because of their inability to ripen well off the tree.

Tree ripened fruit is gradually moving into the marketplace. Obviously, this requires better handling practices and more expensive packaging, which raises the cost, but the consumer does get better tasting fruit. The emphasis in the past has been on longer shelf life, whereas I think the focus should be on growing better tasting fruit.

New varieties of peaches appear on the market each year. They have become redder and deeper in color and shading. However, the white variety of peaches has made important inroads: There is some claim to date of better flavor.

Late varieties from Washington and Oregon are highly regarded for their flavor and beautiful appearance. Local growers in Pennsylvania, New Jersey, Ohio and Michigan are important contributors to their local areas and these peaches bring a premium price because of their proximity to markets and their tree ripening practices.

Do not store peaches in the refrigerator. Leave them out at room temperature either in a ripening bowl or a plain paper bag. That will assure you of better taste.

Real "Tree Ripened" Peaches
When a peach was a PEACH!

When was the last time you ate a juicy, flavorful peach? It has been more and more of a rarity these past few years because the peach itself has been modified again and again, and over time it has lost the flavor of yesterday's peach. Yesteryear's peaches were sometimes not freestone, not as red, nor as beautiful as today's peaches, but they tasted good.

During my produce career in the 1950's and 60's, there were a few outstanding peach growers in both the Northeastern and Western sections of Ohio. I was fortunate to have made a connection with Mr Blackmore, a peach grower from Painesville, Ohio. His peaches were the most beautiful I have ever seen, and probably one of the sweetest I ever tasted. He produced only one variety, the Hale Peach. Since the land in this area was so special for growing fruit, his peaches would all come out highly colored, with a red and yellow mixture that were beautifully shaded.

Nobody could come close to the sizes he produced,

running from 2.5 to 3 inches. (This is a big piece of fruit since two inches was considered average for a peach). Since he was a local grower, he would bring his fruit to market on racks. The peck baskets he packed contained eighteen to twenty large peaches, every one of them as pretty as a picture. I have never seen anything like it, ever since those days! There was a special beautify to those peaches that we will never see again. Interestingly, there is a bathing beach named after the owner of the peach farm, named Blackmore Beach, since he owned the land. Today, the beach is no longer there, having been washed away by the natural forces of wind, rain and the ever-changing lake.

My other peach connection was just as good, but it was an entirely different kind of peach. Petersons Farms in Perry, Ohio grew excellent Elberta Peaches. The Elberta variety was not highly colored, nor did it grow to large sizes; it had kind of an oblong shape rather than a round one. However, it was truly freestone, with a strong coloration of bright yellow.

You have to take note that the land in Lake County had special characteristics that produced great tasting fruit. Peterson was a great farmer who utilized this natural quality and because of his knowledge, he produced wonderful fruit every year. Beginning on Labor Day he would load his truck, double-stacked, and bring in 400 to 500 pecks of peaches, three days a week until September 15th, when he finished his crop. These peaches were much smaller than the Hale Variety, averaging two inches in diameter, but what flavor they had! They were right off the tree, which made more of a difference than anything else.

In western Ohio, a number of growers combined their crops and sent them to a peach cooperative which handled all of the peach harvest from its packing and storehouse. Those peaches were also the Elberta variety. They were packed in bushels, ring-faced, their size running mostly two inches and up; even though they did not have the sharp, bright look of peaches from the Lake County area, they did have great taste and filled the need for good tasting fruit for the average consumer. The storage house was located close to Sandusky. I made many trips in my stake- body truck to pick up loads of peaches. They were not the best looking peaches, but they filled an important need.

One of the best growers I know is in Madison, Ohio on Route 20. The West family is into the third generation of growers today and they still produce one of the best peaches in the Midwest. They are growing the new varieties, such as the Red Crest, the Havens and other innovative specialties. Their roadside market is so popular that they sell all of their fruit through that method.

In Chesterland, Ohio, the Patterson Farms and the Sage Farms carry on the tradition of producing outstanding fruit. Their retail outlet is a haven for anyone who is looking for excellent tasting fruit.

However, I must make the comment that no matter what experts say, I still believe, after seventy years of experience, that there are no peaches that will mach the flavor of the peaches of yesteryear. They are gone forever.

PEARS

We Make A Great Pear

Pears are available most of the year. When they are not available, in early spring and summer, we import supplies from Chile and Argentina. Packhams are a popular variety from these countries. This is a harder version of the Bartlett and ripens much more slowly.

Pears ripen best off the tree. Summer pears generally do well because they ripen more rapidly. Winter pears need more time to attain their maturity. Look for a clean, full colored pear that is firm, free of bruises and discolorations. Markings and black spots should be avoided. It is a good idea to determine quality by checking the color of the fruit. Pears can be stored in the refrigerator for a long time, if they are not overripe. Once they turn yellow, it is best to serve them. Pears are a healthful food. They are an excellent source of food energy and are noted for their mineral content.

Oregon, Washington and California supply us with most of our fruit. Michigan, New York and other states furnish additional supplies. A new variety of pears, the Red Pear has hit the market. There are many varieties of this type that are offered, but they all fall into the softer Bartlett classification. They have gained a considerable following because of their softer texture and because they seem to ripen to a more juicy inner flesh. Their bright reddish color adds impulse appeal as well.

Japanese Pears, also known as Asian Pears, Shinseiki or Oriental Pears, are round, one to three inches in diameter and rusted in texture. Available year round, this fruit is now a standard exotic in the United States. When hard, it has a distinct pear taste; when softer, it tastes more like an apple. Asian pears are crisp and juicy. The brown variety seems to be more popular in the Untied States, whereas in Japan, the yellow variety is more acceptable.

Pears—A Story of Their Origin

During my experiences in World War II in Metz, France, I learned a great deal about pears. While in the reserve, waiting for orders to move out to battle, we were housed in a magnificent French castle. Can you think of three hundred to four hundred men living in one house, even if it was a castle? You can be sure that the place didn't look the same when we left.

One day while I was walking in the orchard behind the castle, I met a Frenchman and I asked him if he knew anything about the fruit trees that were in their first blossoming stage. He told me an interesting story. "Did you know," he said, "all of the popular pear trees you see are of French origin? There is the Bosc Beurre, the D'Anjou and Comice pear. Frenchmen grafted them all! In the old days,

French noblemen grafted fruit for pleasure. It was not uncommon for an owner to develop new grafted varieties. This is the reason that they were able to develop and perfect those three varieties I am talking about." Today, these same grafted varieties, some sixty to seventy years later, still dominate the winter pear market.

I can remember when the Bosc pear was only used for cooking. There were few people who recognized their wonderful buttery flavor when fresh. They are a winter variety that does take longer to ripen, however, once they get that ripe softness, the juice literally pours out. Their disadvantage is the dark brown color that is rather nondescript. It was not until twenty-five years ago that they attained their place as a pear that people learned to love and enjoy.

Harry and David, the gourmet food and fruit company, is the most well known gift fruit packer in the USA. They have created a national and international market for their famous Comice Pears. This is a pear that has a rough green appearance, but it is considered to be the juiciest and sweetest pear you will ever taste. The Comice pear market is guarded so carefully, it is only on rare occasions that you will find them in the marketplace. Ripen at room temperature for best flavor.

In my fruit basket business, we would get our own Bartlett pears from growers in Washington and Oregon from July through October. Then we turn to the Anjou and Bosc varieties, which are available through April and May. Imports fill in the rest of the year from Chile and Argentina.

PEAS
Where Have All Of The Fresh Peas Gone?

Man as far back as the Bronze Age has known peas, some five thousand years ago. They first came into prominence sometime later in Middle Asia. It is interesting that most varieties of peas were originally grown for drying. This is the dry pea that is used for split pea soup and other cooking. Many years later the good eating qualities of the fresh pea were recognized and they became quite popular in France and England during the 17th and 18th centuries.

Today, peas are hardly seen in their fresh form, except in local gardens. There are still large amounts of fresh peas sold, but only as a luxury commodity. Local truck gardens make peas available for a short period at bargain prices since they are not competing with produce processors. Frozen and canned peas dominate the market, but it should be noted that processed peas are equally nutritious as fresh, retaining most of their vitamins and nutrients.

California, Idaho, the Carolinas, Mississippi, New Jersey, Oregon and New Mexico are good sources of supply. Peas are available every month of the year. The difficulty is that they are offered fresh in such limited quantities that they are not always found in most stores.

When selecting peas, look for a firm, bright green pea that is fully podded. The pod must be fresh, for a yellow or overripe pea will prove to be tough. The young, medium pea is the most tender, while the large, oversize pea will be hard. Oftentimes, fresh pods have more green than peas and this should be avoided.

Peas keep well under refrigeration and they will store for long periods in the shell. Like any other fresh vegetable, they taste best when they are used at once. Peas can be eaten raw and many people prefer them this way. Some cooks use the pea pod and enjoy its flavor as well as the pea.

Peas are a good source of vitamins and minerals. They are highly rated for calcium, phosphorus and protein. In studies made by specialists in this field, there is hardly any difference in the fresh and frozen pea in vitamin content if the peas are handled properly. Mexico is an important source of supply for both the fresh and frozen market.

The Chinese Pea is a small tender skinned pea, which can be eaten raw. It is produced primarily in Mexico and the San Luis Valley in California. The other variety known as the Snow Pea is a flat Chinese pea, three to four inches long and one inch in diameter. Both varieties are available year round from Mexico and California.

Snow Pea Pods Have Moved Into The Forefront

Snow pea pods have changed the face of the fresh pea market in the last few years. They have become a standard vegetable crop, with Guatemala and Mexico the leading suppliers. You will find snow peas in many Asian recipes. I've seen them used as a hors d'oeuvre, filled with goat cheese. They are used in stir-fry, salads, and are added to many dishes for color. They store well under refrigeration and can stay fresh for a week or more. The Sugar Pea offers some competition but it is a totally different product; it has a fuller, plump appearance and a mature seed in the pod. Sugar Peas do have a sugary taste and has attracted many new followers, however they have to be fresh and truly green for the best flavor. The Sugar Pea is available all year.

PEPPERS

Does A Pepper Have To Be Green or Red To Be Good?

I have to tell this story and my connection to red peppers. As a purveyor of vegetables to Chinese restaurants during my long career as a wholesale produce merchant, red and green peppers were a staple item for everyday use.

Everyone may have forgotten, but in the early days of the Chinese restaurants, there were limitations on what they purchased and how they used it. The basic items I sold were large Spanish onions, celery leaves and peppers—red peppers preferred. It was common practice at that time to consider peppers that were turning red on the vine to be second rate and overripe. In September and October, green peppers that were left in the field would begin to turn red. This made them less saleable because it was the thinking at that time that the green pepper was the best tasting. It was not until many years later that we learned that red peppers were sweeter. Actually they are a different variety and are bred in greenhouses all over the world.

Peppers that were of mixed color, displaying some red and some green, were discounted in price, even though they were freshly picked and hard. There was a major grower that offered two truckloads of these peppers, packed in full bushels, each bushel weighing about forty pounds. We put them in cold storage, selling them to our Chinese restaurant customers all winter long. In 1950, peppers in winter were imported from Mexico. A small amount of peppers would cost as much as the bushels we had purchased for storage. Green peppers were a rarity. Frozen peppers can only be used for cooking purposes, but that was fine for the restaurants we served. It is interesting that the Chinese restaurants were the only customers who recognized the value of the peppers we offered.

Today the fresh red pepper, along with the yellow, orange and brown varieties have proven to be the king and queen of the pepper industry. Red Peppers have more powerful nutrients than any other colored variety. They have become the engine that has made the pepper into a major force in the perishable produce field. They are available all year, form Canada, The Netherlands, Chile and the USA.

Also: See Chili Peppers

Pickles: See CUCUMBERS

PINEAPPLES

The pineapple is a product of the Americas. Some early records indicate its origin in Brazil and Paraguay sometime before the arrival of Columbus on our shores. This plant is reproduced by its shoots. It has traveled long distances throughout he world and has been transplanted in many warm climates successfully. Pineapples were found growing wild in Hawaii with no record of their growth before this. Hawaii was one of the major producers in the world, but Costa Rica has become the major producer.

Pineapple growing areas are changing and new countries are emphasizing their production. Honduras has entered the field, with Mexico and Puerto Rico also strong sources of supplies for this fruit. Cuba was at one time one of the most important suppliers for this country, but obviously no longer is a producer for our markets because of our fifty-year boycott.

Pineapples are shipped almost every month of the year from somewhere, with peak periods from March through June. The advent of the "Golden Pineapple" from Dole has played a role in the pineapple's continuing popularity. One of the difficulties during he colder months is that the fruit is picked too green, which does not allow them to ripen properly. Generally, though, they ripen well off the bush and should take on full color before they are served.

To select pineapples, look for a clean, fresh appearance. The fruit should have an orange-yellow or golden color. The pineapple should be firm and free of bruising, decay, soft spots and mold. Sometimes you can smell the odor of a fresh pineapple, which will indicate ripeness—this, however, is not always true. Pineapples can be stored for long periods, but they will lose some of their flavor if they are kept too long. Since they are a tropical fruit, they tend to react unfavorably to the cold, so it makes sense to ripen them outside the refrigerator until you are ready to use them. Do not try to ripen a pineapple once it is cut open, it will destroy the entire ripening process. Pineapples are well supplied with vitamin A, calcium, phosphorous and are a great source of ascorbic acid.

A Golden Future

A number of years ago, I met a young man who, having just returned from the Caribbean, wanted to consult with me on the possibility of shipping pineapples from the area. He brought samples, and every one we cut for experimentation tasted wonderful. The pineapples were firm, grew to a good size and were well shaped. Although I was in agreement with him about all of these excellent qualities, I advised him that the perishability of this fruit was too treacherous. He agreed and as a result didn't enter into an agreement with the people he had negotiated with.

A short time later, Del Monte recognized the potential of this magnificent fruit and entered the market with a big promotion and a well planned shipping program for this product. They refer to these pineapples as the "Del Monte Gold" brand. It has made tremendous inroads into the market. Other countries and producers from outside the Caribbean are now growing "Goldens" or a variety of them. In spite of its higher pricing, the consumer continues to support it, and its growth has been an important part of the industry.

Another innovation has been the advent of coring pineapples at the point of origin, by third party processors; also there is in-store coring at high-end supermarkets. This eliminates any kind of hand labor for the consumer and allows the user to take it home in a protected container, ready for use. This is another development that has added a new dimension to this market.

PLUMS

There are many new varieties: The new Star Plum, also called Westerner, has captured the fancy of both growers and consumers. It is an early large plum with good color and excellent flavor and is harvested in May and June. The Laroda Plum is still my favorite, with yellow juicy flesh and a light reddish black skin. The black varieties have proved to be the most popular, with dozens of new entrants. The new specialty plums are finding a niche of their own. Besides the Pluot (30% apricot, 70% plum), there is the Apruim, which is two-thirds apricot and one-third plum. The Plumcot is half plum and half apricot.

Plums can be used in pies, served stewed, scalloped, poached or even sliced into salads. California is the major supplier, with Chile filling in during January and February. June, July and August are the best months for our USA fruit. There are some late plum varieties that do well in September; prune plums dominate the late fall varieties. A plum and a prune are distinguished by this one difference: a plum is not freestone, while a prune is freestone.

RAISINS

Where Have All The Raisins Gone?

I can remember the days when raisins were a part of the daily fare for young and old. They were considered in the same category as fresh fruit, since everyone seemed to know they had a great many vitamins and nutrients. At Passover, the tradition was to give little packages of raisins and nuts in the shell to the children. This was a special treat. There were no miniature packages at that time, so your parents would just put together some raisins and nuts in a small paper bag. The dark raisins were the more popular variety, but we did get little tastes of the golden yellow Thompson variety on occasion. My mother-in-law, Lena Nagelbush, always made a small bottle of homemade raisin wine, which she served during Passover. Everyone seemed to enjoy it because of its overly rich sweetness.

Interestingly, for the home wine maker, dried raisins give the wine its strength and sweetness. The Muscat grape, when exceedingly ripe, will produce a seeded dark raisin that will add a special kick to the wine when pressed. However, they produce little juice.

Muscat raisins are available in limited quantity. However they are seeded, this limits their popularity. If you love wine and eat these Muscat grapes, you can almost taste their wine-like flavor. Sun dried raisins contain heart protective antioxidant compounds. You will also find raisins to be an essential part of Indian cuisine; they are used in rich milk puddings, syrupy cheese balls, and stirred into many fragrant kinds of sauces.

Raisins are harvested in August, then spread on paper trays and sun dried for two to three weeks. This in fact is how raisins are processed commercially today. California is the major producer.

Also: see GRAPES

Raspberries: See Berries

RHUBARB

Rhubarb Comes Back In Style

When I was a young boy, my mother served rhubarb regularly. It grew wild in our back yard and we never seemed to run out of it—I suppose that was the reason she served it so often.

I had performed some special service to a friend and as a thank you she brought over a rhubarb pie. I had never before eaten rhubarb pie and I wasn't overly enthusiastic about it. I said to my wife, "You can either eat this or give it away. I'm not interested in trying it." Bess was insistent. She said, "You have to try it. I'll bet you'll like it." She was right! It just melted in my mouth, just a bit tangy, but the right kind of tang. It has become one of my favorites since that time.

I prefer the garden grown rhubarb, even though it does not have the attractive appearance of the hothouse varieties. For the true rhubarb taste, the outdoor variety has that tangy taste that singles it out. It is also stringier. Shoppers should look for a fresh, attractive appearance. Hothouse rhubarb has a beautiful red color, with long ruby stalks that are generally one or two inches thick; it seems to belong to a separate family, because it is so different in appearance and taste from the outdoor variety.

Grown in Michigan, Washington and Oregon, there are a number of different varieties available. In old time folklore, it was considered to be a spring tonic. I've never been able to prove that successfully. I can also remember when rhubarb strawberry pie was the cats meow, and it still has it fair share of pie lovers. Both hothouse and outdoor rhubarb are available from February to June.

On a trip to New York many years ago, I met a farmer who sold rhubarb juice mixed with apple juice for its cleansing properties; I guess he had his believers who supported him. Rhubarb freezes well and many commercial users store it frozen for year around use.

Strawberries: See Berries

SALSIFY

Is This An Oyster Plant?

I don't think many people are familiar with salsify. I also don't know many chefs who use it—but in the years when I sold wholesale produce, the few old timers who knew about salsify treasured it. It was packed into twelve bunches of six or eight units that were shaped like a long tapered carrot. Each unit was washed carefully and was sold in a half-bushel handle basket.

I don't know why I never tasted it until late in my career. I used it in soup and recognize that it reminded me of seafood, maybe oysters, but I'm not sure. It was referred to as "oyster plant". I haven't thought much about it since that time and the truth is I rarely see it. To make mock oysters, combine two cups mashed salsify, one egg, a bit of salt, a dash of paprika, and one tablespoon of butter or margarine. Shape into cakes and brown in canola oil.

Look for fresh long-rooted vegetables that have a good brownish color. Keep refrigerated. It is a root vegetable that has excellent mineral qualities, high in calcium and phosphorous.

SORREL
Sorrel Is As Sour As Can Be

Sorrel has reappeared on the scene after a long absence. People have discovered its versatility and unique taste: It has a sour taste that gives it a tang you cannot get in any other vegetable. It is more available now, often used as part of a Mesclun mix.

When buying sorrel look for pale to dark green leaves that are fresh and attractive, with no yellowing. It has a shelf life of three days under proper refrigeration, and is available year round.

Sorrel is also known as "sour grass". My mother served it to us as "schav"—a chilled Polish soup—in summer, because of its refreshing taste; she considered it to be a health food!

SQUASH
Zucchini Is The Queen of the Summer Squash

The varied shapes of all kinds of squash, winter or summer always intrigue me. In Central America they grow a long, thick Banana Squash. It can grow two to three feet long with a width of seven to eight inches. It is very popular with Hispanic people.

One of my interests has always been to see that surplus food is not wasted and can be transferred to people who can use it. In the wholesale produce business, there are many instances where there is an over supply. In one instance, a supplier sent a shipment of one or two tons of misshaped winter squash. It was shaped like a plumber's elbow and it was unlike any squash I had seen before, or would see again. The receiver was unable to sell it at any price and he was ready to send it to the dump. When I saw it on the produce platform ready to be picked up, I asked him if I could take it to my business and give it away. Now, I am talking about two thousand pounds of good squash that could stay good for one month under proper storage conditions.

I had my own radio program on WELW AM at that time and I offered it to any institution or organization that fed homeless people. I can only tell you I had immediate success! The calls came in so fast that I almost ran out of product. The people who received it could not thank me enough, because the squash proved to be wonderful eating. I never saw that variety again, but it remains locked in my mind because it was such a memorable experience.

Under the auspices of the Mickey Weiss Foundation, the Cleveland wholesale produce merchants have set up a regular pick-up program of surplus produce. What a success story this has become! In 2003, Mickey Weiss invited Joe Cavalier Jr., another board member of the N.O.F.T., and me to set up a food distribution program. The Cleveland Food Bank picked up two and one half million pounds of surplus produce, which was distributed to needy organizations and institutions; it is still in operation to this day and it is one of my proudest achievements.

Acorn, Butternut, Buttercup, Hubbard and a dozen hard varieties dominate the fall and winter season. Crookneck yellow squash, Zucchini, and Pattypan are the most popular summer varieties. Squash is available all year around.

Star Fruit- See Carambola

STRAWBERRIES

Looking For The Best Strawberries

Today there are two different species of strawberry varieties: Those from Florida have been grafted with those from California, creating strawberries of both great beauty and taste. To select strawberries, look for a bright, clean appearance. The berries should appear to be solid with a fresh looking green cap. Leaky containers indicate over-ripe fruit. Avoid decayed berries, mold, or green looking fruit. Size is not always a factor, although there are many fine large varieties that are exceptional. Heirloom local varieties often taste better, although they may not have the size or appearance. Strawberries are an excellent source of Vitamin C. Store under refrigeration immediately after purchasing. However, remember they must be used in as short a time as possible. Chocolate-covered strawberries are one of the best treats of the season. But what can compare to strawberry shortcake? There is nothing like it.

When you say strawberries, my ears perk up, my eyes open and I say, "I remember." I was the specialist in receiving all kinds of berries in season locally in Northern Ohio. In early June, my berry business went into high gear through the middle of July. First, it was my job to be able to purchase the best strawberries in the market. I was known for that. Once I purchased them I had to be sure I sold them that same day, since they were not pre-cooled and showed the effects of weather as the day wore on. The market opened at 4 AM and our sales closed at 11 AM or noon.

In the 1950's, there were many small family farms. Some of them did not grow enough produce to come to the market to sell their wares, so they would hire a sort of broker who would pick up their berries and bring them to market. He was their agent and he would pick up berries from six or eight growers, whatever they produced that day. Ray Kress and his brother were the agents from the Lake County, Ohio area and they represented the best growers in Perry and Painesville, Ohio. Though they were active for many years, we were king of the berry suppliers. Unfortunately, Ray and his brother went fishing in rough water on Lake Erie one day and their boat capsized and both brothers drowned. They were only thirty years old. It was a great loss, not only for us, but also for the family farmers they represented.

From that point on, our leadership role began to falter. We had difficulty in obtaining the best suppliers. California growers began to ship their strawberries, gradually dominating the market.

Local berry farms were more valuable for real estate development than for farming, so we lost our suppliers gradually. Another factor was the labor process that was so demanding: Every berry had to be picked by hand.

Years ago, before the advent of the fast food chains, the young children of those farms would be in charge of the berry patch, sharing in the profits. But once the fast food restaurants moved in, the economics changed; you could make more as a server than you could picking berries. Today, most berry farmers locally advertise for people to come out to the farm and pick their own berries. This has become a stable part of the business.

See also: BERRIES

SUGAR CANE
I'm Sweeter Than Sweet

The next time you visit a Hispanic grocery, don't be surprised if you see a long, bamboo-looking stick that seems to have mixed colors spaced in between. (It is also available in small 2"– 3" long units in the shape of a flute). It may seem strange to see someone sucking on it, but anyone who grew up in the South years ago will remember chewing and sucking the sweet flesh. Sugar cane does not have many enthusiasts left, but there are still a few remnants of the population who remember it.

SWEET POTATOES

I am always asked to explain the differences between a Jersey Sweet Potato and a Yam. The Jersey has dry yellow flesh, with just a little less sweetness. The Puerto Rican Yam, with its deep red color, has a very rich taste and has come back into favor. The Beauregard, the grafted yam, is grown primarily in North Carolina and seems to dominate the field. It has taken the best qualities of the yam and sweet potato and combined them. The dryer yellow flesh of the Jersey Sweet Potato does not have those unique qualities, which makes a difference to most consumers. There are enough vitamins and nutrients in a yam or Beauregard to keep a person alive for six months, with only water and the potato for food. It would be hard to beat that!

Sweet potatoes are used all year around. They can be baked, French fried, boiled and dried. They remain as popular as ever. Thanksgiving and Christmas bring out the best old-time recipes. Sweet potatoes have become popular in some chain restaurants, steakhouses primarily, baked to perfection and heavily buttered. They sure taste good!

SWISS CHARD

Folic acid is an important element of Swiss chard and has become a byword for pregnant women because of its high folic acid content; it also has many benefits as a nutrient for everyone else as well. Folic acid is known to help build better bones and prevent disease. Swiss chard has taken on new dimensions and acquired many new followers. A major grower has developed a standard package of both the green and reddish-green variety of Swiss chard. The entire chard is edible, from the bottom to the top leaf. It can be sautéed, boiled or steamed; it can be prepared in the same way you prepare spinach. Swiss chard is available all year from some local growers, and California is a major supplier.

See also: BEETS

TARO ROOT

The Story of Poi

After my visit to Hawaii, I learned how important taro root was to native populations. Hispanic people use taro root as a basic food and you will find variations of it used in most Hispanic homes. It is also known as "Dasheen", "Eddo" and "Kalo". It is eaten and served with the skins removed. It is native to Asia and grows primarily in the Pacific areas.

My first encounter with Taro Root was with a Hawaiian guide who did a demonstration of how it was prepared as "Poi". I wasn't too excited about its taste when I tried it, but the demonstration gave me some idea of what it looked and tasted like. When cooked, it has a nutty flavor, with gray and white flesh. Taro root is a starch; it is a potato-like tuber with a brown, fibrous skin.

Today I am not the least bit surprised to find big displays of taro root in regular supermarkets, in part because of the large number of Hispanics using it for their native dishes. In California, with its large Hispanic population, you will find it piled high at grocery stores and markets, along with Malanga, another root vegetable. Most root vegetables, such as the taro root, are loaded with minerals and nutrients.

TEMPLE ORANGES

Years ago, Bess and I would always take a winter vacation in Miami, Florida for a couple of weeks. Fruit juice stands proliferated at all the resort areas, so I would be sure to stop at every juice stand to buy a glass of fresh orange juice. The Temple Orange is one half orange, one half tangerine and though it is the juiciest of all of the citrus family, it does have lots of seeds—maybe that is the reason it never became popular. Temple Oranges are also easy to peel and they can be squeezed for juice quite easily. It seemed as if most of the Florida juice stands used a mixture of Temple and Valencia Oranges. The juice really tasted terrific! Now, fifty years later, you can look high and low for a fresh orange juice stand and you won't even find one. I used to stop at three or four stands before I got my fill of them.

Frozen orange juice dominates the field today, with the exception of the processed, commercial product, which is entirely different.

To select a good Temple Orange, look for solidity, a bright look, no soft spots, no blemishes, and the feel of a thin skin. The season is a short one and the crops are small, so try to find them in January and February. Size is unimportant, but a thin skin is a sign of lots of juice. Florida is the main producer; there are occasional foreign shipments that do not taste the same.

Tangelos now dominate the easy-peel fruit from Florida,

replacing the Temple Orange. This fruit is one half grapefruit, one half tangerine. There are many variations, with the Honeybell making tremendous inroads. Tangelos are available December through February; they are also known as Minneolas, grown in Florida and California.

Also: see Clementines

TOMATOES

The tomato is one of the most fascinating of all the fruit and vegetable families. It is not clear where they first originated, but there is some inconclusive proof that they are native to Peru. The tomato has never been found growing wild. They have been a basic food for centuries for people on the American continents, and of course tomatoes have also been widely adapted in European countries, making an appearance in England in 1596. There was also a period in their history when they were used only as an adornment.

Tomatoes are available every month of the year, with shipments from many states, including imports form Mexico, the Bahamas and hothouses in Canada and the United States. In the US, Florida, California, Texas and the Carolinas are the leading producers, although there are many other states, including Ohio, that play an important role seasonally. Tomatoes are a fruit, considered to be a berry, but in cultivation and most uses, it is a vegetable. Tomatoes are our second most popular vegetable, after potatoes.

The advent of the cluster, also known as the vine-ripened tomato, during the winter months has improved the quality of this type of tomato considerably; it is distinctive because its vine remains attached to the calyx of the tomato.

A good portion of the tomato crop is still ripened at terminal markets and packaged in cellophane cartons for markets that prefer them this way, although this method of retail sale is declining. Many locally grown tomatoes play an important role during their seasonal periods.

Greenhouse tomatoes are a development that has changed the entire concept of tomato growing. Greenhouse tomatoes are sold all over the United States, although the center of the growing activity is in Indiana and Canada. The greenhouse tomato plays an active role in the months when few tomatoes are available from the major shipping locations. They are almost perfectly formed, with good shape, a green calyx and ripen well on or off the vine.

The question of whether pink or red tomatoes taste better is only a matter of preference. The answer pertains particularly to the area where they are grown and the climatic conditions they have enjoyed while ripening. Sunshine brings out the best flavor in this fruit and explains the lack of flavor during the cold, winter months.

A mature green tomato is one that is ready for picking and that can ripen on its own, off the vine. A vine-ripened tomato is one that is colored sufficiently on the vine to attain its full flavor. In both cases, it is the grower who makes the decision.

The consumer is always complaining about tomatoes, mostly because of flavor. To select tomatoes, shop for firm, deep-colored pink or red fruit. The tomato should be bright appearing, free of soft spots, blemishes and scars. It should not be rock hard, however; it should have some give to the touch, but be firm. A well-formed tomato is essential to good slicing. Overripe fruit exhibit cracks and blemishes and should be avoided. Size is unimportant in determining flavor.

Tomatoes can be kept under refrigeration, but they do best ripening at room temperature. Today's tomatoes are less perishable than those of decades ago. They will ripen best out of refrigeration, the taste improving as it ripens.

The tomato is an outstanding source of Vitamin C and is well represented with other nutrients as well. Tomatoes should be on everyone's list of essential daily foods. In a recent scientific study, it was determined that cooked and preserved tomatoes deliver an important phytochemical called lycopene, which is an important ingredient that helps protect the heart.

Cherry tomatoes are small specimens of their larger cousin, with a much sweeter taste. They offer the consumer sweetness of taste, consistency in marketing and are a colorful addition to the salad plate. These miniature tomatoes follow the same growth patterns of the larger tomatoes, but grow only to the size of an ordinary small plum. Also there are grape tomatoes which have zoomed into national popularity.

The yellow tomato is a completely yellow variety of tomato that is non-acidic and grown especially for people on special diets. The plum tomato is oblong and grows small; it is a thick-skinned type that yields well in the field and is harvested in late August. Most people use them for canning and processing because of their distinct flavor. However, they have made a strong impact in the fresh market due to their flavor, firmness and their longer keeping qualities.

Sun-dried tomatoes are available year round and are usually shipped from Italy, South America and California. They have moved into American cooking with great success in the last few years. Used for sauces, pizzas, stews or flavoring vegetable dishes, they have a smoky, sharp taste. The Italian varieties seem to have the most flavor.

The Tamatillo is an egg sized tree tomato from New Zealand. It is deep red in color and is sold in cans because of its high perishability.

The Tomatillo is a small, green tomato that is very hard, but is a prize cooking item. It is shipped in from Mexico and California year round.

Roma tomatoes have become part of the mainstream. Initially, they were used primarily to make sauce. Even though they have a thick, heavy skin they have made inroads into the market, mostly because of lower price, particularly during winter months.

Heirloom tomatoes, which are referred to as the virginal popular varieties of yesterday, have made a comeback, particularly among professional chefs. The Ugli Ripe Tomato grown in Florida by the Procacci family has become one of the accepted standards for flavor, noted for their ridges and odd shape, they seem to hold their own because of their fresh outdoor taste. The Campari variety has become known for its true tomato sweetness.

New hope for tomatoes

The tomato during off-season has been and continues to be a source of dissatisfaction among tomato lovers everywhere. It is sad that a fruit that is so loved has so many dissatisfied customers. However, there are some changes in the marketplace that may improve this situation. In fact, there are many improvements already taking place.

The cluster or vine tomato, which is grown primarily in Holland and Israel, has made a tremendous impact among tomato lovers. For some reason, no one in this country recognized that a cluster tomato would help retain some of the original sweetness of the tomato when it is ripe and mature. This genetically engineered tomato has moved into the forefront of retail sales because of its flavorful qualities, its beautiful appearance and its ideal shelf ripening abilities.

In the interim, Canadian greenhouse growers have entered the field as well as some large Colorado greenhouse producers, with additional shipments from Texas, California and the Carolinas. The question still remains to be decided: who will be able to produce the best tasting tomato of this kind?

Now we turn to the Israeli growers. Fifteen years ago, I visited the scientific laboratories of a well known agricultural college in Israel. While touring the exhibits and discussing the merits of the tomato projects that were going on, I was pleasantly surprised to hear of a program that was to take place in the future: The scientists were discussing the possibility of producing cherry tomatoes shipped on a vine, with the tomatoes still attached to them. I thought it was an impossibility at the time, but said nothing. Today, Israel ships a Desert Cherry tomato, grown in the Negev desert, on the vine with the tomatoes attached! It is probably the sweetest tomato you will taste anywhere. Packed in twelve one-pound bags to a box, they are flown to many destinations.

Interestingly, Mexico is also a major producer of tomatoes and has an identical product to that of Israel, packaged in the same way. The two packages look so very much alike that it is important to see what country the tomatoes came from. The Grape cherry tomato, grown in the United States and

Mexico is another addition to this category. This is a cherry tomato shaped like a tiny, oval shaped grape; it does have a distinct sweetness of its own and should capture a share of America's insatiable appetite.

WATERCRESS

Watercress Can Soothe Your Nerves

On a camping and hiking trip in Buena Vista, California many years ago, I came upon a bed of wild watercress growing along the river. When you talk about true watercress flavor, once you've tasted outdoor watercress, you know how good it can be. Most watercress is grown in hothouses under controlled conditions, however in my produce purchasing days, there were farmers who grew watercress outdoors in season.

For as long as I can remember, when you ordered a steak or a filet in a restaurant, it would have some watercress leaves for contrast as a decorative touch. Oddly, it is no longer seen or used that way, except by a few old time restaurateurs.

Watercress can often be found along streams and damp meadows. It has small white flowers in the spring, with only the leaves and stems being edible.

Watercress is noted in alternative medicinal circles for its benefits in some kidney disorders and for its soothing qualities. It is rich in iron and Vitamin C. Arugula has similar qualities and seems to have replaced watercress in restaurant circles. It is grown in greenhouses and it available year round.

Goat cheese and watercress tea sandwiches can make an interesting combination. Watercress soup has made some new friends and has an ardent group of followers.

A Final Word on Buying the Best, Most Delicious Fruit

When we think of fruit, we picture juicy peaches, crunchy red apples, plump strawberries, refreshing grapes and red and black raspberries that melt in your mouth. However, the real thing doesn't always meet our expectations. We all know the disappointment we feel when we bite into a hard, dry peach, a cantaloupe with no flavor, or a tasteless honeydew.

The problem lies mostly with transportation and the time the fruit was picked, purchased and then used. Picking too early or too late, delays in shipping or mishandling in the warehouse can make a big difference. Studies have shown that seventy percent of consumers have been dissatisfied with their peaches and nectarines. The so-called tree-ripened fruit shipped from long distances have failed to meet most consumers' requirements. Again, it is also a race against time and human errors.

Ripening Fruit

Fruit should not be left on the windowsill to ripen, because heat from the sun can cause it to over-ripen and turn mushy. Placing fruit in the refrigerator before it is ripe can ruin its flavor. Cold temperatures damage the internal natural ripening process. Fruits and vegetables are living, breathing foods. They absorb gases and the fruit gets sweeter as it ages, storing its sugar. Once it has ripened, it is more susceptible to bruising, punctures and spoilage.

The use of the newly developed ripening bowl, the ripening bag or just a plain brown bag can be of great help in obtaining better tasting fruit; check the contents daily for progress. Using your refrigerator as temporary storage will be your greatest asset. Long-term storage of fresh fruit detracts from its benefits. Don't refrigerate fruit until it is ripe, then store half of it and keep the remainder at room temperature.

Good ripe fruit may be able to remain in the refrigerator up to one week. If the fruit starts to over-ripen, mash or freeze it and use it as a puree for fruit drinks or for dessert toppings. Bananas can be frozen. They make terrific chocolate-coated banana desserts. Strawberries freeze well but lose their appearance and most of their flavor. Blueberries and black raspberries seem to be the best fruits to freeze in the berry family. Red raspberries do almost as well while peaches do not. If you refrigerate fruit, do not transfer it back and forth in and out of the refrigerator.

Tree-ripened fruit offers the best taste. Shop at local farm markets whenever these fruits come into season. There is a healthy trend toward more produce stands featuring their own homegrown products. Freshness is the key.

INDEX

A Few Family Memories

Maury at 20 (top left), Bess at 20 (top middle); Maury
and his son Alan (bottom middle).

Maury in a pensive mood, late 1960's.

Shelley Feren Yonas, Maury's daughter, hiking.

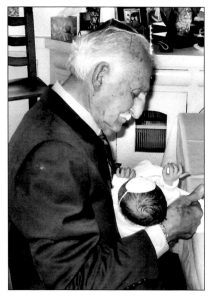

Maury's first great-grand child, Michael Feren.

Maury and Bess Feren happily celebrate their 50th wedding aniversary.

1939 Ford Convertible Sedan

1941 Hudson Station Wagon

"I thought when I retired that I'd just be doing some writing. But then I started doing it, and well, I saw what I could do, and that there was so much out there that needed doing."

— Maury Feren, produce expert, radio personality, and sculptor, on successful aging.

M Myth Busters
Defying The Myths of Aging.

Sculpture - a retirement hobby.

Fly, Baby, Fly

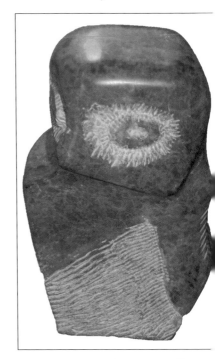

The Owl Knows All

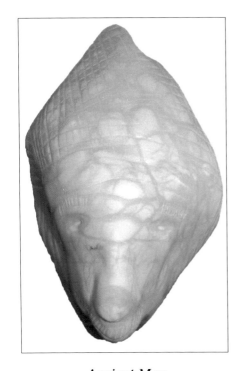

Ancient Man

Unicorn, Truth or Myth?